ALGONQUIN STORY

BY

AUDREY SAUNDERS

DEPARTMENT OF LANDS AND FORESTS

HON. H. R. SCOTT
Minister

F. A. MACDOUGALL
Deputy Minister

ACKNOWLEDGMENT

The author wishes to express her gratitude for the aid rendered in the preparation of the manuscript of Algonquin Story, to the following members of the committee who supervised its preparation on behalf of the Ontario Department of Lands and Forests.

MR. A. G. NORTHWAY and MR. C. A. G. MATTHEWS, leaseholders in Algonquin Park; MR. TAYLOR STATTEN, camp director and operator; PROFESSOR CHESTER MARTIN, Head of the Department of History, University of Toronto; PROFESSOR R. M. SAUNDERS, Department of History, University of Toronto; PROFESSOR J. R. DYMOND, Director of the Royal Ontario Museum of Zoology, Chairman of the Committee.

AUDREY SAUNDERS.

TABLE OF CONTENTS

Introduction

BY SELWYN DEWDNEY

Can anyone who has seen it forget the sudden glimpse, as he paddles quietly along the lakeshore, of a deer drinking at the water's edge? — the quick graceful lift and turn of the head, the soft inquiring eyes, the curve of the glistening black nostrils; the great sensitive ears searching the air for sound, the delicate poise of the tense lithe body, the twitch of the short, white-tufted tail?

Whoever has experienced such a moment will want to read this book.

Others, old and young, will want to read it too: all Canadians and others who love the northern wilderness; all people who have wondered about its future.

And yet, it is neither a specialized study of Canadian wild life, nor an analysis of the value of Canada's northland. It would be wrong to call it a history of Algonquin Park, though that idea gave it birth. Neither, though the Park is a tourist's paradise and reveals itself as such, is it tourist propaganda.

Rather, and quite simply, this book is the story of Algonquin Park. It is a story that hitherto has appeared only in fragments: in the reminiscences of gnarled old lumbermen in Killaloe or retired Haliburton trappers, in the dry pages of history books and dusty government volumes of departmental reports. Some pages of the story lie buried beneath the pile of sand and scattered rotting logs that mark the site of an old camboose camp; some hang, for all who come to see, on the walls of Canada's National Gallery.

When Audrey Saunders was commissioned by the Ontario Department of Lands and Forests to collect from every available source material for the story of how Algonquin Park came to be, and the consistent expansion of its usefulness since the day it was set aside, it is doubtful if she realized either the extent or the direction of what she afterwards described as the Park's "flow of activity". For out of this conscientious study has come a character as well as a story: the character, if one may speak so, of the Park itself. Somehow the beauty of its landscape, the vital energy of its animal life, the warm humanity of the old Park residents and rangers, the big ideas of the old lumber kings — even the apparently casual activities of the summer visitor—add up to one total impression. One cannot help feeling when one has read this book that Algonquin Park, both as a place and as a background of expanding activity, is uniquely significant for Canadians.

This is a tall statement, or sounds like one. How can any one area in one Canadian province be so significant?

We have recently ended the physical battles of a war in which nations of limited natural resources gambled for control of the world's wealth—and lost. Hostile eyes have stared covetously across two oceans toward the great undeveloped wilderness of northern Canada, noting how its population — except where the western prairies sweep northward — huddled in its cities close to the American boundary.

Let us look for a moment at this country of ours in which we do not live, known to geologists as the Canadian Shield.

Sweeping the shores of Hudson Bay in a great arc, bordered on the north by the Arctic Ocean and along its outer edges by an almost continuous chain of freshwater seas, it is a land like no other on the surface of the earth: a land of rocks and lakes, forests, and Arctic prairie, stretching interminably north from the shores of the Great Lakes. A prehistoric Paul Bunyan might once have leaped into Hudson Bay, splashing its water over half a continent, leaving a million haphazard puddles to overflow the hollows they filled, and trickle back to the ocean by ten thousand devious routes. Standing on the Arctic coast today the same Paul Bunyan would see about him nothing but reindeer moss, hardy grasses, and a few dwarf trees covering the clay, gravel and patches of rock. But, looking south, he would observe increasing masses of dark green spruce, beyond that a sprinkling of lighter-hued birch and poplar, and the emerald pine; and finally — if he strained his eyes toward the region that lies between Lake Huron and the Ottawa River, and if the month were September — he would glimpse the glorious scarlet and gold of the Algonquin Park maple tree.

This vast area, extending to Ungava Bay and the Atlantic Ocean on the east, to the prairies and Mackenzie River on the west, is the Canadian Shield.

Wedged in the centre of its southernmost extension, like the keystone of an inverted arch, with English-speaking Ontario below and French-speaking Quebec to the east, lies Algonquin Park. Here the northern spruce and the southern maple meet in the native land of the pine. This was the historic barrier that separated the old settlements of the east from the great undeveloped reaches of the west. Even as a place the Algonquin Park area is significant.

To the eyes of the city dweller crossing through the Shield country of Northern Ontario on any one of the transcontinental railways, it is a bleak, inhospitable looking land — even in summer. Hour after hour the weary passenger stares out at the endless panorama of trees, water and rock, muttering gloomily to himself, "Why don't they give it back to the Indians?" Occasionally he looks down from his comfortably appointed coach at a shabby group of natives standing idly on the station platform. An isolated section-man's shack flashes by, or a little lake on which a lonely "kicker" put-puts its way. The train thunders over a bridge, the stream below choked with pulpwood, or whistles brief greetings to an abandoned sawmill. Always the miles of wilderness in between; nothing but rocks and water and trees. Who would want to live in such a God-forsaken country? he asks himself, glancing in disbelief at the woman and child who stand waving at the speeding train from the door of a little log cabin miles from nowhere. Over the crest of a distant hill the shafthouse of a mine reminds him of the country's buried mineral wealth; but he snorts contemptuously at the unimpressive second growth bush along the trackside — hardly big enough to make decent fenceposts!

Is it a dreary wasteland, good for nothing but a meagre living for the sprinkling of Indians, trappers, prospectors and pulpwood cutters that inhabit it?

The reader who has lived in the land will vehemently disagree. No one can step into a canoe and paddle through the country for a week or two without becoming a violent partisan for its value and possibilities. Turning a bend in the stream the traveller comes upon a great cow moose, fattened on the vegetation of the land, and watches her stalk into the brush, followed by a month old calf. The stream widens into a swamp where acres of wild rice nourished by the rich black muck beneath, push their graceful shoots out of the water. A brood of ducklings splashes frantically ahead and disappears in a succession of little plopping dives. He leaves the swamp and crosses the lake, landing on a clean white beach scattered over with the tracks of deer and bear. Up on the hill is an old fire-burn where he stops to stuff himself with luscious blueberries, the whole hillside blue with the fruit. On the portage he climbs over the trunk of a windfallen spruce, three feet thick at the base;

and passes, a hundred paces beyond, through a park-like stand of stout red pine. A barren land? The distant roar of water filters through the trees, and he drops his pack by the trail to make his way through the bush toward the sound. He stands at last, staring at the amber-clear flood arching powerfully over the bed rock ledge, splitting in vivid greenish yellow sheets over the air pockets beneath projecting rocks, and smashing itself on the boulders below, to froth away in creamy splashes of sunlit foam.

No one who knows the country wants to give it back to the Indians. But, to be honest, we Canadians have set too small a price on its value, and taken too shortsighted a view of its use. Our forefathers, coming into a land of incredible wealth from the crowded islands and mainland of Europe, developed a philosophy of materialism which still shocks the visiting European. Like children around a candy barrel they ate themselves sick. Farmlands and forests alike were "mined" of their best and abandoned for richer lands beyond. The rivers of the settled south were polluted with industrial waste and sewage; water-conserving forests were cleared, and wide streams reduced to a mere summer trickle. In the Canadian Shield country billions of cubic feet of the best white pine were cut into squared timber. The forests were recombed for smaller saw logs, and cut over again for pulpwood. Today the plastic and plywood industries are looking hungrily toward deciduous trees the others despised. Let the man who is skeptical over the decline in our forest wealth take a walk down King Street West in Toronto, where the wear and tear of eighty years have exposed the inner construction of a few old buildings. Planks two feet wide were common then; today, even if our lumber yards were full, he would look in vain for such boards.

If this were the total picture we should have desperate cause for shame, and we have cause enough. Against this gloomy background Algonquin Park stands bright as the splash of yellow birch leaves against the sombre autumn forest in a Tom Thomson sketch. Among the few men who saw beyond the narrow horizons of their generation was Alexander Kirkwood, the man in whose brain the idea of the Park was born. With the establishment of this Park in an area so typical of Canada's northland, a movement was begun fifty years ago which is, in its implications, of national significance. For here an attempt has been made to answer the question: what's to be done with our Canadian wilderness?

Great stress has been laid on our tourist industry, on the

international goodwill to be created by luring visitors into our country and giving them the time of their lives. Mention too is made of the dollars and cents they spend within our boundaries. Economically, we live by trade, and the unique attractions of our northland are something we have for sale. But in these postwar days when commercialism is all too ready to swamp us again, it is heartening to read of a place which does not pay for itself in mere dollars and cents. In fact we learn that, during the two periods when its administrators were asked to make the Park financially self-supporting, the very purposes for which it was founded were endangered. Logically, nothing else could have happened. It is the idea that counts, and if the idea is to make money, the more permanent values must suffer.

Like a good serial, this book leaves off at its most exciting point. Intended though it is merely to show the background and development of the Park idea, it leaves us at the end with the feeling that this is only a beginning. The basic purposes of the founders, wild life and forest conservation, have been realized — at least to the layman's satisfaction. But the phenomenon of Tom Thomson's brief brilliant appearance was something they never foresaw. Nor did they dream of the new horizons in education and scientific research that would open up before Park workers today.

This much is clear to most Canadians, from reading the story of the Park: the Canadian Shield country cannot support the conventional type of Canadian community. Neither is there any basis for permanent use in unplanned commercial exploitation. If we are going to build permanent homes for our children in the northern wilderness, some new approach must be found.

Perhaps the workers in Algonquin Park are, in the unconscious direction of their total activity, cutting this new portage. Already it stands as a unique kind of community, a large, apparently aimless, floating summer population, and a small permanent and purposeful resident nucleus, each stimulating and stimulated by the other. Is this the prototype of a new kind of communal life in the Canadian future?

A hundred questions throng the reader's mind as he closes this simple story of Algonquin Park. What will come out of it? Can the solid benefits of summer camp life now enjoyed by the favoured few be extended to the many? Will the adult and youth education movements now developing in the Park grow into a great "University of the North", scattered in scores of units over the Shield country, forming the nuclei of similar communities?

Is there in the old depot farms, as in so many other early Park activities, the seed of a future development? Could scientific study and research, now directed largely toward forest and animal problems, include the uses to which the pockets of fertile soil that are scattered through the Canadian Shield might be put? Is it possible to develop a domestic blueberry that will grow where other berries find the soil too sour? Could our swamps yield harvests of wild rice that would be profitable to gather?

These are perhaps idle questions, with no basis in the hard facts of economics. It is, after all, a waste of time to speculate over what *may* happen. But one fact is made clear in this book. We Canadians, so long content to follow our neighbours' examples at a safe distance, are now beginning to recapture the pioneer tradition in a national sense. In growing to maturity, we are discovering our own way of doing things, and finding that we can do them well. This is the exciting point in the story of Algonquin Park where it must stop, until the next instalment is written by the hand of the future.

In the eloquent quotation that closes these pages Dr. Scott remembers Algonquin Park as "a place apart". Whether the Park's wider sphere of usefulness impresses the reader or not, he will agree with that. And he may also feel, when he has met the Dufonds and the Dennisons, when he has eaten sea pie in the camboose camp, enjoyed the inexhaustible store of Mark Robinson's reminiscences, and stood silently before Tom Thomson's cairn overlooking the blue waters of Canoe lake, that this is a place he knows well; and that somehow, even though he may be a stranger who has never seen the Park or visited the province in which it lies, it belongs to him too.

CHAPTER 1

THREE CENTURIES AGO, in the year 1615, a Frenchman of gentle birth and fierce ambition, his Vandyke beard pointing the way like a spear, craned his neck to see past the sweating Indian paddler ahead of him. The broad expanse of Allumette Lake stretched south; then turned like a goose's neck northward again and west. It was here, two years before, that he had turned back, weary and disillusioned, the plausible fantasies of the opportunist Vigneau exposed for what they were.

This time he would go on.

But when and how would he reach the Western Sea? Had he known what every school child knows today, he would have realized the only Western Sea he would ever reach was the fresh water body we now call Lake Huron. Had he known what every Park ranger in the region knows now, there were three routes over the highlands that separated him from this Sea, each of them less roundabout than the Nipissing-French River approach.

Champlain, for of course he was the Frenchman in question, might have ascended any one of three tributaries of the Ottawa River. First was the Madawaska. Up in the heart of the Algonquin highlands lay its largest lake, Great Opeongo. This same lake could be reached without much portaging by ascending the Bonnechere River to its source in the highlands. A third ascent was more difficult: a long portage past the lower rapids, good going after that, up the Petawawa, called in early times the Nesswabic River, into the northern section of the highland area itself, so pitted and channeled with hundreds of lakes and streams that one could travel by canoe in almost any direction, always provided he was willing to carry his canoe and its cargo overland from time to time. Issuing from the highlands and descending westward into Georgian Bay in Lake Huron, were two streams, the Magnetewan to the north —but well south of the French River — and the Muskoka system of rivers and lakes draining the southwest corner of the highland area.

If his Indian guides knew of these shorter routes they were silent. Champlain's canoes ascended the Ottawa past the mouths of the Madawaska and Bonnechere tributaries, past the mouth of the Petawawa, and reached the Mattawa River approach to Lake

Nipissing. Here he had one last chance to take a shorter route. Descending northward from the Algonquin country into the Mattawa, was the Amable du Fond River, from whose sources he could have reached either the Magnetawan or the upper Muskoka waters. But Champlain and his Indians went past the mouth of the Amable du Fond, crossed over to Lake Nipissing, and descended the French River to the north shore of Georgian Bay. Returning after an unsuccessful two years of Iroquois campaigns with his Huron friends, Champlain used the same route. He had not found the fabulous Western Sea he dreamed of; he had even missed the very real paradise of the Algonquin Lakes and height of land country.

It may be he was not altogether unconscious of the latter loss, though his reference is brief to the lands lying west of the Ottawa River. He says:

> "Moreover, it is quite a wilderness, being uninhabited
> except by a few Algonquin savages who dwell in the
> country and live by the fish they catch in the ponds
> and lakes with which the country is well provided."

As a result of Champlain's finding the first map of this region was compiled in Paris by the King's map-maker, Sanson, in 1653. Across the Algonquin Park region of this early map is the phrase *"Grand chasse de cerfs et de caribous"* — "a fine place to hunt stag and caribou". Whether he surmised this from observing the abundance of game along the south bank of the Ottawa, or whether he learned it from the Indians who actually hunted there, we have no way of knowing.

There is no doubt, however, that he met Indians to whom the region was an open book and an earthly happy hunting ground. Each year, when hunting and trapping was at its best, family groups of these Algonquin bands would pack their kit into light birch-bark hunting canoes to travel up the water routes into the interior. When Champlain came upon them first they were on their summer camp sites along the sandy shores of Lake Nipissing. There the men could catch a plentiful supply of fish, while the women and children could pick and dry the blueberries that Champlain says were used in the same way as dried currants in southern France. This hardly means that any of them could be called natives of the Park region. None of the Algonquin bands had any fixed abode. They wandered about from hunting grounds to fishing regions, from blueberry plains to the shallow lakes where wild rice grew; as the spirit and the state of their larder moved them. A journey of two hundred miles would be nothing for one of these family groups, since they travelled light and took all their worldly belongings with them in their bark canoes. So they might travel in and out of the Park area several times in a single year.

However, in spite of a nomadic existence necessary in a country that could never support more than a few wandering bands at a time, most of the land was regarded as the particular property of some special Indian group. Most early records agree that the Ojibways looked upon all the lands east of Georgian Bay, up to the height of land in the Park area, as their special preserve. The Ottawas claimed hunting rights on the slopes falling toward the Ottawa River. Usually these Indian peoples preferred to live along the main water routes, but at certain periods of the year they would move inland to replenish their stores. For this reason, while there were never any Indians who made their permanent homes in the Park itself, there were frequently Indian groups in that district. Then, as now, it teemed with animal life, and was also an excellent summer camping spot for fishing parties.

From the prairies to the Gulf of St. Lawrence the paper birch grew in abundance, and the Indians who used its bark developed into a language group known variously as Ojibway or Chippewa in the west, Missisaugas and Nipissings in the centre, and Montagnais in the east. But the name most familiar to readers of Canadian history, and that favoured by Champlain himself, is the name borne by the Park today — Algonquin.

Perhaps, being less accessible, the white or paper birch grew to a greater size here, before being stripped of its useful bark. Certainly no other forest product was quite so useful for these Algonquins. Birch bark was an absolute necessity in their way of life, and from early days there were great stands of birch in the Park district. There the Algonquin families could find the raw materials that they needed for their own immediate use. Both the graceful fishing canoe, with decorative rounded ends, and the more practical hunting canoe, smaller and not so well finished, were made of cedar frames covered with birch bark and sealed with spruce gum. As for their homes, these took the form of bark-covered wigwams, distinctly different from the skin-covered tepees used by some of the other Indian tribes. For this wigwam a framework of poles fastened together at the top was first constructed. Then sheets of bark were stretched across the poles. Since these sections have a natural tendency to curl at the edges, they would stay where they were

placed. The whole structure could be set up at a new camp-site
in a matter of twenty minutes, and when it came time to move on,
the dismantling process could take place just as quickly.

Champlain was a soldier and geographer; no anthropologist.
As a gallant Frenchman, however, he has left us one tantalizing
glimpse of Algonquin dressing habits — a tid-bit for the gorgeously
attired beauties of the court of Louis XIII.

> "Above all others our Montagnais and Algonquins
> are those that take most trouble with it; for they put
> on their robes strips of porcupine quill which they
> dye a very beautiful scarlet colour; for they value
> these strips very highly and take them off to make
> them serve for other robes when they wish to make a
> change."

In spite of Champlain's silence, it is not difficult for anyone who
camps in Algonquin Park today, with only a dash of historical
background, to recreate a typical summer camp of these original
Algonquins, situated, let us say, on the shores of Opeongo Lake.
Across the bay on that rocky tree-clad point, where a gusty northwest
wind blows the flies to shelter in its lee, a little group of bark
wigwams stands among the jack-pine. A bark canoe shows up
against the blue-grey rock, drawn high into the shore brush so that
only the graceful stern is in the water. A young woman clad in
doeskin stands beside the fire, leaning over to throw another stick
on the fire from time to time; or turning the racks, supported on a
tripod of poles, where fillets of fish and strips of caribou meat
hang in the rising smoke. Suspended in the shade, on a sturdy pine
trunk, is the tight-laced moss-bag of an Indian babe, sleeping in its
vertical cradle. An old woman sits on her heels pounding strips of
fish and meat already dried, into the pemmican that looks like
saw-dust. Not far away a young girl is lacing the seams of a birch
basket, with sturdy threads of barked spruce root. A boy of five
sits on the rock, thoughtfully munching a piece of dried fish that
fell from the rack.

Down the lake two black dots appear against the sparkle of
the waves. A woman runs out of the second wigwam and shouts.
An ancient crippled creature, with a thousand wrinkles on her old
brown face, hobbles to the doorway and squints out.

Before long the men are paddling close, the gunwales of their
bark canoes low in the water. Three men and a lad of sixteen, their
faces beaming with typical Algonquin good humour — the fishing

Tom Thomson, Canada   Courtesy Art Gallery of Toronto

THE WEST WIND

MAGNOLIA WARBLER.

has been good! Quick gesticulations — a joke about the young lad in the second canoe — happy shouts across the water! The canoes reach shore and eager hands unload the catch, flinging the silver harvest up on a grassy hollow in the rocks.

Change the sinewy Algonquin's hue to a lighter tan, change the yellow bark of the wigwams to the white of canvas tents, substitute modern speech for ancient Ojibway or Ottawa dialects, and we have leaped from pre-history to the present. The contrast of feast and famine, as they knew it, is gone; but fish swarm in Lake Opeongo now as they did then, and the same primeval urge of the fisherman still thrills the boy from Chicago and the girl from Montreal, as they reel in their first lake trout. The doe no longer lies bleeding on the ground, her eyes glazing in death. But the breathless moment of the chase, when the buck stands tense and beautiful in the clearing, still comes to the doctor of New Orleans, pointing his movie camera lens with the same shiver of ecstasy that paralyzed the arm and aim of the Algonquin stripling on his first hunt a thousand years ago.

No modern white Algonquin could have long endured a winter visit with these Indians. Within a winter bark lodge the central fire provided adequate warmth. But the stench of sweaty leather, unbathed bodies — and worse; the eye-smarting fire smoke that did not always find its way out of the hole in the roof; and the confusion of old skins, bones, baskets, hunting equipment and small children, would have driven the modern winter camper, used to a tidy log cabin, into hysterics. Yet no modern sleeping bag has been devised that can rival for pure luxury and comfort the Algonquin rabbit skin robe.

When March came, it was invariably a hungry month. Up to that time some of the supplies prepared during the previous summer, could still be counted on. Usually besides dried blueberries and raspberries, some fish had been smoked, and occasionally there was a cache of game prepared. In the winter, however, it was difficult to go very far afield in search of food. The Algonquin people made snowshoes by bending white ash bows and stringing them with moose or caribou thongs, but otherwise their equipment was very primitive. They were still living in the stone age and had no iron, and only a very little copper. The larger animals had to be killed with stone-tipped arrows, and then skinned and scraped with knives and scraping tools made of stone or of bone. For fishing they used nets woven from willow roots, spears, or bone hooks. Even the task of chopping a hole in the ice in winter, using only a stone axe, would be tedious.

With the Hurons to the south and west, occupying the region between Lake Simcoe and Georgian Bay named after them "Huronia", Champlain was more familiar. Already they had been his allies against the fierce Iroquois of what is now New York State, and neither he nor they needed much persuasian to set out on the long expedition south to Lake Ontario through the Trent River system. All the satisfaction Champlain got out of the affair, was an arrow through the knee. Wanting to get home quickly, he asked his Huron allies whether there was not an eastern outlet to Lake Ontario; but they brought him all the way back to Georgian Bay, and entertained him in their villages.

There, for the winter of 1615-16, Champlain continued to live. During that time, he became aware of some of the difficulties of his own situation. His friends, the Hurons, were not always on the most amiable terms with their Algonquin neighbours to the north. True, they occasionally traded with one another — Huron corn for Algonquin furs — but sometimes wandering war parties raided the settled Huron villages. Champlain undertook to patch up one such quarrel since eventually, to return home to Quebec, he would have to pass through Algonquin territory, and he preferred to be regarded as their friend.

Back in Quebec at last, Champlain had a rich fund of stories, and his published report fired the imagination of the Recollet Fathers. Within a few years the black robes, and white, bearded faces of French priests lost much of their strangeness for the Algonquins camping along the Ottawa-Nipissing route to Huronia. The kindly fathers regretted that they could not take time to preach the gospel to these scattered groups whom they encountered along the way, but these Indians' way of life and their linguistic variation, presented difficulties that the first missionaries found hard to overcome. Instead, the Recollets, and the Jesuits who carried on their work after 1632, concentrated on the settled Huron lands lying betweeen the Georgian Bay and Lake Simcoe. As time when on, occasional workers were sent from the great mission headquarters at Ste. Marie to establish dependent outposts for some of the wandering Algonquin bands.

To convert these people to Christianity, and then to keep them in the fold, was no easy task. One of the Fathers, writing his annual report in 1648, made mention of this problem when he said:

"All these tribes are nomads, and have no fixed
residence except at certain seasons of the year when
the fish are plentiful, and this compels them to
remain on the spot. Therefore, they have no other
church than the woods and forests; no other altar
than the rocks which break the waves of this lake.
However . . . the sky is as good as the vaults of a
church; and not for one day only has the earth been
the footstool of Him Who has created it."

In spite of these obstacles, the Jesuits had at this time at least
two missions on Lake Nipissing.

One further ray of light on the lives and manners of these
Algonquins is shed by an early account of friction between
Christian priests and the native medicine-men.

"Last summer an Algonquin, a Sorcerer by trade, or
at least one of those who make profession of invoking
Manitou, that is the Devil, who found himself worsted
in an argument by the Father, fell on him in a fury,
threw him down, and dragged him by the feet through
the coals and ashes, and had not the Savages hastened
to his assistance, this man would have ended by mur-
dering him. That is what one has to fear, even from
friends."

In spite of all these difficulties, the Jesuits continued to do what
they could for these wandering Algonquin bands, as long as they
were able to maintain their missions in the Georgian Bay district.
And though we have no record of it, a black robed Rocellet father
or recently converted Algonquin chief may have said the first
Christian prayer under the pines on the shores of an Algonquin
lake.

But neither priest nor chief could have realized that before many
years had passed, the seeds of the gospel of love would fall no
more for many years on Algonquin ground; nor could they have
heard the war drums beating far to the south, where the implacable
enemies of the Hurons were preparing to reap the red harvest of hate.

Just three hundred years ago, the Indians who hunted and
fished, picked berries, and peeled bark from the birches of the
Algonquin region, their bellies pinched with hunger or distended
with meat according to the vagaries of their nomad life, were
suddenly confronted with war. Where Algonquin mothers had bent
in love over their papooses, the fierce Iroquois bent in savage

triumph over his fallen victim, grasping his hair with one hand, dexterously circling his head with an iron scalping-knife, and wrenching the limp skin and hair from the still breathing body of the Algonquin brave. There is little doubt that beside more than one of these peaceful lakes, where the water lies calm as glass and the sun shines warmly overhead from the bluest of skies, there once lay such a body, gasping its last tortured moan, as the blood slowly oozed from the bare red skull-top, clotted, and turned black in the sun and wind. Where now the bear and the fox live unmolested, the blood of men, murdered by their fellow-men, once trickled to the ground.

In 1648 and 1649 the Iroquois from northern New York State attacked Huronia, burning Huron villages to the ground, torturing their captives, martyring the heroic Jesuit fathers Lalemant and Brébeuf.

The Iroquois confederacy, known commonly as the Five Nations, was in existence at the time when Dutch traders first set up a post at the mouth of the Hudson River. From the Dutch and from the English who took over the settlements along the Atlantic seaboard, the Iroquois obtained firearms in exchange for beaver skins. The European demand for furs was so great, that within a few years the whole region south of Lake Ontario had been almost denuded of beaver, while at the same time the Indians had become accustomed to the goods which the trade brought them. In consequence, the Iroquois began to look to the regions north of the lake as a hunting ground for themselves.

At the same time they became aware that French priests, and, in their wake, French traders, were making contact with the Indians of this region. That meant that if the Iroquois were to gain control of the rich fur-bearing lands lying to the south of the Lake Nipissing route connecting Luke Huron with the Ottawa River, they would have to get rid of the Indians who were friendly with the French. It meant also that they would have to get rid of the Algonquin trade route. Their campaign in Ontario, beginning in the winter of 1648, showed careful planning.

They first crossed over Lake Ontario in the Trenton district, and then, travelling on snow-shoes, came northwards along the Trent River system. The Jesuit records of their attacks on the Huron missions show that the first post seized was that called St. Joseph, between the present towns of Barrie and Orillia, and since these were surprise attacks, it is probable that the raiding bands had come from the northeast. It is quite likely that the Iroquois had spent the previous winter in the Algonquin Park-Haliburton region, where they would find a plentiful supply of game to tide them over between the time they came north on the frozen rivers and the time they attacked the Hurons in July.

We learn of their subsequent actions from the next year's account in the Jesuit Relations. In the fall of 1648 the Iroquois must have returned to the Algonquin Park region, and, as a matter of fact, they must have travelled all through it, because they went as far north as Lake Nipissing and as far east as the Ottawa River itself. They spent the whole winter in that region, and returned in the next summer to complete the destruction of the Huron villages, and to carry on the massacre of the French priests stationed at Ste. Marie. Late that year, when the remnants of the French band retraced their steps back to the Quebec settlements, they found that the familiar Lake Nipissing route had been laid waste by the marauding Iroquois.

The Algonquin Indians, too, must have suffered at the hands of the invaders. The returning party of Frenchmen and their Indian friends found Algonquin wigwams destroyed all along the shores of Lake Nipissing, and evidence that some of the Iroquois had spent the previous winter there. From that time on, for a period of almost a hundred years, French traders using the Ottawa route knew they were running the gauntlet of a hostile tribe. Twice the French challenged their sway — once when Dollard and his brave band of comrades stopped the Iroquois' attack on Montreal itself in 1660, and again when Frontenac, the fighting Governor, was brought back to New France to deal with this menace. Frontenac was able to make peaceful arrangements with the Iroquois, so that there were fewer raids along the Ottawa River route after 1701, than before that time.

However, the Iroquois did not entirely disappear from the Algonquin Park district until well on in the Eighteenth Century. We learn this from stories of French fur traders who dared to venture north again along the Ottawa River route, which had been so effectively blocked by the Iroquois. One reason why the trip taken by Radisson and Grosseilliers was regarded as so epoch-making, was that they managed to get through this Iroquois-controlled route. However, these, and other French traders, did not attempt to penetrate into the Algonquin Park country itself. Why they did not can be seen from a map of that period, dated 1720, where the

Algonquin Park region is marked as "*Chasse de castor des Iroquois*". At that period the Iroquois still used the district in order to hunt the beaver for the English traders, whose headquarters were in New York State. The first English maps printed after Canada became British, show that the Park area was still under Iroquois control. On a map of 1763, the Algonquins are shown in the neighbourhood of Sault Ste. Marie, while the Iroquois are located in the Park. The Missisaugas, north of the French River, were the only Algonquin tribe left in the district.

Finally war, that had driven the Algonquins from their native haunts, made it possible for them to return. The Iroquois warriors whetted their scalping knives and moved south again to fight with the British against the French, in the Seven Years War. Quebec fell, and the Treaty of Paris was signed. The American colonies revolted, and Joseph Brant with his followers, threw in their lot with the Loyalists. The settlement of these peoples along the valley of the Grand River in southern Ontario meant that they had become a peaceful agricultural nation, and that they were no longer interested in their previous hunting grounds to the north. Then it was, that the Algonquin bark canoes appeared once more on the placid waters of the Park.

There were three outlets for furs from the Algonquin Park region in the nineteenth century. The first was by way of the fur trading posts operated by the great companies along the Lake Nipissing-Ottawa Valley route; the second by way of the Muskoka Lakes and Penetanguishene; and the third was that used by a private trader, Charles Thomas, who set up his post on the lower Bonnechere River at the favorite Indian gathering place at Golden Lake. All three of these groups of traders operated independently, but all looked to Indians trapping in the Park area as one of their chief sources of supply.

The North West Company, which was founded in Montreal soon after the British took over the French colony, found in the Ottawa River route its main artery to the west. Up the old Champlain trail, and out by way of the Lake of the Woods route to the western prairies, went the French-Canadian voyageurs; who carried the company's supplies over thousands of miles into the interior, and returned in the following year with their freight canoes laden with precious furs. All along the way was a chain of forts acting as supply bases and trading centres, from which the company's employees could contact the neighbouring Indians. Early records show that along the Ottawa route, there were at least five of these posts which could have been reached by Indians bringing their wares down the rivers that flow out of the Algonquin Park district. That French traders went into the area themselves, we know from the names of some of the lakes that are found on very early maps such as Lake Lavieille, but in general they preferred to have the Indians bring their season's catch out to the posts along the great water route.

When the North West Company amalgamated with the Hudson's Bay Company in 1821, most of these Ottawa Valley posts continued to operate under the latter's name. Of these the most important was the one called Fort William, situated on the north bank of the Ottawa, opposite the mouth of the Petawawa River. There the Hudson's Bay Company continued to trade with the Indians who lived in the surrounding country. When we examine the records of the trip taken by Alexander Sherriff through the Park district in 1829, we shall find that the company officials knew little about the country from which these furs had come, and that the Indians living on the shores of the Ottawa River had never travelled inland from the main route. On the other hand, the Indians whom Sherriff later found hunting on the upper reaches of the Petawawa in the Park, told him that they took their furs out to the Ottawa Valley posts in order to trade them for the goods that they needed. These particular Algonquins likely traded at the Mattawa fort since, according to their own accounts, they were accustomed to travel from their winter camping grounds in the Cedar Lake district, by way of the Amable du Fond River, in order to dispose of their catch.

Once Sherriff had crossed over the height of land, in his journey through the Park, he found that the Indians along the Muskoka waters marketed their wares at Penetanguishene. Independent traders who had their storehouses at Penetanguishene, travelled all through the Muskoka Lakes from about 1825. One of them, by the name of Thompson, was the founder of the store at Penetanguishene which still bears his name. The Lake of Bays district became so well known as a fur trading centre that one of the neighbouring lakes was called Trading Lake, and some of these independent traders set up posts in the area.

A later development came in this same region with the opening up of a Hudson's Bay post at Orillia in the 1860's. Then the Ojibway Indians who had their headquarters at Lake Couchiching could bring their furs from the Oxtongue district, in the southwest corner of the Park, right down to this post. As an offshoot of the Orillia trading house, and as a way of intercepting some of the free traders who still came into the Lake of Bays from the Georgian Bay coast, the Orillia factor, Mr. Thomas Goffatt, set up an outpost on Lake of Bays, where Bigwin Inn now stands. These posts were all abandoned when the coming of settlers into the Haliburton region turned the channels of the trade in the opposite direction, to the buyers who came into Minden at the end of steel.

In the southeast area of the present Park, in the Golden Lake district, a parallel development was taking place. There, too, independent traders went inland to meet the Indians before they could bring their wares out to the posts of the Hudson's Bay Company along the Ottawa Valley. Charles Thomas, who established a post at Golden Lake about 1832, is typical of these free traders. Thomas was a man with a wide and varied experience in the fur-trading business; in fact, he had been born into the trade at the Hudson's Bay post at Moose Factory on James Bay, where his father was stationed in 1793. He was sent back to the old country to school, and afterwards acted as Inspector of Forts for the Hudson's Bay Company on Great Slave and Great Bear Lakes. Travelling by canoe, he brought his wife and family down to Montreal in 1822, and after several years of working intermittently for the Company on the Ottawa and the Bonnechere Rivers, he finally decided to enter business for himself in that same region.

But the great days of the fur trade in the Algonquin region were nearly over. Each year the great stands of red and white pine farther down the Ottawa valley were falling one by one; each year the ominous thud of steel axe on pine trunk shattered the winter silence a little closer to the ancient Algonquin hunting-grounds. Down the Ottawa, never to return, floated the great square "sticks" of timber in thousands; and all along its shores lay the heaps of "slash", while great gashes in the forest showed like wounds.

It was Charles Thomas at Golden Lake, who presuaded his naturally suspicious Indian friends to allow the first Algonquin timber cruiser, Alexander Macdonell, to enter the country. With the traditional courtesy of the north, he even wheedled the Indians into making for him a rough sketch map on birch bark, of the route between the headwaters of the Bonnechere and Madawaska Rivers. Therefore, it was only a matter of time, before axes were heard in the very heart of the land of the Algonquin.

CHAPTER 2

TWO HUNDRED YEARS after Champlain's canoes first pushed their graceful bows up the Ottawa River, neither Indian wars nor Jesuit missionaries, nor even the fur-trapping Algonquin, had disturbed the primitive grandeur of the country that would one day become Algonquin Park. Perhaps fires had become more numerous, though even on his first expedition Champlain had used the word "brûlé", to describe such areas along the upper Ottawa. In little marshy ponds the swamp grass had grown farther out from the shores; up on the hills a forest giant had crashed to the ground from time to time, split by the lightning of a passing storm. The trout tribe still swam supreme in the deep lakes and rushing streams, undisturbed by the black bass introduced in modern times. Caribou were getting scarce, as were the coveted fisher and marten. But fundamentally, there had been no change in the land for twenty thousand years.

Soon the eyes of the curious Canada jay would bulge with amazement at the sight of a "camboose" camp in the heart of the Algonquin forest. Soon the chickadee would call pert greetings in the winter woods to the faller, as his axe bit into the base of a great white pine.

But before, and during, the development of the lumbering industry in the region, there were other white pioneers with other axes to grind.

Over in Europe the Napoleonic wars had ended; and so had their echo in North America — the series of skirmishes along the Canadian-American border, known as the War of 1812-14. This latter war had made the British guardians of the colony of Upper Canada, acutely conscious of strategic weaknesses in their system of defence; and obsessed with the necessity for an alternative water route from Lower Canada to the upper Great Lakes, so that military supplies from the seaport of Quebec could safely reach the inland bases at Penetanguishene and Michilimackinac.

Now that peace had come again, land-hungry British immigrants and war-weary British veterans were finding that the easily-reached border lands along the Lower Lakes were already settled. Land companies, as well as government officials, began to wonder what kind of land the interior of present-day Ontario held, and exploration parties were sent far afield, to bring back reports on the agricultural possibilities of the border land to the north of old Ontario.

Beginning in 1818, and continuing for the next fifty years, the Algonquin Park country had its share of canoe-trippers, who passed to and fro along the Park highways. These travellers were sent there for specific purposes. There were army officers seeking transportation routes to bases on Lake Huron and Lake Superior; there were government and private surveyors sent to report on the soil and vegetation of the region, and to trace out the courses of the many rivers flowing out of this height of land. All these men have left some record of their visits to the Park, but very few of these stories have ever reached the public eye.

Information about the first three travellers in the district, depends chiefly on a hand-drawn map of Lieut. Walpole's route from Lake Simcoe to the Ottawa River. This map has an inset which shows where the two other Royal Engineers, Lieut. Catty and Lieut. Briscoe, had journeyed during the preceding ten years. All three of these men were seeking new ways of linking the older colonies with outposts at Fort Michilimackinac and farther west.

Catty's course touched the southeastern tip of the present Park. He went inland from Lake Simcoe, and travelled by way of Balsam, Gull, and Kennisis Lakes in Haliburton, through into Pen, Rock, and Long Lakes (where Whitney is now situated). Finally he made his way by means of the Madawaska through to the Ottawa River.

Briscoe's journey in 1826 took him through a much larger section of the Park. He went up the Oxtongue River into Smoke Lake, and then across, by way of Hilliard Lake, into Cache Lake and the Madawaska River. It is interesting to note, that of the three ways of crossing from the Muskoka waters to those of the Madawaska — by way of Source Lake, by way of Kootchie Lake, or by way of Hilliard Lake — the last mentioned, which is the least used to-day, is the earliest on record. From the Lake of Two Rivers, Briscoe's party travelled by means of a series of portages through Sundan, and other small lakes, into Opeongo. From there, he passed north into Hogan's, and thence by the little Madawaska River, into the Petawawa proper.

Walpole's map shows that he went by a route that carried him slightly to the south of the Park, in his journey from Lac des Chats, near the present Pembroke, to Lake Simcoe, but he, too, made use of the Madawaska route. Fortunately, we have some first-hand information about this trip, which was taken in 1826. One of his canoemen, by the name of Croteau, was along some nine years later on another expedition conducted by Lieut. Baddeley in the Black River area, and when Baddeley's party was marooned at camp during a series of rainy days, Croteau began to recall what had happened on his earlier trip. He spoke of the Black River as the route by which Lieut. Walpole had travelled on his way to the Ottawa, and of the journey that he himself had taken from the head of the Chats Rapid, by way of the Bonnechere River, to meet Walpole at the dividing ridge between the Ottawa River and Lake Huron. Croteau says that this meeting took place on September 12th. From the ridge they travelled on down to Lake Simcoe, which they reached on the 27th of September, by way of the Talbot River. Although there is no official record of the finding of this excursion, Croteau may have been echoing Walpole's own sentiments when he described what they had seen along the way. He says:

> "The land through which we passed was in general very good, but the best we noticed was on the Madawaska River where there was large prairie and very little rock. The height or dividing ridge consisted of land covered with a fine growth of maple. The longest portage met with was nine miles on the Talbot River through excellent land. In the spring of the year you may pass by canoe from Lake Simcoe to Bytown (Ottawa) in eight or nine days."

By the 1820's the Ottawa Valley below Bytown (now the City of Ottawa), had been opened up as farming land to incoming settlers. Lumbering activities, begun during the Napoleonic Wars to provide materials for the ships of the Royal Navy, had helped to clear the land in the first place, and as usual the lumberman was giving way to the farmer. On the upper Ottawa, it was to be expected that the same shift of occupation would take place, and promoters were beginning to wonder what this district held in the way of agricultural lands. As early as 1825, pine was being cut on the Madawaska and the Bonnechere Rivers, but as yet few permanent settlers had taken up land.

It was because Charles Sherriff of Quebec City was anxious to find what the chances were for settling immigrants in the Ottawa-Huron tract that his son, Alexander, undertook his trip through the district in 1829. In his report, which was published two years later in Quebec, we learn that he wanted to find out whether transportation on the upper Ottawa River made it feasible to bring settlers into that region; and if the land was fertile enough to justify settlement.

Sherriff, as a result of his earlier experience in the south along the St. Lawrence, had a bee in his bonnet that misdirected popular conceptions of the Park region for nearly half a century. He had found that the presence of hardwood forests was an almost infallible sign that the land, when cleared, would make excellent farm country. The luxuriant stands of maple and other hardwoods along the ridges of the Park district convinced him that the area would be ideal for settlement, and his whole report glows with the enthusiasm of a man astride his favourite hobby-horse.

Sherriff travelled up the Ottawa almost to the mouth of the Mattawa. Beyond Arnprior, settlements thinned out quickly, but Sherriff was convinced the land was fertile, and was eager to penetrate the almost unknown hinterland.

The only route known to him was Catty's, and he eagerly questioned everyone he met on the way, trader and Indian alike. Near Fort William, a Hudson's Bay Post almost opposite the site of Pembroke, Ontario, he encountered a large canoe bearing a man of substance.

"Here Mr. Simpson, the Governor of the company, passed us on his return trip from a northern tour, impelled by the strength of the stream and ten or twelve stout paddles that carried him with the velocity of the wind."

Immediately after that he was amazed, on turning a bend of the river, to find a whole family newly deposited, with all their household goods, on the river bank. The head of the house calmly watched Sherriff's canoe turn in, and strolled over, his hands in his pockets, to meet him as he landed. He was the first of the group of settlers who were to take up land in the Pembroke area, and told Sherriff that

"his intention was to clear the land and to lumber some, and in addition to keep a rum and whiskey shop when he could obtain a supply."

Sherriff felt that he had chosen a good spot to carry on all three of these occupations.

Finally, by repeated questionings, Sherriff decided on the best course for his party to follow. Neither of the lower tributaries, the Madawaska or the Bonnechere, appealed to him as a way into the interior, but Indians and private traders whom he encountered told him of "the largest of the Upper Canada tributaries — the Nesswabic". This was the name by which the Indians called the main branch of the nearby river, although one of the smaller inland branches seemed to bear the name of the "Pittoiwais". How to make his way up this river presented a major problem, since it was known to be very full of rapids close to its mouth. At length, however, he learned of a portage from Deux Rivières, and he decided to travel by that route. An Indian gave him a chart of the way they should go to preserve their bark canoes, and they set off overland to strike the Petawawa farther up its course.

Their own Indian canoeman and guide didn't seem to know very much about the country through which they expected to pass. From him, and from others, Sherriff had learned that

> "the lands of the Algonquin Indians frequenting the
> Ottawa do not extend quite to the height of land, at
> least on the Nesswabic; and the traders on the Ottawa
> have no communication with the Missisaugas who
> hunt beyond the Algonquins".

Sherriff had to be content with this guide who had never travelled through the district, but who claimed that he could act as an interpreter for any other Indians whom they should encounter during their trip.

When the party left Deux Rivières it was already late in August, and they were anxious to get across to Penetanguishene and back again, before the winter closed in. They found their first portage a difficult one. For about eight miles the trail led inland through a wilderness country. Sometimes they seemed to be following a path, but at others they lost it altogether. Finally they arrrived at a stream where they were able to launch their canoes. A paddle of about twelve miles brought them out to an expansion of the river which they were seeking. There at Trout (now Radiant) Lake, they found themselves on the Petawawa waters, and so they went on upstream to Cedar Lake.

At Cedar Lake, Sherriff camped for three days. One of his men had injured his leg on a portage, the weather was bad; and they met a party of Indians who had just arrived. These Indians who had chosen this spot to set up a winter hunting camp gave him directions for the next leg of his journey. Constant Pennaissez, son of an Algonquin chief and head of the party, drew for Sherriff a sketch of the best route up the Nessswabic (now the Petawawa) nearly to its source; though he would not, or could not, direct him over the height of land into Muskoka waters.

Constant, whose name seeems to have been preserved in Constant Lake and Constant Creek in Renfrew County, also told Sherriff of an alternate route from the Ottawa to Cedar Lake. According to him there was a much better way that the Indians usually used themselves

> "by a stream entering the Cedar Lake from the north
> and communicating with another called by the
> Indians who hunted on it Map di Fong (Amable du
> Fond's) Creek. This, though the longest, is much the
> smoothest route and is always followed by the
> Indians passing between the Ottawa and Cedar Lake
> with loaded canoes."

Apparently the Indians themselves preferred to take their furs out of the Park by making use of the chain of lakes linking Cedar Lake to Kioshkuqui. From there the journey down to the Ottawa was much easier than either the way Sherriff had come, or the way he was to return — that is, by going right down the main stream of the Petawawa River.

When he had learned all he could Sherriff made his plans. The man with the game leg would be left behind with the smaller of the two eighteen-foot bark canoes, and instructions not to go any farther afield than Trout Lake for thirty days. In the meantime, with the help of the friendly Constant, it was felt that he would be able to fend for himself and give his leg a chance to heal. The others — four in all — were to go on towards the Georgian Bay coast in the other canoe. For this trip they were to take only twenty days' provisions, so that they could get to and fro as quickly as possible. If they did not return at the appointed time the injured man was to make his way back to the Ottawa as well as he could.

Sherriff and his men continued on south from Cedar Lake, along what is now one of the most travelled canoe routes in the Park. Even at that time there was a good portage road to avoid that part of the river that the lumbermen afterwards called "The Five Mile" because of the rapids covering that distance. When Sherriff describes this road we can identify it with the one that is still there today, for he says,

> "It has been formed north of the channel, through a
> hardwood tract in which three small lakes are crossed,
> and this at length brings us to elevated country."

In that district Sherriff made particular note of the tree growth, since he found white pine everywhere prevalent with very little of the red pine he had seen elsewhere. On the whole, however, he felt that maple made up about half the forest — a sure sign, in his estimation, that the land was fertile.

As for the fishing in that region he declared that
"the waters of the Nesswabic surpass those of any
other river I have seen in this country."

He found the eels and catfish to be of a size rarely seen in the Ottawa, and the white or lake trout he learned could be caught in great abundance both in the winter and in the summer. These latter were of a light silvery hue, cream-coloured in the flesh, and frequently as much as forty pounds in weight.

All along their way the party had Constant's chart to guide them; but after three days, as they approached the height of land, they found that they were once more entering unknown territory. Now they were in the Missisauga hunting grounds, and their problem was to find the portage that would lead to the head-waters of a river flowing towards the Georgian Bay. Once they lost their way, but were lucky enough to meet another Indian, the first human soul they had seen since Cedar Lake, by whose directions they were able to cross into the Muskoka waters via Otter Lake, now called McIntosh Lake.

Oddly enough, this Indian was an interloper in the district, one of a group of Iroquois who resided on the Ottawa at the Lake of Two Mountains. Actually, he was poaching extensively on the territories controlled by other Indians. He told Sherriff that he had not interfered with the furs in the lands of his friends of the Ottawa Valley, the Algonquins, but had passed on through to the country of the Missisaugas. He had been wandering around in those parts for the best part of a year, and described it as "Bonne terre, partout, partout". Besides knowing about the existence of the "South River" flowing into Lake Nipissing, he told them of the Muskoka route through to Georgian Bay. He had just come back along that way himself, since he had been down to Penetanguishene to market his goods and lay in his winter's supplies. In doing this he must have passed right through the territory controlled by "Muskeekee", also called "Yellowhead", the Ojibway chief who regarded the Lake of Bays district as exclusive Ojibway hunting grounds. The name "Muskoka" comes from the name of this Indian leader.

With the Indian poacher's help, Sherriff had no difficulty in
finding the right portage across to the first small lake that lay on
the Lake Huron side of the watershed. At that lake he noticed that
the beavers had built a dam across the outlet, with the result that
they had "nearly affected a junction of the Huron and Ottawa
waters". His passage down the Muskoka, for which he said the
Indians had a name, but which he could not discover, was
comparatively simple. All along the way he continued to remark on
the nature of the rock formations and the type of soil, and he noticed
that there was very little limestone in the area until he reached the
neighbourhood of Penetanguishene. In order to get to the trading
post at that point, he went down the main stream of the Muskoka
instead of going by way of the Severn River portage, the route
taken by the Indian hunter he had encountered in the Park district.
He and his party finally arrived at their destination on the 17th
of September, eighteen days from the time they had left the Ottawa.

At the little outpost they visited the naval station in the cove,
and they noticed the

> "small new inroads into the forests with buildings
> apparently of a few days' standing".

Then they set out on their return trip to the Ottawa. This time they
passed up the Severn River, which Sherriff described as the common
route by which fur traders from that point crossed into Lake
Muskoka. As yet none of the lakes and rivers in those parts had
been named, but the geographers have been able to reconstruct
their route. When they reached the height of land between the
Muskoka and the Madawaska waters, they crossed over through
Source Lake along a portage which is supposed to be one of the
best travelled of Indian paths through the Park area. From there
they passed down the Madawaska almost to Rock Lake, and thence,
by a series of portages, some of them as much as three miles long,
into the south end of Lake Opeongo, then called "Abeunga".

Sherriff's description of this lake is the earliest that we have,
and in view of later stories about a Hudson's Bay post on the shore
of the lake, it is interesting to note that he mentions that there was
a building there in 1829, which might answer to that description.
Four miles up the lake near the place where they passed into the
eastern arm, he says, "there is a trading house occupied by the
Company in the hunting season". In actual fact, although we have
seen already that to Sherriff "the Company" meant the Hudson's
Bay Company, it seems quite improbable that the Company went

YOUNG FAWN.

BEAVER.

against its long established custom of encouraging the trappers to bring their wares out to them at the trading posts.

The party went on through the East Arm to "Lac Clair" (now Dickson Lake) which was described as "a pretty piece of water but with sterile looking shores". From there they passed into Lake "Lavieille", also named previously by French trappers or lumbermen who seem to have travelled all through that part of the country. In all, Sherriff felt that this return trip was a most harassing one, and that the route that they had followed on their way out had been much easier. At length, on the twenty-fifth day after leaving Cedar Lake, they returned to that spot in order to pick up the man that had been left behind there. They found him fully recovered; and, once more in their two canoes, they set off for the final lap of the homeward journey to the Ottawa. When they reached the mouth of the Petawawa at Lac des Allumettes, they found that the return trip had taken only twelve days from Penetanguishene. At that time, they reckoned that for anyone knowing the route, the time could be reduced to ten days by the Petawawa-Muskoka River waterway over which they had originally travelled.

In Sherriff's report, it is interesting to see what general conclusions he draws about the district through which he had been journeying. Along the courses of both the Petawawa and the Muskoka Rivers he felt that the soil was sufficiently light and highly elevated to be useful as agricultural land. In addition, he pointed out that the region was without rival as a health resort for

"its considerable elevation, and pure waters ensure it
    as being unsurpassed by any other section of the
    country in the important requisites of healthiness".

Although it took the better part of fifty years to convince Government authorities that the land would never really be any good for settlement and farming, no one has ever contradicted Sherriff's praise of the bracing air and crystal-pure waters of the Algonquin area.

In 1835 the Government of Upper Canada secured two British officers to conduct a survey of that section of the Province lying between the settled regions fronting on Lake Ontario and Lake Nipissing. To Lieut. Carthew, a naval officer, and Lieut. Baddeley, of the Royal Engineers, was given the task of surveying a line from the northeast corner of the Township of Rama, near Lake Couchiching, northward to the shores of Lake Nipissing. The authorities had originally intended that this line should serve as a base for later surveying parties when they proceeded to open up these townships for settlement. In actual fact, however, the line that Carthew and Baddeley ran was not sufficiently accurate for this purpose. On present-day maps, it is possible to follow its course to a point about eight miles south of Skeleton Lake. Beyond that point, the numerous lakes and rough terrain adequately account for the inaccuracy of this first survey.

In fact, when one considers the hardships of these early surveyors, one wonders at their patience. To crouch over a surveyor's transit and sight accurately down the line while a swarm of mosquitoes or blackflies suck savagely at one's neck, behind the ears, and at the tender skin of the wrist, demanded the faith and philosophy of Job himself. To this was added the heart-breaking task of carrying every last ounce of food, shelter, and equipment on human backs. Here in the wild fastnesses of the Algonquin wilderness even a mule was useless.

When Carthew and Baddeley set forth from the capital at Toronto they were charged with two tasks; they were to run this survey line north, but they were also to carry on lateral excursions up all the large rivers flowing into Georgian Bay, in order to report on the agricultural possibilities of the district. Baddeley, who was a competent geologist and a student of natural history, was equipped with a copy of Sherriff's earlier account as he journeyed into this same region, so that we may infer that the Government was seeking to confirm or refute his optimism over the farming possibilities in that area.

The technique then employed was to establish a base for supplies at Penetanguishene, and then to conduct survey parties, in two separate groups, up the different rivers that could be reached along the Georgian Bay coast. In this way, one or other of the leaders ascended the Severn, the Black, the Muskoka, the Shawanaga, and the two branches of the Magnetawan Rivers. Whenever one of these parties returned to the shore of Georgian Bay, it would be met by Mr. Beeman, a trader and storekeeper from Penetanguishene, who was to bring additional supplies up the coast in his sloop. In this way a preliminary survey of the whole area was conducted between July and November of that year.

Although neither of the parties actually penetrated into the present area of the Park, Lieut. Baddeley in his excursion up the Magnetawan very nearly did so. This trip is of interest to us for two reasons — because of the information that he gained from an Indian whom he encountered as he travelled upstream, about a route across the Park to the Ottawa Valley, and because the obstacles which he encountered and overcame were typical of those which all travellers into the Park district faced in the early days.

Baddeley's diary of his October trip gives us a good idea of how these surveys were conducted. Early in the fall when he and his party were out at the coast of Georgian Bay, he had a difficult time with his Indian canoemen. They told him that the season had arrived for them to lay in their winter's supply of fish, and that they wanted to return to their families. However, Baddeley was sufficiently persuasive to overcome their concern, and the party was able to continue its exploratory trip up the Magnetawan River. Once this journey was well under way, a spirit of adventure descended upon the whole party. They seem to have lost all desire for a speedy return to their families, and completely forgot the arrangements made previously to connect with other members of the survey party at a meeting place on the Georgian Bay coast. Instead, they determined to push on up past Ahmic Lake into the headwaters of the Magnetawan River, and thence, across the height of land into another stream, which they learned flowed out into the Ottawa Valley.

This scheme grew out of a conversation with an Indian whom they met on the river. He gave Baddeley a "carte du pays", told him about a cache of provisions that he had stored on an island in one of the lakes along the way, and persuaded him that it was quite simple to cross through to the Ottawa River. Baddeley gave him a "wampum of acknowledgment which would enable him to secure a gun or a pair of blankets at Toronto" for his information, and tried, without success, to persuade the Indian's boy to accompany them as their guide. When this attempt failed, the party decided to go on through to the Ottawa by themselves. For two days they continued up the south branch of the Magnetawan until gradually they found the navigation more difficult. Then they started to have qualms about the Indian's honesty, and to wonder if there really was a cache as he had said. Added to those doubts was the lateness of the season, dramatically brought home to them when one of the party got a ducking and nearly froze in his dripping clothes. Finally at a spot which they judged to be

> "within ten or fifteen miles of the dividing ridge which throws the waters one way into Lake Huron and the other into the Ottawa."

they decided to go back by the way they had come.

Then the real privations began. They had no ammunition left for their guns, and for some strange reason the district which usually abounded in both game and fish proved barren. When they met some of the other members of their party on October 31st they were still a long way from their supply base, and their total stock for twelve men consisted of six pounds of flour and a little pea soup. By November 2nd conditions began to look serious, and Baddeley decided to take one canoe in order to push on towards Georgian Bay, to see if he could make contact with the sloop that was supposed to be waiting for them there. On their way they were so hungry they even tried some of the pond lilies which the muskrats usually eat. These they found to be impossibly bitter. At length, on the evening of November 4th, after they had devoured the last crumb of the bannocks they had previously made from the flour, they came upon the sloop near the mouth of the Shawanaga River. When the other canoes came along soon after they were saved a return trip with supplies, and the whole group proceeded by boat back to their original starting point at Penetanguishene.

Baddeley, in his report, completely disagreed with Sherriff's estimate of the Ottawa-Huron Tract as good farm land. Referring directly to Sherriff's survey, he said:

"In passing we beg to call the reader's attention to Mr. Sherriff's communication as well deserving his perusal. We think, however, generally that he has drawn too favourable an inference from level and quality of timber, neglecting the more important consideration of the soil, which almost everywhere throughout the country appears to be excessively light and sandy, and often very shallow."

Later on he says more definitely, "The growth of hardwood on land is by no means a *positive* indication of good soil."

However, with a view to the future development of the district, he gave to the authorities two other pieces of information that were to prove valuable. He spoke of transportation routes through the country, and made it clear that it would be much easier to penetrate into the area by way of the Ottawa Valley than by way of the south or western approaches. In this connection he says:

"It seems reasonable to suppose that it will be by way of the Ottawa and Rice Lakes, rather than by Lake Huron that its good lands will be settled eventually."

In addition, in order to give an idea of the climate of the region, he drew up a meteorological table to show the variety of weather and temperature that the group encountered during the months they were working in the north. This is of interest to us even today, for from this record we can see that the first fall of snow came to the Algonquin Park region on Hallowe'en, October 31st, in the year 1835.

Within the previous ten years, the Government of Upper Canada had become involved, in one way or another, in the construction of at least three different canals in the Province — the Welland, the Rideau, and the beginning of the St. Lawrence waterway. Naturally there was keen interest in the possibility of linking the Ottawa River with Georgian Bay by a water route that would take the larger boats. To investigate this matter a commission was appointed with F. H. Baddeley, now a Captain, as one of its members, and it in turn assigned the task of determining the best route to a group of three men who were to report on the alternative courses. Trips covering each of these routes were made during the summer of 1837 —through the lakes and rivers of the Timagami country by David Taylor; through the French River-Lake Nipissing, and also the Magnetawan-Petawawa route by William Hawkins; and through the Muskoka-Madawaska district by David Thompson. The latter also reported on the measures that would have to be undertaken to get past the Calumet Rapids on the Ottawa River near Hawkesbury. For our purpose the records of the findings of Hawkins and Thompson are of prime interest, although anyone interested in the Timagami region, and the post of the "Honourable Hudson's Bay Company" there, should read Taylor's account.

The survey parties led by Thompson and Taylor made the naval store at Penetanguishene the chief base for their supplies. But long before the trips started off, David Thompson, who had won fame in the far west as an official of the Hudson's Bay Company and as the explorer of the British Columbia river which still bears his name, had been given the task of supervising the construction of the canoes that would be needed. When Taylor came north on the Yonge Street stage-coach on July 22nd, he found Thompson at work at Holland Landing, and the paint on the canoes was not yet dry. As indication of the interest that the Government of Upper Canada was taking in the whole venture, no less a person than the Surveyor-General himself, Hon. John McCauley, accompanied the party as far as their jumping-off spot at Penetanguishene.

The first of these three canal surveys was submitted by William

Hawkins, who had been along on Baddeley's previous expedition as a surveyor, but who was now Deputy Provincial Surveyor. His report of the levels along the Magnetawan-Petawawa route gives an admirable picture of the difficulties that would have to be overcome if a canal were to be built to make use of these water courses. His information shows that the total ascent from Lake Huron to the height of land was 340 feet, and that the distance between the head-waters of the two rivers was a matter of less than a quarter of a mile. However, his account of his own trip shows that he thought that the building of a canal there would be a foolish undertaking. At one place he points out that,

> "For fifteen miles from the height of land the Pittoiwais is but a comparatively small stream and in many places, even at the distance of ten miles from the height of land, its channel will scarcely admit a passage for canoes. We were frequently compelled to cut the banks before our canoe, although only four feet in width, would pass through."

On the whole, Hawkins' conclusions seem to favour the idea of making use of the old fur trading route through Lake Nipissing for the projected canal.

With reference to the Petawawa country in the Park district, Hawkins made several observations that tie in with what Sherriff had found some eight years before. Both men came upon traces of Indian hunters and trappers, although neither encountered many actual people along the way. As yet there seemed to be no signs of white trappers or of lumbermen, in this region. Of the appearance of the country along the Petawawa course he says,

> "There are four things strikingly peculiar to this section of the country — its timber is red; its soil is red; on the banks of the lakes and rivers its rock is red; and its waters are also red — deriving their colour from the soils and rocks over which they pass."

On the lower Petawawa River he mentions in particular a great wall of this rock along the shore: according to him it was 200 yards long and 150 high, with animals and other devices engraven by the Indians. Later travellers mention Indian huts scattered at intervals along this section of the river, so that this district may have been used for a long time as a general gathering spot for adjacent wandering groups of Algonquins.

David Thompson does not seem to have submitted a report for

his section of the canal survey, but he did turn in to the Commission what was probably more important in the long run, a series of four very beautifully drawn maps of the region through which he had travelled in his cross-country trip from Penetanguishene to the Ottawa. To geographers these maps are of great importance, since they provide them with the first accurate picture of the entire system now known as the Muskoka Lakes. The maps were drawn first on paper and then mounted on linen backing so that they are still in an excellent state of preservation.

The second map of this series shows the section of the Park through which this famous explorer travelled. To a man who had lived for the greater part of his life in the Athabaska country, this trip through the comparative security of the Ontario wilds would be a holiday jaunt. During the fourteen years which he spent in the employ of the Hudson's Bay Company before he came east in 1797, he had several times penetrated into the Rocky Mountain passes and on one occasion, when he came down the turbulent tributary of the Fraser, now called the Thompson, had accomplished one of the most difficult feats in the history of canoe navigation.

From Lake of Bays, which he called Forked Lake on his map, Thompson travelled up the Muskoka River to Oxtongue Lake, by him called Cross Lake. All along the way the actual course of his canoe is marked by a dotted line, so that one can see where he paddled to get the best view of the lake edges, traced on his map with such skilful accuracy. The present South Tea Lake he labelled as "Canoe" Lake, perhaps for the same reason that the name was applied to the lake so well-known now by that same name — he may have had to pause there to build or repair his craft after the initial stage of the journey. The trip through to the Madawaska waters was made by way of Ragged, Black Bear and the Bonnechere lakes, and thence through Head and on into Cache, but none of these are named on his map.

Today David Thompson's route is one of the most travelled sections of Algonquin Park, and the greenest of young tyro canoeists who "catches a crab" with his paddle on the glassy surface of South Tea Lake, can boast that a hundred years ago the intrepid western explorer dipped his paddle into the self-same waters.

CHAPTER 3

IN SPITE OF BADDELEY's attempt to straighten out the impression created by Sherriff's report, the legend persisted that the area was good farm land. Not till long after the camboose camps had come and gone, did this legend finally die.

Year by year, settlers established pioneer homesteads closer to the land of the Algonquins. In government circles the Huron tract, comprising the whole hinterland south of Lake Nipissing, was the goal of an extensive road-building project to open up the Haliburton area and beyond to settlement. Concurrently, the lumber interests were pushing farther and farther up the Ottawa and its tributaries in search of new supplies of the profitable red and white pine. Behind the lumbermen, as well as south of the Park, settlers were moving in. Unconsciously, the two movements, one from the south, the second from the east, converged in a race to occupy the height of land where the Park now stands.

The Haliburton settlers penetrated the Park area as early as any, since they eked out their scanty farm living with winter fur trapping; but it was the lumbermen and eastern settlers who first occupied the land.

Dan McLachlin was one of the first. Dan was a Glengarry man who had taken up land near Arnprior, on the Ottawa River. He may originally have intended to farm, but before he could begin, it was necessary to clear the land. Mr. McLachlin soon discovered it was far more profitable to concentrate on marketing the timber on his holding, than to depend on plough and hoe for a livelihood. The great lumber business operating for so many years in the Park area under the name of McLachlin Brothers, had as simple an origin as that.

Alex. Macdonell of Sand Point, the first cruiser to enter the region, took up limits on the upper Bonnechere. So did Alex. Barnet of Renfrew village. Along the upper Petawawa River cutting rights were reserved by Messrs. Perley and Pattee. Others followed till the Park area came to be known far and wide as a top-ranking square timber district. Each year their men came up into the camboose shanties along the old wagon roads from the Ottawa Valley. Each spring brought increasing thousands of logs down the Petawawa, Bonnechere, and Madawaska tributaries, into the mainstream of the Ottawa.

Without railways, these early lumbermen depended entirely on the rivers for marketing their logs. Consequently, all the leases were let along the river banks. The old licenses all read that the limit should extend for so many miles along the banks of a certain river "following the sinuosities of the said river" and should reach back to a depth of five miles. That was considered the maximum distance to haul a log profitably from its point of cutting to the water. On a contemporary map of the Park timber limits it is still possible to pick out these old leases. Most of the companies with holdings on the Ottawa tributaries, such as the Gillies and the J. R. Booth Companies, still operate on limits laid out in this way.

The mainstay of the business was the British export trade, and only the most select pine was cut for this market. Hardwoods could not be floated downstream, but pine, the cleanest and straightest and tallest of the softwoods, was in constant demand by British carpenters and shipwrights. Only the largest of these could justify the expense of cutting, squaring and rafting timber to the ocean ports, and its shipment overseas from there.

All these old companies were cutting "square timber", the product of a particular way of cutting the logs, and trimming them for market. Only the soundest and straightest red or white pine could be used to make a "stick" of timber. When such a tree was felled, trimmed of its branches, and cut flat on four sides, it made one timber, or stick, perfectly square, and measuring the same at the top and both ends.

In order to make one stick of this type, several highly specialized woodsmen were employed. The axe was their only tool, the horse their only source of power for lifting and hauling. The whole process required skilled and hardy woodsmen.

Before a stick could be cut, however, the timber limits had to be found, staked out, and leased. The man who determined the direction and extent of new operations was the timber cruiser. Usually in summer, sometimes in winter, alone, or with a small party, he ranged the forest, facing every kind of weather and hazard; making his estimates in the knowledge that the whole success of the operations to follow depended on his good judgment. The timber cruiser's report, as will be seen a few chapters later, could ruin a large company when larded with too much enthusiasm.

Once the area was leased, the road built, supplies hauled in, and the camp set up, the specialized axemen were ready. The fitter came first, selecting trees large enough to make a stick, and sound from top to base. The faller laid axe to tree, making it fall in the most convenient direction for the next operation. The log maker took over next, trimming the log of its branches, and cutting off the top to the specified length. After him the scorer peeled the bark from the upper sides, stretched a cord the length of the log and marked the thickness to be sliced off to make a flat side. He then "scored" each side with an axe at close intervals, so the hewer could hew to the line. The hewer, standing on top of the log, wielded a broad axe with a large head and razor-keen edge, trimming first one side and then the other, till *each was almost as smooth as a planed board.* Finally the log was rolled over ninety degrees, the scorer and hewer repeated their operations, and the stick was finished.

At a later date "waney" timber was made by the same method, only in this operation the edges of the log were left rounded instead of squared off. In this way the good outside boards, that were previously wasted, were sliced off at the mill into narrower pieces than the actual square would have allowed.

The pathways to the Park were being cleaned out of the best white and red pine at an alarming rate. T. C. Keefer, Assistant Engineer to the Board of Works on the Ottawa River, reported in 1847 that two and a half million cubic feet of pine had floated down from the Madawaska alone. At Quebec this quantity of timber brought in £90,000. Keefer's report, incidentally, reveals that it took two years for the timber to reach Quebec: he pointed out that with improvements at High Falls on the Madawaska, and on the lower Ottawa it would be quite possible to take the timber out in a single season. His figures in the report for 1846 show that nearly two thousand square miles were under license along the Madawaska, less than a thousand on the Bonnechere, and a little over a thousand on the Petawawa. Down these three rivers, that same year, floated a total of four million cubic feet of red pine and over a million of white. More than a third of the red pine came from the banks of the Petawawa. Since the "traverses," or cross-beams, for rafts all down the Ottawa were cut from red pine, and the Lake Traverse region was an excellent source of this timber, this is probably how it got its name.

Information about the route these lumbermen travelled to get into the upper reaches of the Petawawa in the 1850's and afterwards, is very difficult to obtain. However, we know that there was a "tote" road along the upper Ottawa for quite a distance above Pembroke by the middle of the century. Supplies would likely have to come in to the Park camps by this way, rather than up the Petawawa watercourse itself. As we have already seen, even the Indians found this route too rough for ordinary travel by canoe, so that the lumbermen would hesitate to bring in heavily laden canoes or flat bottomed "pointers" by that way. Instead, the roads, used later when the Canadian Pacific Railway Company constructed the section of its trans-Canada line along the south bank of the Ottawa River between Ottawa and North Bay, must have been opened up at this time. The lumbermen were not able to bring their supplies in by the railway until after 1880, but there were many companies operating along the Petawawa, and also farther north on the Amable du Fond, before that date.

In the northeast corner of Algonquin Park, a whole network of roads was cut overland from the upper Ottawa to the "Peetawaway", as the old-timers called it. The jumping-off point for the Lake Traverse district was the village of Bissett; from Deux Rivieres the lumbermen took in their supplies for the Cedar and Trout Lake areas; and, to reach the Amable du Fond, tote roads were cut from Mattawa and Eau Claire. These roads were eighteen to twenty-five miles long and exceedingly rough. Tough men, sturdy horses, and stout sleighs, were needed to cover the early trails. It was not until the Canadian Northern Railway line through the Park was completed in 1915 that the companies in this region had easy transportation brought to their doorsteps. To this day some of their winter roads may still be picked out from the air, but on the ground they have become so overgrown they are hard to find, except where the "corduroy" of logs over a gully or soft ground lies rotting among the second growth.

At several places along the roads leading from the Ottawa in to the Petawawa limits, there were "stopping places" where the teams could be fed and watered, and where the men could be put up for the night if necessary. One such place is marked on an old map as "Halfway P.O.", situated midway between Deux Rivières and the farm at Cedar Lake. Another was "Captain Young's" place in Edgar Township to the west of Lake Traverse. *Old-timers describe the appearance of these buildings.* The Captain had made the lumber for them himself by standing the logs on end in a scaffolding and then slicing them into boards by means of a "whip" saw. The surveyor who reported on this region for the Township Survey in 1887 said that Captain Young's was a busy stopping-place at that time.

There was another way of getting into the Petawawa camps, by means of the White Partridge Road from the south. Although this route into Trout Lake is marked on some of the early maps, it is very difficult to determine just who used it and when. When one starts to trace out its lengthy course, one finds it hard to believe that teamsters could have made the long haul up the wild bush trail that led from the Ottawa settlements to White Partridge Lake. This road passed up the Bonnechere River, past a supply base at Basin Depot and on by way of "McIntyre's Clearing" to White Partridge Lake. It may have been used by the firm of Perley and Pattee who operated at that place in the early days, but it is difficult to find out whether the road was constructed for their benefit, or whether it was a continuation of sections that had already been opened up to reach the upper Bonnechere limits.

A hand-drawn map in the possession of Mr. Dan McLachlin, of Arnprior, the grandson of the founder of the McLachlin lumber firm, affords some information about the southern part of this road. This map was made in 1855 to show the McLachlin holdings on the upper Madawaska River. To the north of the McLachlin limits is marked the "Basin Depot", so someone must have been operating in that region in 1855. Whether Thomas Barnet was in as early as that, or whether this was a stopping place for the White Partridge Road, is difficult to determine. We do know that William McIntyre had cleared some ten acres at a point now within the Park boundaries by the time the surveyors arrived in 1889, and that he was then operating a farm and a stopping-place for lumbermen. This farm was situated fifteen miles beyond Basin Depot on the Bonnechere River, at the point where the teams turned off to go north to White Partridge and the Petawawa limits.

All these old square timber companies housed their men in shanties built of logs which were cut on the spot where the camp was to be constructed. These shanties were built with a "camboose" in the centre, and came to be known as camboose camps. All through the Ottawa Valley and in the Algonquin Park district, this was the usual sort of building in the early days of lumbering. From old-timers such as Charles Macnamara, who worked for many years for the McLachlin Company, we learn of life in these camps. Mr. Macnamara provided the material for two articles written by

Harry Walker for the Ottawa Journal; and his own photographs, taken in 1900, give us an authentic picture of how one of the last of these buildings was constructed, and how the men were fed.

According to Mr. Macnamara, the name "camboose" was originally the French *"cambuse"* — a store-room, and as in so many other cases where French words were used in Canadian lumber camps, its true meaning had been changed because of the new environment. To the lumbermen the camboose was the central fireplace in the log shanty, but since this shanty was the place where the cook made the meals, stored some of his provisions, and fed the workers, the French meaning of the word would still apply. The camboose shanty was more than a store-room in the early lumber camps, since this one building served as dining, sleeping, and recreation centre, throughout the winter's bush operations.

Paddy Farrell of Pembroke, who for many years was a "walking boss" for camps operated by the Gillies Company, recalls the first time he ever "went to shanty". His father was one of those Ottawa Valley farmers who journeyed into the camps each winter with his team of horses, and who, during the course of many years spent in the bush, had become well known as an expert axe-man. Ever since he could remember, Paddy had seen his father go off into the woods in the fall, and finally, at the age of thirteen, he was to be allowed to go along with him. In those days there were many jobs that a husky lad, accustomed to handling horses and to swinging an axe on the farm at home, could do in the camps.

When Paddy and his father arrived at their destination, their winter quarters had not yet been prepared. Paddy helped to cut the logs that were to go into the building that was to be their winter home. On the first day they cleared the site, and cut the logs that were to be used for roofing. Then, while the more experienced men went on with the felling of the trees to be used for the construction of the walls, some of the others were able to scoop out the logs into long wooden tiles for the roof. On this particular shanty the walls went up very quickly, for the sides were made of three great logs that gave sufficient height for the roof when they were set one upon the other. The door in the front, and the small window beside it, were cut out afterwards.

When the roof was put on, a great hole, some six feet square, was left in the centre, open to the sky. This was the chimney for the fireplace that was erected in the centre of the floor space directly underneath, and it also provided light and ventilation for the occupants who lived and ate in this building. The fireplace, the actual "camboose", was built on a square foundation of stone and sand. When the camp was first built, a fire was kindled in it, and from that time until the river drivers departed in the spring, that fire never went out. It provided warmth, light, and heat for the cooking, during the whole winter season.

Today, in the Park, all the traveller may see is a pile of sand with a few rotten logs lying around, usually close to the water's edge. But earlier visitors saw them in a better state of preservation. C. H. Irwin, of Carnarvon, remembers one on the Little Nipissing River which his party came upon during a timber survey in 1921. Philip Roche of Killaloe located another built in 1894 on Pine River, a tributary of the Bonnechere. On Crow River near Big Crow Lake, according to James D. Pennock, Supervisor of Scaling for the Ontario Department of Lands and Forests, is another. Mr. Pennock also ran across the camboose pile and old *"cramiere"* of another camp, which he says may still be seen on the north-east bay of Shirley Lake.

Mr. E. Thomas of Kishkaduk Lodge tells us that an old-timer recalled the building of a camp in 1878, when the Hawkesbury Lumber Company was cutting on Cedar Lake. At this site it is possible to take measurements in order to determine the exact size of the original building. The actual rectangle formed by the walls still remains, because the earth was dug out on the outside in order to bank up the walls to prevent draughts along the floor. The foundation logs are still intact, and they show the length of the building to have been forty-one feet, while the width was thirty-six. The single door was cut in the front, facing the lake. The mound of earth in the centre of this space shows the location and the size of the camboose fireplace. In this particular instance the square in the centre measured twelve feet on each side. This had been built up with logs on the outside to hold the sand in place. On the far side of the fireplace, away from the door, there appears to have been a shallow pit, lined with stones. This was likely used by the cook as storage for potatoes and other supplies that he would need to have on hand. The floor itself seems to have been made of small poles, set close together to make a corrugated surface.

In passing, it is interesting to note that the use of this central camboose type of fireplace is coming back into fashion in Canadian architecture. Visitors who bask in the warmth of the famous central fireplace at the Seigniory Club, in the Province of Quebec, likely do not know that French-Canadian lumbermen long enjoyed the same kind of comfort from the old shanty fires. In the Park, too, several new buildings have recently been constructed on this model. The new dining hall at Camp Wapomeo, and the main lodge at "The Arowhon Pines" at Baby Joe Lake, are both heated by a camboose-style fireplace.

As for the original camboose fireplaces, old-timers will tell you that they were responsible for the excellent health of the lumber-jacks who spent the long winter in the bush. The roaring fire in the centre of the building not only threw its warmth into every corner, but it acted as an excellent ventilating system. Through the great hole in the roof the uprushing air currents took off the smoke from the fire, the odour of cooking, the smell of drying woolens, and the penetrating incense of green tobacco, smoked by weary labourers at the end of the day. At the same time this upsweep of air was strong enough, and hot enough, to prevent snow or rain from coming into the camp through the large aperture in the roof. All shantymen agree that there was very little sickness in lumber camps in their day.

From Mr. Tom Pigeon of Madawaska, we were able to obtain an excellent picture of the way the life in these camps was regulated. For many years he was cook in camboose camps located both in the Park area and along the upper Ottawa River. Now, at the age of eighty-five, he has vivid memories of the life led by the men in the early days. Then, as in modern camps, the power of the cook was second only to that of the foreman himself. A good cook was an ornament to any camp, and in return he was treated with true deference and respect by bosses and men alike. Tradition has it that the famous lumber camp habit of silent, speedy eating, dates from the time of the camboose camps. Then, when cooking, eating, and washing up had to be done in the same building, where the men sat and slept, a rule of order had to prevail. It was the cook who imposed the rule of "no talking at meals".

Mr. Pigeon started his training as "cookee", or cook's assistant, as a boy of sixteen. That was in the 1880's when the square timber trade was in full swing "up the Kippaway" north of Mattawa. Later, as a "McLachlin man" he cooked in many of the camps established by that firm on their limits in the Park district. He was, for a number of years, at the White Trout Depot as well as other places on the upper "Peetawaway", as he and many other old-timers call the lumberman's paradise. When we talked about the old days, Mr.

Pigeon's conversation was mostly about the food supplies, and the methods of cooking in the camps, but he did have many other stories of the time when the great square timber rafts floated down the Ottawa to the seacoast. One of the heroic figures in the annals of those days, was the cook who continued working in his cookhouse on a timber crib, as the whole affair went sliding down one of the Ottawa chutes.

All the supplies for the bush camps in the Park area had to be toted in by wagon or sleigh from the Ottawa Valley. The old companies, with headquarters along the Ottawa River, had to solve the problem of how to get equipment and staple foods into their limits at the lowest possible cost. It is really no wonder that the cooks found only very limited equipment at their disposal when they came to cook on the camboose fireplaces in the backwoods shanties. They were provided with two kinds of iron kettles — a tea kettle, which was suspended from an iron crane, or *cramière;* and a bake kettle, with a tight-fitting lid that was set in the sand along the edge of the fire. A sturdy knife, kept sharpened to a razor's edge, a few ladles, an iron fork and a shovel fashioned by the camp's blacksmith, usually completed this equipment.

As for the men, their eating utensils were also of the simplest type. Each man was provided with a small tin bowl, a "shanty-mug" from which he drank his soup or his tea, and a tin plate. From home he brought with him a knife of his own, and with this he carved out a wooden spoon for himself. If he lost this knife, he could buy another from the clerk who was in charge of the "Van". When he went to bed in the "muzzle-loading" bunks that lined the walls of the shanty, he stuck his knife in a niche of the wall at his head. At meal times each man brought out his own plate and his "shanty mug", and helped himself to the food he wanted from the great kettles along the edge of the fire.

When Mr. Pigeon first began to cook in the shanties, the food supplied by the companies was of the roughest sort. There was absolutely no variety in the menu. Only the staples were hauled in over the bush trails: beans, salt pork, flour and blackstrap molasses. From these ingredients the three meals of the day were made. Breakfast was eaten at about five o'clock so that the men who had to tramp out to the bush could begin work at seven o'clock. This meal consisted of beans, fried salt pork, known as "grillades", bread, and strong tea. The mid-day meal was eaten in the bush at eleven o'clock. For it, each man had brought the ingredients with him in the morning. To quote Jim Campbell, now foreman on the Park highway, who has vivid memories of these meals in the bush, "You dropped the meat, cold salt pork, into a long linen bag, tied it with a string in the centre, and then put a loaf of bread in the top half. In the other hand you took a pail containing blackstrap, and away you went. At the dinner time you made tea, *and by God, it was tea!* When you ate your meal you gouged a large hole into the bread and poured the blackstrap into it, unless the weather was too cold, and then you cut out a hunk of blackstrap and put it into the hole. Then you took your fat salt pork in one hand, and your bread and molasses in the other, and ate them bit about." In the evening when the men came back to camp after a long day's work in the bush, the six o'clock supper was the same as the breakfast menu.

When there was a depot farm run in connection with the camp, it was sometimes possible to obtain a limited supply of fresh vegetables. Even then, there was not much variety in the meals because, since it was hard work to clear the land and to farm on these bush clearings, the depot farmer usually limited his crops to potatoes for the camp, and oats for the horses. In this way, the cost of the long haul of bulky supplies from the outside world could be cut down. However, even in the camps where it was possible to obtain these slight additions, Jim Campbell's account of the standard diet held true. According to him — "You never seen a cake, you never seen a cookie, you never seen a pie" — in those early days. In spite of these limitations, though, he was emphatic in his statement that there is nothing nowadays that can compare with beans baked in the sand for a long period of time, or with bread cooked in the same manner in the great iron "bakkittles".

Many are the stories told about "Chicago rattlesnake", as the salt pork was affectionately called by the shantymen, whose mainstay it was. According to these old-timers, the pigs that were used for the product were very old — from five to seven years — and consequently tough. In fact, the "gristle" on the hunks that were carried out to the woods was so hard to cut that it resembled shoe leather, rather than a form of food. The story is told of one man who carried the same piece out to the bush in his lunch bag for a whole season, without being able to make any impression on it. Finally, when he gave up struggling with it, he turned it over to the blacksmith who found a good use for it by making it into harness for the camp horses.

It is interesting to trace through the changes in lumber-camp fare, to our own time, and to see how the meat courses particularly have altered because of improvements in transportation facilities. The reason why salt pork was formerly the only kind of meat in the camps was that it was shipped in barrels, and could be hauled in during the previous spring while the winter roads were still good. There it could be stored through the summer months so that when the busy season came after the first autumn snowfall, the meat supply would already be on hand. About forty-five years ago the first change in camp fare came with the introduction of corned beef, which was also packed in barrels. Then some firms found it possible to ship live cattle in on the nearest railway, and to drive them along the bush roads to the camps. This was done in the Park in the early 1890's, when the Gilmour Company drove cattle north from Minden and then slaughtered them at the end of the Dorset Road at Tea Lake. Nowadays, whole quarters of beef are shipped into the bush, and the men are served the choicest cuts in the camp dining rooms.

Mr. Pigeon remembers how a similar change came about in the baking of the cakes, cookies and pies, which are now made in large quantities in the camps, but which Jim Campbell says were entirely lacking in the early camboose shanties. First came the discovery that the camboose fire could be used for baking pies and cakes by setting up a sheet of tin to act as a reflector oven. In Mr. Pigeon's own camp, when the men asked him if he could bake them some buns or pies, he pointed out that his standard supplies did not include the essential baking powder. The men replied that that was a small matter, and took up a silver collection amongst themselves for the purchase of five cans of the "Cook's Friend". After that, the Sunday meat dish, called "sea pie", was augmented by buns sweetened with blackstrap. When one of the walking bosses visited the camp he complained about this extravagant use of syrup. However, the will of the men prevailed and in after years baking powder was added to the list of regulation stores. Further changes came with the introduction of dried apples, pails of minced raisins and other commodities that could be used to form the filling for pies in the camps. Nowadays, pie forms a standard part of at least two meals a day in most lumber camps, but all these varieties of food have been introduced since the early days of shantying in the Park.

Although there was very little time for anything but work in the old camps, the week-end break brought a slight change in the usual routine. On week nights, after supper, the men would sit around for an hour or so, playing cards, fashioning axe handles out of ironwood, or sharpening the blades of their axes, but soon after the evening's pipe they would roll into their bunks, and shortly after eight o'clock everyone was in bed and asleep. However, on Saturday night, everything was different. There was always someone in the group who could produce a mouth organ, an accordion, or even a fiddle, and then would come a great "rattling of the bones". Mr. Pigeon talked about these "step dances" with great delight. There were no women in the camp, but that didn't dampen anyone's spirits. Half the group would turn themselves into female partners by pulling their shirt tales out over their trousers, and everyone would cavort with great glee. In the ordinary shanty there was room for two squares at a time, and everyone else would sit around on the benches or lounge on the bunks until that group was exhausted. Then it would be their turn — and so the dance went on until twelve o'clock brought in the Sabbath, and everyone turned in for the night.

On Sunday morning, breakfast was a little later than usual, and the day was given over to resting, writing the occasional letter home, and cleaning up. The business of washing clothes was a solemn rite, undertaken in turns and at lengthy intervals. Each man, when he came into the camp in the fall, brought his winter supply of clothing and his own bedding with him. The former consisted of a supply of extra woollen socks and some heavy outdoor clothing; the latter of a couple of quilts. Usually a supplementary supply of a pair of blankets was available at the camp. When you went to bed you simply took off your cowhide mocassins and covered yourself up. From the "Van" you could purchase mitts and socks if necessary, as well as tobacco and matches, but because your storage space was limited to the niche in the logs at the head of your bunk, or the space on the floor underneath it, there were no extras in the camboose camp.

Wash day, however, was a memorable occasion. Pork barrels, cut in half, made excellent wooden tubs. Snow could be melted over the open fire. There was room on lines around the fireplace for a limited number of socks, but the larger garments were hung outside where they would immediately be frozen stiff. By the next week, however, the wind would have blown the moisture out and they would be ready to put on again.

Twice during the winter months there came visitors from the

outside world to bring in the news, and to break the monotony of this existence. One of these visitors was the local priest or preacher; the other was the jewellery pedlar. These visitors were welcomed into the camps, and shared the same fare as the men themselves. In this connection, there is one tradition of the lumber camps that continues down to our own time. No visitor ever dropped into a camp who was not welcome to stay for a meal — and there was no charge for this hospitality. However, no visitor who knew anything about the etiquette of the camps, would stay for a longer period than one day. The wayfarer was welcome to the food that was available, but he would not cause his host to run short of supplies when these same supplies were so hard to obtain.

The visiting clergyman was usually in camp when the men returned after a day's work in the woods. No one could tell in advance when he would arrive — he didn't know himself, because that depended on the weather and the travelling conditions. He would have to drive from camp to camp all through the district, and there was no way of letting people know of his visit in advance. However, some time after Christmas he would pay his pastoral call. Then the men would be awakened an hour or a half hour earlier on the following morning. A service, attended by Catholic and Protestant alike, would be held at that time so that the work in the bush could begin at seven o'clock as usual.

Some of these travelling ministers must have been exceedingly hardy men. Stories told about Rev. P. S. Dowdall, who was the first parish priest at Whitney, confirm this fact. Even before the Booth Railway line went through the south part of the Park, there were priests who came into that district from Maynooth, and from settlements along the Opeongo Line, but information about their comings and going is difficult to obtain. Father Dowdall's parish, however, extended from Whitney right across to Dorset, and he visited all the camps in that area from 1896 on. From Father Hunt, who was Father Dowdall's successor and his close friend, comes the story of how this large parish was established. Before that time there were only mission "stations" in the district, but when the St. Anthony Lumber Company's mill was built, the Bishop decided that there should be a resident priest at that place. Father Dowdall applied to E. C. Whitney, the owner of the mill, for a grant of money, and for land for the church building and the cemetery. Father Dowdall had some trouble persuading Mr. Whitney to grant this request, but finally one evening he agreed to help in the construction of the church. Then he wanted to know how far this new parish was to extend. The story has it that Father Dowdall replied, "As far as I can walk to-morrow". The next day he set out from the village at about two o'clock in the morning. All that day he kept walking westwards so that by the end of the day he had covered fifty-eight miles. The next morning he continued on into Dorset, where he offered Mass. According to tradition, that is the reason why the whole of the south part of the Park was set aside as part of the Whitney parish. Sceptics may doubt the actual truth of this tale, but it well illustrates the sort of work that was undertaken in the early days by these hardy preachers of the gospel.

The other visitor to the camps from the outside world was the jewellery pedlar who brought his store of watches, rings, and ornaments, right into the bush. Ever since their first arrival in the fall, the men had been talking about what they planned to purchase from the pedlar when he made his annual call, and great was their excitement when they returned at the end of their day's work to find him installed in the camp with his wares. Everyone examined what he had to offer and made the purchase of the objects that took their fancy. Many diamond engagement rings, expensive watches, and other pieces of jewellery found their way into back country communities in this way. In fact, it was frequently the case that, when a man was paid off at the end of the drive and had spent a few days in town celebrating with his pals, there was very little else besides these souvenirs to take back home with him in the spring.

These shantymen, then, were the people who knew every inch of the Algonquin Park region in the early days. In the fall of the year they would trek in along the bush roads to the spot where the camp was to operate for the winter, and in the spring before the break-up, they would drive their teams back along the same way, or else go with the logs down the tributary rivers flowing eastwards to the Ottawa and the markets of the outside world. Men from all up and down the Ottawa Valley, yes, and from farther afield than that, too, came up into the camps in the Park. One of the favourite stories told about the McLachlin firm illustrates this fact. One of the members of the family was once travelling along the Gaspé coast in lower Quebec. There he saw, hanging on a fisherman's family washline, a dress made of two pieces of cotton flour bags. The front of the garment was decorated with great red initials "McL". It had come out of one of the McLachlin camps on the upper Ottawa River.

In the settlements in the Ottawa Valley itself there is, even today, scarcely a family whose father or cousins have not at one time or another worked in camps in the Park. The older people pass on to their sons stories about the time when they first "went to shanty" and tales of the wondrous deeds that were performed in the far off days in the past. These tales are of how this one was so nimble at running the logs that he could "cross a river on match sticks"; and how that one could tote a pack consisting of a barrel of pork, a bag of flour and a keg of molasses, over long distances. Even Paul Bunyan visited the Park in these early times, but this was a French-Canadian Paul Bunyan, and he was carrying on his back a great bag of dried peas. At the end of a portage he fell, and the whole load tumbled into the lake. He was furious with himself for his own clumsiness, for of course the peas could not be salvaged from the water. However, he was resolved not to be done out of his pea-soup. Consequently, he set fire to the forest along the edges of the lake, and when the fire had died down he found that the lake was bubbling and boiling in the form of the delicious soup that was his national dish. For once in his life he had enough pea-soup for supper.

From down along the Opeongo Line come other tales about the men who travelled by that route into the camps in the Park. At frequent intervals all along the way were the "stopping places" where the thirsty shantymen could "wet their whistle". By the time many of them reached the Booth Farm at Kitty Lake they had to "stay put" for several days until they could sober up. Old-timers say that the great stone heaps along the edges of the clearing at that place, were made by men who were put to work at this task at a time when it would have been suicide to allow them to swing an axe. After that respite they were taken on into the camps, and their drinking days were over until the next spring.

For the men who took the square timber out of the Park, as well as for those who later drove saw-logs down the tributary rivers, the trip to the Ottawa was a hazardous undertaking. Still as one travels along the watercourses in the north part of the Park, one is made aware of the dangers of the river drive. With the break-up of the ice in May the swollen streams would start to rampage, and then would begin the long trip downstream. For many weeks the men who were following the drive would camp out along the shore wherever they happened to find themselves at dark. The rate of their journeying depended on the speed of the water current — on the rivers when the dams were opened, the logs would swirl along at terrific speed, but on the lakes the movement was a long, slow business. There the individual logs would have to be fastened into booms in order to be towed across by primitive "alligators". A raft, such as the one still to be seen on the beach at Radiant Station, served instead of a modern tug for this purpose. A team of horses was hitched to a windlass in the centre of the raft. These horses walked round and round in order to wind up the rope that gradually hauled the raft to the spot where the anchor had previously been dropped. This stage of the journey was a tedious one, but it gave a little respite to the riverman's hectic life.

There were many of these river drivers who never did return to their homes along the Ottawa, and in places along the Petawawa the traveller can still see the wooden crosses which mark the places where men were buried as a result of river accidents. At the end of the first portage upstream from Cedar Lake, there is one such grave. The upright piece of the cross has recently been replaced by some thoughtful passer-by, but the cross-piece bears the carving of the riverman's comrade who cut it when the accident took place. It bears the lettering, "A. Corbeil 9 Juin 1888". Like a well-known shanty song that tells the story of young Monroe, who never did return to his sweetheart, Miss Clara Dennison, this French-Canadian shantyman lies buried by the shores of the river where he met his death.

Today the camboose camp lies in ruins, and the old-time shantymen are old — many of them gone over the last height of land. But the Park is filled with these reminders of their hey-day.

On the portage between Porcupine and Ragged Lakes still stand some sections of the old Porcupine Chute, scene of the kind of tragic accident that illustrates the hardy, sometimes reckless, humour of the early lumberjacks.

About the year 1900, the lumber firm of J. D. Shier of Bracebridge was cutting in the Ragged Lake section of the Park. Their operations extended down into Porcupine Lake, just outside the southern boundaries, but all their logs came through the Park on their way to the Muskoka mill, by way of the Oxtongue River. All along this route the company's employees had constructed a great series of slides and dams, some of which have been maintained or rebuilt until the present time. The dam now standing at the outlet of Ragged Lake is built on the original Shier site, but all signs of some of their other improvements have been lost altogether. Only if you search with special care, will you see the remnants of the enormous timber chute that formerly carried the logs down the long incline between Porcupine and Ragged Lakes.

Jim Campbell is one of the few men who remember the time when this Porcupine Chute was built, and who recalls the disastrous occasion when logs first dashed down it to the lower level. Jim Campbell was a foreman for Shier's, and was working at a nearby camp when the chute was under construction. He and the man in charge of this undertaking had had an argument about the best location for the slide and about the proper grading of the curves. Said Jim, "It ought to be built like a railroad, banked on the turns," but Mr. Piper, the boss, did not agree with this theory. Jim was convinced, even before the trough was tried out, that the logs would break through the sides when they were hurled downwards by the great force of the water.

When the project was finally completed, it was regarded as quite an engineering feat. On Porcupine Lake a dam had been built to control the flow of the water, and the chute itself was nineteen hundred and fourteen feet long. Together they had cost in the neighbourhood of $5,200.00 to build. Naturally the owners, as well as the men, were very anxious to test out the new slide.

One day soon after its completion, J. D. Shier himself paid a visit to the camp. He decided that it would be well to try out the system while he was there, and he gave instructions for the test to be made. After dinner, Jackson, the carpenter, who had been in charge of the building, and the eight men who were detailed to look after the slide, reported that they were ready for the trial. It was all arranged. The key log in the dam above would be released so that a supply of water could flow through the trough, and then, when it was full, a series of logs would be fed into the slide at the top to be carried down to the next lake by the flow of the water.

When all the preparations had been made at the top, the men who were to occupy key positions along the side, started down the pathway to take their places. However, two of them, Louis the flag man, and another by the name of Sam, conceived the idea of running down on the surface of the slide itself. The man at the top could not see what they were doing, and he opened the dam to start the stream of water. At first it came very slowly, and Sam wisely climbed out over the edge. Louis, instead, thought it would be rather amusing to be pushed down as though he were taking a sleigh ride, so he sat down and allowed the water to carry him along.

The men whom he passed at first, laughed and called out, "Are you having a wash?", but very soon they stopped laughing, and ran to the side of the trough to see if they could haul him out. They could hear the main flow of water descending in a gush, and they realized that its force would rush him irresistibly into the pothole at the bottom.

All their efforts, however, were of no avail — they were not able to grab him out in time. He was swept along at great speed and disappeared into the boil below. For some time they waited, but there was nothing they could do — he didn't come up again. Two of them had to make their way to the railroad, where they travelled by jigger along the line to Headquarters in order to get a certificate from Mr. Bartlett to get the body out.

When the first logs finally came down they shot through the outside curves of the trough. Jim Campbell had been right, and whole sections had to be rebuilt, banked at the proper angle.

In spite of this inauspicious beginning, all the logs driven from the area south of Ragged Lake came down this chute on their way to Muskoka River mills. It was not until 1912 that the old companies stopped cutting in this region, and the Porcupine Chute, like the camboose shanties, fell into neglect.

The time will come when only a few huge rotting stumps, with the unmistakeable mark of the axe in the moss-grown wood, will show that once the Algonquin forests rang through the short winter days, with the shouts of the shantymen, and the bite of their axes into the stout Algonquin pines.

CHAPTER 4

IT WAS THE FIRM CONVICTION of Government and people alike in the 1850's, that once the forest was cleared of its timber, a large percentage of the area where the Park now stands would be available as farming land for prospective homesteaders. Consequently, lumbering was looked upon only as forerunner of the more important and permanent industry of agriculture.

For a time it looked as if this development would follow. Settlers in the southeast established "depot farms", and managed nicely growing potatoes and oats for the lumber camps, sometimes adding to their income by winter cutting. But the Haliburton farmers, lacking any local markets, did not fare so well. Only by winter trapping were they able to carry on.

The Government, however, went ahead with its ambitious plans. Yonge Street, already an established road to the north, was to be extended north of Lake Couchiching; the road to Bobcaygeon was to parallel it through the heart of the Ottawa-Huron Tract; and the Opeongo Line was to pass from Renfrew County clear through to the mouth of the Magnetawan River on Georgian Bay.

The Yonge Street extension, known as the Muskoka Road, brought travellers no closer to the Park area than Lake of Bays. But the other two roads promised to pass through the very heart of the region.

Neither achieved its goal.

The Opeongo Line stopped short at Bark Lake, between Barry's Bay and the present borders of the Park. Another primitive highway, called the Peterson Road, furnished the only land passage from the Ottawa Valley over to the Muskoka Lakes, and it was rough to say the least. According to Mrs. E. W. Lockman of Dorset, who came into the district as a school teacher in 1888, the Bobcaygeon Road never even crossed the Oxtongue River where it had originally been surveyed. Instead, it was diverted in a northwesterly direction around the shores of the Lake of Bays, in order to link up with the Muskoka Road near Huntsville. The modern highway still follows this early road, named in the old Colonization Road Reports the Muskoka-Bobcaygeon Road.

All four of these were of prime importance to the families who moved into the Park borderlands during the thirty years prior to the Park's establishment. Many of the men who work in the Park today as rangers, guides, or lumbermen, are descended from these families.

Government reports of this period show a steady exodus of homesteaders from northern Haliburton. Those who remained turned to trapping for a living, making long trips up into the rich fur-bearing region of the Algonquin height of land, where the few Indian trappers were soon discouraged from competing. In the 1870's the railway pushed through to Haliburton village; and twice a year, on the fifth of November and the twenty-fourth of May, dealers arrived for the Haliburton fur auction, which attracted trappers from far and wide.

By this time at least five of the families who were to figure so largely in the later history of the Park had taken up land in the Haliburton district. Most of these were from old Ontario, and had accepted the Government's offer of free homesteads in the newly opened regions. In this way, three adults of the Sawyers family were able to take adjoining lots, which they still hold, at Maple Lake. The Sawyers had previously lived in the Peterborough district where they, along with other Irish families, had cleared farms for themselves. Now they were sufficiently enterprising to pioneer again. When others moved out, and they discovered the impossibility of making their farms pay, they took to trapping.

Of these it is known that James Sawyers definitely trapped in the Park region. Four other original trappers, and the areas their traplines covered, are still known. Jack Archer, who lived at Dorset, and later at Boshkung Lake — where his son Tom still lives — trapped around Dividing Lake and the Bonnechere Lakes. His main camp was on the old clearing at Porcupine Lake. Joseph Mossington, also from Dorset, trapped on the north side of the Oxtongue River. His son Archie's lines, today run southeast of the Park in the Crown Lake country; which he reaches by way of the Bobcaygeon Road and Smoke Lake, going out through Kimball and Hollow Lakes, now known as Kawagama Lake. James Sawyers and Isaac Boyce (also spelled Bice), each with his sons, moved in from Maple Lake. Jim worked up beyond Canoe Lake to Doe Lake and the Otterslides. In 1895 he was taken on as a Park ranger, and remained in that post for twenty-six years. His sons, Long Bill and Hank, kept the Maple Lake farm, and have since been working as expert guides in the Redstone-Kennesis district south of the Park, where both have built widely known deer lodges. Isaac Boyce had three sons, William, Wes and Fred, all of whom worked with him in the Misty Lake-Pine River country. Wes is still on the Maple Lake farm, but Fred moved to Kearney, from which he traps today, in a zoned area south of the Park. His son Ralph, and his grandson, still help with the trapping in the winter, but guide in the Park in summer. All we know of the fourth original is that his name was Durham Radnor, and he trapped up through Cache Lake.

The sons of these originals are now themselves reaching their seventies, and a chat with any one of them reveals how from childhood the whole countryside was an open book. All tell much the same story of the early trapper's routine.

Among the trappers themselves, there was a friendly arrangement about the area each man could call his own private trapping preserve. Thus, though he might need to travel through another's territory to reach his own, each trapper could return year after year to his own trapping grounds, and find his trapping gear undisturbed where he had cached it at the end of the previous season. Before the Park was set up in 1893, the whole district had been divided up in this way amongst the families in the Lake of Bays and Haliburton regions. White trappers had taken over the Indian hunting grounds, and the area yielded a rich harvest annually.

Early in the fall they would go north to their traplines; and be out again before the freeze-up, for the Haliburton fur sales. The men from Dorset—Mossington and Archer regularly, and sometimes Tom Salmon and Sam Vanclief as well — would come down through St. Nora and Kushog Lakes by canoe; while the Maple Lake families usually toted their pelts on their backs, along the section of the Peterson Road that led to Haliburton Village. There, all of them gathered to sell their furs, and spend the proceeds on necessities for the coming winter.

In the main, Archie Mossington and Hank Sawyers agree on the way these sales were conducted, although they, as youngsters, never had a chance to attend one — that was the special privilege of the father of the family. There would be eight or ten buyers in town by the time the trappers had arrived, and the bidding was conducted somewhat after the fashion of a fur auction, except that the bidding was a secret affair. Each buyer would examine the furs in the presence of the owner, and then write on a piece of paper the sum he would give for the lot. In this way no buyer could know what the other was offering, and was forced to arrive at his price independently. When the trapper looked over his offers, he turned over his pack to the highest bidder. Old-timers are sure that they got a much fairer price for their furs by this system than they do today.

Figures on a season's take are interesting, although money values have changed so much that it is difficult to compare them with prices today. Tommy Archer remembers one season when he and his father, working together, took out eighty beaver, forty mink, forty marten, and ten fisher pelts. One fisher skin sold then for five dollars, a beaver for three, and mink and marten at a dollar each: so the season's catch totalled $370.00. This might not amount to much these days, but then, in a country where there was no rent to pay and one could almost live off the land, it was a tidy sum.

Naturally, with all this ready money in his pocket, a man would want to celebrate in town a day or so, especially when his cronies were on hand with stories to swap of exploits up in the back country. But, in a few days he would be off for home once more, carrying with him the supplies the family would need for the coming season: shoes, tea, sugar, and other staples that were not produced on his own clearing.

During the early winter the men would remain at home, but in January, when the fur was at its best, and the winter at its coldest, they would set off again for their traplines. Moccasins, toboggans and snowshoes, carried them and their supplies through the silent, snow-laden winter forests. Sometimes they could take shelter at a friendly trapper's cabin for the night; but often they slept wherever night overtook them. On such nights they would scoop away all the surface snow from the site of their tent, and fireplace. Otherwise the fire would melt its way down out of sight. Often for shovelling away the snow they brought along a homemade cedar shovel. This, and the broad end of a snowshoe, made short work of the task.

Wes Boyce has vivid memories of such a trip into the Park area, when he and his brother Will went with their father for their first winter in the woods. They had been up in the Misty Lake district by way of McIntosh's in the fall, for the short five-week season, but they were home in time for the November fur sale. It was March before the three of them were on their way again. If the first trip had been exciting, this second was to be even more so. Wes was then a boy of fourteen, and his brother was two years older, but the intervening sixty-two years have not dimmed the memory of his excitement then. They had looked forward to setting their first trap line in the Misty Lake country ever since they could remember, and now they were actually on their way.

Their father, Isaac, believed in giving the boys a chance to work independently, and he set them up in their own camp with their own trap line. They went off in one direction and he in another; it was only on Sundays that the three got together to exchange information about the number of animals each had taken, and the methods that had worked best. When Monday morning came the two boys would go on with their work, he with his, until the spring season of 1882 had passed, and it was time to go home.

Although they had come out on snowshoes, they planned to return by canoe. This time they could travel light. Even coming in they had not been too heavily loaded, having picked up supplies at the Barnet Company's depot, already established at Burnt Island Lake. On the other hand, the Boyces had the farthest to travel of any of the Haliburton trappers, since they were the farthest north in the Park district. Above them the country was trapped by men from the Mattawa.

Just before the break-up Isaac had built a birch bark canoe. Early in May the lake was clear of ice, and the party set forth. This time, because the water was high with spring floods, and the days were long, they were able to return home in a fraction of the time it had taken to trek north. One trip took them over each of the portages, and in three days they were home at the Maple Lake farm.

Jim Sawyers, their neighbour, was reputed to be one of the best bushmen ever to work as a Park ranger. He knew every inch of the Otterslides area, and in his later years, when he was stationed at the rangers' cabin on Manitou Lake, he could be seen almost any day busy making a bark canoe. His son Hank remembers that once when he helped his father build such a canoe in the Park, it took the two of them only two days to finish the job.

Jim Sawyers' other son, Long Ben, is well known as a trapper and lumberman in the Haliburton district, and as a guide in the Park; and now, although he is over seventy, he is a difficult man to find at home. In summer he is busy with tourists; in the fall he arranges hunting trips for American deer hunters, and in the winter he is in charge of a lumber camp back in his own Redstone district. Long Ben's memory of the Park must often go back to the time he trapped there with his father. His brother Hank tells several stories of trips which they took in the old days, before the Park.

Once he and his brother were paddling through Lake Opeongo on their way home, with a large load of beaver skins. They had been out for some time, and they were carrying just about all their canoe would take without shipping water when, just as they reached the Narrows, they spied a beaver swimming quite close at hand. It seemed too good a chance to miss, even though they had a full load and were in a hurry. While they were wondering whether to stop, the beaver suddenly made up their minds for them. Desperately the frightened creature swung around and attacked the canoe. One of the brothers slugged him on the head with his paddle, while the other, dexterously avoiding the wicked front teeth, grabbed him by the hind legs. It was the work of a minute, once they had got him ashore and finished him off, to skin and scrape the hide, and get on their way again, with one more pelt to their hoard.

While the Haliburton settlers were either leaving the country or turning to furs for a livelihood, a different development was taking place along the famed Opeongo Line. Here, along with the advance of the great lumbering outfits, a dozen small communities were growing together into a district conscious of its own character and achievements, even to the point of creating a ballad, sung by the youngsters, with variations, to this day:

> Take me back to Renfrew Valley
>   Where the Bonnechere winds it way
> Through the perfumed fields of clover
>   And the scent of new-mown hay;
> Where the foothills frame old shadows
>   On the Opeongo trail;
> Where the people are good farmers
>   And their work shall never fail.
>
> Killaloe to Letter Kenney,
>   Barry's Bay to Camel Chute;
> Golden Lake to Mount St. Patrick,
>   Combermere to old Maynooth;
> Petawawa to the Bogie,
>   Eganville to old Smith's Creek;
> You will find exiles returning
>   To revisit every week.

Into the country back of Renfrew, by way of the Opeongo Line, a great number of Irish newcomers poured when the road was opened up. One can detect their origin by the names they gave their villages, including the famous shrine of Mount St. Patrick, whose sacred well draws pilgrims from afar to this day. At first, settlement by way of this road developed quickly; by 1857 there were 166 settlers who had cleared some 1,092 acres in all; but soon after that there followed a period of stagnation. The coming of the big lumber companies changed conditions again. When J. R. Booth started his men working on the upper Madawaska, the Opeongo Line became a busy thoroughfare. All along the way were "stopping places" where the teamster could rest his horses, and refresh his own weary body with a stimulating drink. Then prosperity came to the people of the district. Whatever they could produce was easy to market, and if they didn't want to farm they could work farther up the line on timber limits, which are now inside the Park boundaries.

The old village of Killaloe in those days was a thriving community. It may still be seen, a mile and a half down the road to Brudenell, from the present village. There, by the side of Brennan Creek, a grist mill and school still function. But the store has long been closed, and the woollen mill is gone. Old Killaloe is almost deserted. But for the fact that some of the Park rangers still live there, where their children can go to the same old school, it would probably have disappeared. Harry Stack's comings and goings are typical of the Killaloe resident today: the fire season as a ranger at Brent, a few weeks of leisure at home in Killaloe, then a job in a lumber camp near South River until May comes round again.

By the 1880's, the Government had begun to see the Ottawa-Huron tract for what it was: a wilderness of trees and lakes with only a few pockets of fertile soil which could not be farmed profitably unless there were a permanent industry nearby to provide a market for their produce; a land where only the lumberman and trapper could make a seasonal living. Gradually the dream of populating the area faded, and one by one, as their usefulness disappeared, the new roads were allowed to grow over. Many were still used by the lumber companies, but when the railways finally penetrated the area, even these fell into desuetude. Nowadays, in the region bordering the Park, one still comes upon sections of the original roads that have become modern highways; but in general the roads themselves exist only in the memories of the old-timers, and in the stories they tell about the first settlement of the district.

Black Bear.

YOUNG SCREECH OWLS.

CHAPTER 5

Two Families, the Dennisons and Dufonds, established themselves in the Park area even before the lumber men came. These two families, with the McIntyres, McGueys and Garvies, have given rise to many tales that circulate in the Park to this day, and must be included in the story of its development. They reflect the spirit of the times; they show the sturdy courage of these hardy individualists; and they provide a vivid insight into the way the people of the area lived, in the days before the railroads penetrated into the region.

The reader must inevitably ask at this point, what became of the original Algonquins — the Indians who had hunted and fished through countless generations in the land, whose name the Park now bears? Unfortunately there is no clear-cut answer. During the days of the camboose camps, no doubt, the Indians found that game was scarce and trapping brought no returns. In the areas untouched or abandoned by the lumbermen, the pioneer white trappers from the south had established themselves. The Indians here, as elsewhere, had simply been crowded northward by the more aggressive, systematic, and better-equipped white pioneer from the south. Only in the north they continued to come into the region on occasional hunting trips.

There was, however, one notable exception.

Alexander Sherriff, the explorer responsible for the myth of Algonquin soil fertility, wrote in the account of his travels in the northern Cedar Lake section, that the area was the hunting territory of an Indian called "Map di Fong". Algonquin Indians told him that their favorite route to the Ottawa was by way of a river named after this man, the river marked on maps today as the "Amable du Fond". Peter Ranger, a Park ranger at Kiosk today, knew the Dufonds well.

When Ignace and Francis Dufond first settled in the Park area, they made a small clearing at the south end of Lake Kioshkoqui (Lake of the Gulls). The logs from the house that they built at that place were afterwards used for the first ranger cabin, established near Kiosk by Peter and Telesphore Ranger in 1912. By that time the Dufonds had moved to the next lake farther south, Manitou Lake, where they had cleared quite a bit of land, had built a substantial log house, and had set up a fairly large barn, as well as other outhouses.

The first lumber companies in this section of the Park were glad to buy whatever the Dufonds could produce on their farm. William Mackey, who cut square timber on limits in this area, and J. R. Booth, who afterwards took out saw logs, were both on friendly terms with the Dufond brothers. In this way the Dufonds grew so prosperous that they came to be regarded by Indians and white settlers alike throughout the Mattawa district, as persons of conse-quence. At one time, Peter Ranger says, they had a cash reserve of six hundred dollars in the bank, and, as he himself remarked, "I think I never heard of any other Indian with so much money."

"The Old Susanne," as Peter always calls the wife of Ignace Dufond, was a skilful worker and a thrifty housewife. When Peter knew her she was old — about eighty years of age. He describes her as being short and square in build, with a face like a man's and a slight beard. Susanne was a full-blooded Indian, and had learned the arts of her ancestors as a young girl. She could tan leather better than anyone else in the district — and make better mitts, and mocassins, too. Peter always depended on her for his own leather equipment, and she showed him how she prepared the skins for use. First, she would scrape the hides; then, when they had been smoked, she would work them until they were soft and pliable. Finally, when the pattern had been cut, she would sew up the article with strong thread made from the sinews along the deer's back.

Sometimes this same thread would be put to other use as well. If Peter found a button loose on his jacket when he stopped by at her cabin while making his rounds, she would sew it on again with her sinew thread, and then it would stay for good.

Susanne was an expert also at making maple sugar. In one season she could produce as much as three hundred pounds, a readily marketed crop, since what the Dufonds did not use themselves they could easily sell at nearby lumber camps or at the town of Mattawa. Some of her produce, however, she loved to give away as presents to anyone she particularly liked. When the Ranger children lived in the Park with their parents, Susanne used to make fancy moulds out of birch bark as containers for her gifts. The children were always delighted with these novelties.

Since Susanne was in the habit of smoking a pipe, Peter used to ask her to join him in a smoke whenever she called around to see him at the Ranger cabin. One day when she arrived Mrs. Ranger and the children were on hand. That time she refused to come indoors for her pipe, lest she should offend them. She and Peter adjourned to the wood-pile for their smoke.

When Peter called around at the Manitou farm he was always greeted warmly and invited to share the next meal. The Dufonds were clean as well as hospitable, and Peter was usually glad to accept their invitation. However, he recalled at least two occasions when he would have preferred not to, but was afraid of offending them: once, when they served a groundhog for the meat course — placed on the table roasted whole, head and all; the second time, when a gallon of pure alcohol had been brought in along the wagon trail from Mattawa. Peter had seen the "Old Susanne" before when she had had something to drink. Sometimes she became "mad like a bear." This time all the guests sat around in a circle and passed a dipper of the alcohol mixed with a little water around the ring. Each person took a drink before passing it on to the next.

But the best stories about the Dufonds centre around the young girl, Pinonique. Peter's eyes still twinkle when he speaks of her: "not bad looking at all, a good girl, with straight dark hair, and not pure Indian." Susanne was not her mother, but adopted her as a baby, and loved her as her own. When Peter knew the family, Pinonique was almost twenty years of age. Susanne was very jealous of the girl, and would allow no one to come near her. When the old lady went off to Mattawa to get her liquor, the girl would be left at home. Pinonique used to hide the knives after Susanne was gone, having good reason to fear that the old lady would be "mad like a bear" by the time she returned. At the same time "the old Susanne" was good to her adopted child. She used to bring back from these trips all sorts of pretty things, clothes and ornaments; and once she even bought a gramaphone, one of the very latest, that played wax rolls for records.

At last, of course, the inevitable happened. His name was Baptiste, he was young and good looking, and he came to work for the Dufonds one summer. Pinonique was cute — she didn't let the old lady know anything about her feelings. The summer over, Baptiste took the team to town one day. He never came back. Neither did Pinonique, who disappeared that night. When Susanne followed her tracks in the morning she read the story on the road. That blackguard, Baptiste, had gone only a short distance and then had turned back to wait for his sweetheart. When night came she had walked down the road to meet him — and they had gone off together.

This time "the old Susanne" was really "mad like a bear". She came to Peter Ranger at Kiosk in a frenzy of frustrated wrath. "What can I do?" she wailed when her anger had died in the knowledge of her loss. Peter did his best to console her. There was nothing she could do — the girl was of age, these things happened, sooner or later. He himself thought privately that it was all for the best. But the old lady was inconsolable.

All the pretty things that she had given Pinonique remained at Manitou Farm until the day aged Susanne herself left. As far as Peter could learn, Pinonique and her Baptiste settled down happily in the outside world, and — as the old nursery stories say — for all we know they are living there yet.

When Francis Dufond died—Ignace was already gone—Susanne was left alone on the farm and had a hard time of it. One of the relations from Mattawa came to run the farm, but finally Susanne gave up, sold her belongings, and moved away. A government pension kept her going for the remaining few years of her life. After she left, some of the buildings were torn down and rebuilt as ranger quarters, and even today there is still a considerable clearing to mark the old Dufond farm at the north end of Manitou Lake.

The best bear story ever to come out of the Park, and one that throws into harsh relief the hazards of pioneer life in wild country, is an intimate part of the history of the Dennison family.

Almost every old-time ranger or traveller in the Park has spent a night in a ranger's cabin known as "Sunnyside", built on the old Dennison clearing, and has heard the famous story of old Captain Dennison's encounter with the bear. Of the many versions, Jack Smith, the ranger now stationed at Lake of Two Rivers, tells one of the best.

According to Jack, old Grandfather Dennison was an Englishman by birth who had come to this country to take up land. He had settled first at Combermere, about ten miles south of Barry's Bay. But old Mr. Dennison had the pioneering spirit in its most adventurous form, and became much more interested in trapping than he had ever been in farming. For that reason, he decided to move his family farther north into the wilds, and set up the beginning of a farm at the Narrows on Opeongo Lake.

One day, when he was starting off on his rounds to examine his traps, he took his eight-year-old grandson with him in the canoe up through the North Arm of the lake. He had been up that way the week before, and had set a bear trap on the Green Lake portage. When the two of them reached the appointed spot they beached the canoe, and went up the portage to look at the trap. The old man led the way.

The particular trap that they were about to visit had been skilfully set. It was chained to the far side of a great log and baited with rotten meat. As they approached the log there was no sound at all, and the old man decided the trap had not been sprung. However, just to make sure he stuck his head over the log to take a look. With that, an enormous bear, whipped into fighting madness by the pain of the steel clamp, leaped at him, clawed him, and dragged him over the edge of the log. The old man screamed, but was powerless in the mighty grip of the great beast. He called out to the boy to go for help.

The little fellow rushed down to the canoe, and paddled the long eight miles back to the farm as fast as he could. When he got there he found his father had gone out on an overnight hunting trip, and there was no help to be had. Days later, when he and his father returned to the spot, they found evidence of a terrific struggle. All the old man's clothes but his boots had been ripped to shreds. Both he and the bear were dead. The son carried the body back to the clearing for burial, and there the grave may be seen today. A fence made of split rails sets it apart from the encroaching forest, and marks it as hallowed ground.

In one of the Park Newsletters information was published which was gathered from an interview with Mr. C. B. Dennison, a grandson of the old man:

"Capt. John Dennison, of English birth, was born at Penrith, England, in the year 1799. He was a literary man, possessing a high degree of education. He was of military mien, and landed in Montreal in 1825, and rather distinguished himself in the Lower Canada Rebellion of 1837.

After a lapse of a few years he had a son, John, and settled in Bytown (now Ottawa) in 1854. The Dennisons pushed on up the Ottawa River as far as Arnprior, then followed the tortuous Madawaska for many miles, settling at a spot that was known for many years as Dennison's Bridge, which is today the

charming village of Combermere, in the year 1869.
The Captain, charmed with the beauty of the virgin
forest, renewed the voyage with his two sons, John and
Henry, to the Great Opeongo Lake, where in the month
of June, 1881, Captain John Dennison at the age of 82,
met a tragic death."

From Mort Findlayson of Barry's Bay, another of the Captain's
grandchildren, has come some additional information about the
Dennison family, and the famous incident with the bear. Mort's
mother was Mary Dennison, a sister of John and Henry, and as a
young man Mort had frequently visited the Opeongo farm. For
many years he worked as a fire ranger on the Booth limits in the
Park.

Mort has it that Captain John Dennison obtained his commission
serving with the Beach River Volunteers in 1837. When he moved
to Combermere he kept a stopping place, but in the 1870's, when
his wife died, he decided to go farther inland to open up land at
a spot where the Opeongo Line would eventually strike. At the
Opeongo Narrows his two sons, Harry and Jack, decided to make
their clearings. Harry's was to the left of the Narrows as you pass
through them from the main body of the lake; Jack's to the right.

Mort says that when the family first came to the point on the
left, which they afterwards named "Sunnyside", they found a small
clearing already cut, and were told the Indians had used it for a
summer camp in the old days. Close by were the ruins of a log
cabin, said by Sherriff to be the remains of an old Hudson's Bay
Company trading post. The Indian camp site checks with the stories
of the Golden Lake Indians, but there are no records in the Hudson's
Bay Company archives of any such post. Probably the building had
been the headquarters of early white trappers who took their furs
out to "The Bay" posts in the Ottawa Valley.

When the Dennisons moved in their household belongings to
the Opeongo farm site, they came from Combermere by the river
route. This journey through the Egan Estate limits of the Booth
Company was, before the coming of the railroad, one of the best
known ways of getting in and out of the Park district from the
southeast. From Bark Lake the travellers went up the Madawaska
River, across to Victoria Lake, and then through a chain of lakes
to the Opeongo River. Mort remembers travelling this route when
he went in to the Dennison farm, and he recalls seeing an abandoned

log building at Crotch Lake that roused his curiosity. It was twenty feet square, and had been built long before timber cutting had begun in that region. His uncle, Harry Dennison, told him it had been built by hunters in the 1850's.

Mort has further details of his grandfather's tragic end. It was a very windy day when the old man set forth with his grandson, eight-year-old John Dennison. According to Mort's story, the old man had left his grandson at the boat, with instructions that if he wasn't back in two hours the lad was to go home. The child became frightened when the old Captain failed to show up, and went home for his father. That evening the father searched the shoreline, shouting as he went, but there was no answer, nor any sign of the missing man. In the morning he found the trap — the bear was still alive, but the old man was dead. They took the body back to the farm and buried it in the small fenced-in spot back of the barns. As far as Mort knows, this is the only grave in the plot; the little Dennison girl who died later was buried farther down towards the shore.

About the lumber companies in the Opeongo district when the Dennisons first moved in, Mort Findlayson has some scattered information. He thinks that Alex. Graham, from down Renfrew way, was the first man to cut square timber in these parts. At one time Annie Bay, at the eastern extremity of Lake Opeongo, was called Graham Bay after this man. This bay was renamed after Annie Dennison. The old winter road running through the woods from here to the farm may have been cut by Graham's men. Fraser and McCoshen were the names of two other Lake Opeongo operators who may have been cutting as early as the 1870's. Mort once saw McCoshen getting some of his square timber through the Narrows. His "cadge crib" was a raft worked by horses, and it took a long time to drag the heavy booms out through the East Arm to the flowing waters of the Opeongo River. From there Mort recalls it used to take two years for the trip to Quebec, although there is a record of the logs having gone down in a single season.

About 1882 the Dennisons decided to move, and by 1885, when the survey of Bower Township was completed, the Sunnyside clearing had been taken over by the Fraser Lumber Company, and was being operated as a depot farm.

Today the full extent of the old Dennison clearings is still visible from the air. On the ground, the passage of time and succession of different occupants have brought about great changes; but it is still possible to trace out the foundations of the first log buildings, and to visualize the general layout of the farm.

A faint trail, marked by ingrown blazes barely discernible now, still leads from the lake to the first clearing. In what was once a well-worked field, small evergreens are growing now, twelve feet high and more. Near the old farm site two magnificent birches catch the eye — planted to mark the grave of the little Dennison girl. Farther up, on a piece of rising ground, is the fenced-in grave of the old Captain.

Beyond lie the remains of the farm buildings, for which Mort helped to cut some of the timbers: a storehouse on the top of the hill, a milk-house down by the spring, the barn and stables, and a large woodshed. Of the house itself, very little is left — the logs have been carted away by lumbermen, rangers and campers — but one pauses to admire the magnificent view across Great Opeongo Lake that the old Captain must once have loved.

Although the Dennison family moved out of the district ten years before the Park was established, it would be a pity if their memory were not retained in some way at the Sunnyside farm clearing. Here was a family in the best of Canadian pioneering traditions. Daring to push ahead into the wilderness miles beyond any settled region, they chose their location, cleared their land, hewed logs for buildings, and constructed a comfortable and substantial home in the heart of the Algonquin forest. Algonquin Park may well be proud of the Dennisons.

Today the section of the Park to the extreme southeast, drained by the Bonnechere, is rarely travelled by canoe trip parties. However, in the old days it was one of the most frequently travelled sections of the Park. Year after year the Ottawa Valley lumber companies poured men into their limits up the Bonnechere.

From the 1850's on there had been a supply centre at Basin Depot, a stopping place about twenty miles above Round Lake at a point now well within the Park boundaries. This centre was used by all the old companies that cut in the region, by Barnet's, by McLachlin's, and by the companies that went into the north of the Park along a lumbering road leading into White Partridge Lake. For over fifty years the families at Basin Depot, at the stopping places later established at Sligo, and at "The Village" where the road turned north, were known to all the lumbermen who came into the Park country. "Dinney" McGuey and Paddy Garvie who lived at Basin Depot, William McIntyre, whose clearing was farther up the Bonnechere River, and the Widow McDonald who raised her family at Sligo near the present Park boundaries, were among the earliest Algonquin Park residents.

Of Dinney McGuey more will be heard when the story of the Park's establishment is told. Mike Garvie, now living at Golden Lake, has fond recollections of his father, Paddy Garvie, "the pioneer of the Bonnechere". For sixty-five years, till his death in 1916 at the age of eighty-five, Paddy worked on his farm at Basin Depot. Mike says that Paddy was first employed by John Egan, and later by Alex. Barnet, both of whom operated square timber companies in the district. Paddy ran the stopping place at "The Depot" as the old-timers called it, and sold whatever produce he could raise on his farm to the camps. Finally, when the square timber was gone, and the limits sold to the McLachlins for saw-logs, Paddy's allegiance was transferred to this firm.

When Mike Garvie was a boy his father's farm was a flourishing concern of some two hundred acres. On this homestead clearing there were about forty head of cattle and a number of sheep. In most matters the family was self-sufficient, but there were two commodities at least that had to be obtained from the nearest settlement at Eganville, some thirty miles away. From an old store ledger, kept by Daniel Lacey who ran the Eganville store, has come interesting data about Paddy's shopping habits in the very early days. The heading for one page reads: "Mr. Paddy Garvie, Little Bonnechere." Two items are marked down as follows:

Aug. 22 (1866) — To one pair calf boots for self......1/10/0
July 13 (1867) — To two gallons hard wine 18/0

Although the women and children could be clad in soft home-made or Indian-made mocassins, heavy shoes had to be purchased for the men working on the land or in the bush. The hard wine was likely for consumption at Paddy's stopping place.

Jack Wilson, the ranger at Park Headquarters, and other old-timers who have cut timber along the Bonnechere, have a host of stories about Paddy Garvie. There is one about the time when Paddy needed some new shingles for his house at Basin Depot. He was quite put out when he went to the McLachlin foreman to ask for the necessary supplies and was told that the shingles on hand would all be needed for the company's buildings. He would have to make his own with a drawknife and some chunks of "corky" white pine, the foreman told him, if he expected to have any shingles that year. Paddy went home grumbling. Wasn't he a "stiff" McLachlin man and shouldn't they look after their own employees? But Paddy was to have his revenge. Only a few days later the big dam above the Basin broke, the company's store yards were flooded, and all the shingles came floating down to Paddy's farm three miles below. Well, Paddy was not the man to waste time wondering who had sent him this magnificent present. When the McLachlin foreman came downstream looking for his lost property, the company's shingles were adorning Paddy's roof.

There are dozens of Paddy Garvie's stories, all illustrating his ready wit, his kindly shrewdness, his rugged common sense, and his rather naive way of doing business. Dr. Reeves at Eganville, who knew and liked Paddy and his family, used to visit him when he went up the Bonnechere on hunting trips. One time Paddy had an organ brought all the way to his stopping place at the Depot. When asked how he could afford to buy such an expensive article he protested, "All it cost me was a piece of paper." It was not that he was dishonest; he simply knew nothing of business methods, and trusted other people as he expected them to trust him. Many a man enjoyed a pint of whiskey "on the house" at Paddy's bar, and the walls of the old place were covered with the names of these passers-by.

Speaking of whiskey brings up a story which has nothing to do with Paddy Garvie, but illustrates how highly hard liquor was valued by the men in the camps. Today in the Park there are stringent regulations against the sale of intoxicants within its boundaries. The early lumber companies were just as strict in keeping liquor out of their camps. But they did not always succeed, and the story of how Whiskey Rapids got their name is almost a case in point,

In the late spring one year, a group of men on the tail end of a drive through the southwest corner of the Park, were camped for the week-end rest on the Oxtongue River below Tea Lake, now named Waskigomog Lake. They had been working for some time, and soon they would be on their way downstream with the last of the logs that were being floated down to the mill on the Muskoka Lakes. Since they felt that this called for a celebration, they had made arrangements with some of the railwaymen to bring in a keg of whiskey for a party on Saturday night. A keg, holding three gallons, cost three dollars and eighty-five cents, a sum the men had all chipped in to pay.

At first everything happened according to schedule. Two men

paddled up the river from the camp near the Three Sister Islands, close to the Park boundary. They portaged around a series of rapids, and then proceeeded on up through Tea and Canoe Lakes to the spot where the keg was to be dumped off the train. The train was on time, the keg was delivered, and the two men started off back to camp with the precious load in the bottom of the canoe.

Then the inevitable happened. One of the paddlers suggested to the other that the first drink was really their due. Hadn't they travelled all this way to pick it up? And besides, who would miss the odd drop from a whole barrel? His companion recognized the force of these arguments, so they pierced a hole under one of the hoops and drained off a little of the contents. It didn't take long. Soon they were on their way again, feeling much better.

However, when they reached the river itself it was getting dark. They had better hurry — after all the others couldn't start their Saturday night celebrations until the whiskey arrived. By now they were both feeling fine, the river was high from the spring thaw, and they were slipping along at a good speed. Suddenly the man in the bow realized they were approaching the rapids, and turned to warn his friend that it was time to land for the portage. "Oh letsh shoot them," replied the other, and in a moment they were in the white water.

It was too dark to see the right channel, even if they had been sober enough to pick it out. Into the river they went with their precious cargo. By the time the two men had dragged themselves out of the river the whiskey was gone. For hours they searched, before they gave up and returned to the camp, sober and empty-handed. Then the whole camp turned out for the search. Alas, the whiskey keg had disappeared forever, but to this day this treacherous stretch of the Oxtongue River has been known as "Whiskey Rapids".

To return to our friends of depot farm days, Dinney McGuey and Paddy Garvie were not the only Bonnechere settlers in the old times. Along the stretch of road used by the stage that drove in three days a week from Eganville to Basin Depot in the 1890's, lived the Widow McDonald and her family. Their home was at Sligo, now just within the Park boundaries. Mr. McDonald had been employed originally by the lumber companies, but when he died his wife stayed on at his small clearing, where she valiantly struggled to make a living and bring up a large family of small children. Sometimes the lumber companies would contribute a bag of flour or a barrel of salt pork to the family's larder, but for the most part times were very hard.

From Mrs. Harry Stack, one of the widow McDonald's children, has come the story of how this courageous woman carried on. She had a few cows of her own, and the family's sole income came from the butter that she was able to sell at the nearest village. One summer, after she had sold her whole season's supply, she found that she had only realized forty dollars. With this money she had to purchase all the provisions for the coming winter. It is little wonder that the McDonald children were all needed at home to gather wood and to help with the work. As for schooling, it was impossible to spare the children even for as long as it would take them to go as far as the Depot, where their neighbour Paddy Garvie had established a school for his own family. Only one or two of the McDonalds were ever able to continue at school long enough to learn how to read or write.

Up the river past Dinney's upper farm was the last stopping place on the Bonnechere River. There, about twenty miles above Basin Depot, William McIntyre had cleared a ten-acre patch of ground by the time the township survey was made in 1889. One of his sons, Jack McIntyre, was brought up in this Park homestead. Jack McIntyre is now Deputy-Chief Ranger in the north of the Park at Achray.

From several different sources comes word of another family that lived in the Park once. On Lake Clear, now Dickson Lake, the surveyors reported in 1888 that there was a clearing of fifteen acres and a log house. Here, on the west shore of the lake, there lived a man, his wife, and two little girls. No one seems to know today either their name, or how they came to live so far from other settlements. Mark Robinson says that when he first joined the Park staff in 1907, he used to hear from the other rangers about an English family living there. Bob Balfour and Steve Waters had both called at the place and reported that the sixteen-year-old daughter couldn't remember anything at all of the outside world, having spent almost all her life in the Park district. The rangers said that there was a piano in the house that had been hauled in along one of the lumber tote roads. The mother of the family died at the homestead and was buried there. Afterwards the family moved away and nothing further is known of them.

When Park visitors ask today whether anyone ever lived in the Park, there are few who can give them accurate information about this almost-forgotten chapter of Algonquin Park history. Actually, none of the land in the Park area was ever granted by the Crown for settlement purposes. The farm at Manitou Lake had been acquired originally through a mining patent, but all the other clearings in the Park were made by families who came into the country to work the land in conjunction with the lumber companies who were cutting in the district. Here and there were patches of fertile soil sufficient to supply some of the food and fodder in the camps. When the companies stopped cutting and the railways came, the depot farms became superfluous. After all, if the Dennisons could not make a go of it, no one could.

Now the locations of the old depot farms are marked only by a few small clearings, and by the remnants of the log dwellings which originally housed the Algonquin Park pioneers.

CHAPTER 6

TWO STORIES remain to be told before we come to the crisis in the larger story of the Park, the historic letter of Alexander Kirkwood to the Ontario Commissioner of Crown Lands. Both have their setting in the days when the lumberman was absorbed in the practical problem of getting his timber to the mills. How one man brought the mills to the timber is an important part of lumbering history; how another brought the timber to his mill, is one of the Park's most fantastic stories.

By the eighties, the days of square timber cutting were numbered. All along the Ottawa Valley sawmills had been established, and limits that had been regarded as cut over by the square timber men could now be developed profitably, in view of the shorter haul to the mills. Trees which had been passed by during previous operations as too small, unsound in parts, or inaccessible, were now prospective sawlogs. Improvements that would have been too costly for twenty-foot logs, could now be undertaken for the shorter fourteen-footers. Even the older companies who did not contemplate adopting the new methods, profited from the change. Mackey's limit on the Amable du Fond is said to have been worth $655,000 when it was bought by J. R. Booth. Barnet's limit in the White Trout, or as it is now called, the Big Trout district, which was sold to the McLachin's, was valued at $750,000. In both cases these later companies operated for many years on limits that had previously been cut over for square timber. Booth's logs were floated out of the Park to the mill at the Chaudiere Rapids just above Ottawa, while McLachlin's went out by way of the Petawawa route to Arnprior.

What was even more significant was the arrival of the railways. With the completion of the Canadian Pacific Railway between Ottawa and North Bay, the stations of Bissett, Deux Rivieres, and Mattawa had become favourite jumping-off places for companies operating along the Petawawa. To the west the Grand Trunk Railway reached Huntsville in 1885. Before long stations north of there, such as Emsdale and Sundridge, were starting points for tote roads into the Park. From the railway terminus at Minden to the south, teamsters drew supplies up the Bobcaygeon Road to camps on the

Oxtongue. Finally, in 1888, J. R. Booth and a group of Ottawa associates decided to build the Ottawa-Arnprior and Parry Sound Railway, to provide a short direct transportation route between Lake Huron and the Ottawa Valley.

John R. Booth was not the only lumber king to have substantial interests in the Algonquin region, but wherever Park old-timers gather to "swap" stories of the old days, "J.R." is the central, almost legendary figure. They delight particularly in telling how the great lumber king used to arrive in his camps at all sorts of odd times to see how the boys were doing. He had learned his business the hard way by working in the mills and camps; and to the end of his days he loved to pick up an axe or a cant hook and demonstrate that he was still one of the boys at heart. To many men who worked in the Booth camps in the Park the Old Man, wearing felt boots and a padded jacket, as unpretentious as any of his workmen, was a familiar and respected figure.

His son, Jackson Booth, who retains his connection with the firm, tells us how his father got his first limits in the Algonquin Park area. "J.R." was born in 1826 in the eastern townships of Quebec, where his parents had settled when they first came to Canada from Ireland. In the 1850's, when American lumbermen from the New England States first brought their novel techniques into the Ottawa Valley, young Booth moved north to work in one of their mills. Before long he had set up a shingle mill of his own at the Chaudiere Rapids, and had begun to acquire limits along the Ottawa and its tributaries. Just at this point, the great limits along the upper Madawaska River, known as the Egan Estate, and said to contain the finest stands of pine in the country, came up for sale at public auction. Characteristically, "J.R." took a shrewd gamble and outbid all competitors.

For a time the Opeongo Line sufficed as a means of supplying Booth's camps on the Egan Estate beyond Bark Lake. But Booth was a man who took the long view. The advantages of a railway were obvious. Already he had played a part in building a railway from Ottawa to join the Central Vermont Railway at Coteau, on the St. Lawrence River. It is altogether likely that the lumber king was looking beyond the needs of the lumber industry, and had visions of a great transportation system to be added to his empire.

Booth and his associates went ahead with their plans. Obstacles were brushed aside. When a legal conflict developed with the Canadian Pacific over the right of way through Wilno Pass, Booth secured the services of the famous Ottawa lawyer, Dalton McCarthy, and won. To this day, the C.P.R. line involved goes only as far as Eganville.

Through the years '94 to '96, construction gangs sweated summer and winter laying the grade and tracks. By September, 1894, the line had reached Madawaska Station. Before long it was within the Park itself, bringing with it E. C. Whitney, owner of the St. Anthony Lumber Company, to build a sawmill at Whitney. It was alleged that the new line was the cause of several fires; in fact, the following year two of Whitney's camps were burned out, giving point to the growing consciousness for the need of systematic fire protection.

In October, a year later, W. P. Hinton, the traffic manager, made a trip in to the end of steel at Cache Lake. In November, supplies for the new Park headquarters arrived there, including lumber from a mill at Eganville.

A Dr. A. S. Thompson looked after the health of the Whitney lumber camps at the time, and from May till October of 1896 was employed by the railroad construction firm of Ferguson and O'Neill, then working on the completion of the line. One of his most vivid memories of his stay in the Canoe Lake district has been preserved in his own words:

> "On one occasion, August, 1896, I got into camp in time for supper. After supper the foreman, Jack McLeod, an experienced rock-man, asked me to go with him to a rock cut 200 yards distant to have a chat while he fired two shots. As soon as he made the proposal something within me said, in tones of authority, 'Don't go. It's none of your business!' So I excused myself on plea of being tired. I knew something about rock drilling and the use of dynamite, but just why this warning voice came to me, I know not. There must be something in the belief of guardian angels.
>
> "We heard a shot, a deep rumbling noise indicative of large masses of rock being upheaved, and waited until dark for the second one, which did not come. I was just turning in when a man rushed into the camp, saying that an accident had occurred in the rock-cut. I ran along the crooked path between rocks and stumps to the cut, and groping in the

RANGER'S CABIN, ALGONQUIN PARK.

SUMMER SCENE, ALGONQUIN PARK.

dark I felt a man's hand, struck a match, found a
man lying on his back, arms extended over his head
with a huge rock lying on his legs and the power part
of his body. He was quite dead. On further search
we found the bodies of Jack McLeod and O'Brien,
blown thirty feet out of the cut, both dead. The
blast had ignited their clothes and their faces were
burned . . .

"A man living in the shanty nearby heard the noise,
investigated, and brought word to the camp of the
accident. The man I found lying with the rock on
top of him had been ordered to go home some time
before the accident occurred, but he delayed too long.
The accident cost the lives of three men and if I had
accepted McLeod's invitation, without doubt I would
have been the fourth. It was a sad duty to inform
Mrs. McLeod, living in the camp, of the death of her
good man."

From Scotia Junction, on the Grand Trunk, tracks were being
laid toward the western boundary of the Park at the same time as
the line from Ottawa Valley was under construction. When these
two sections came together the job was finished. On December
the twentieth, 1896, the first through train on the Ottawa-Arnprior
and Parry Sound Railway ran from Depot Harbour, on Georgian
Bay, to the City of Ottawa. This was a trial run: the line was not
officially open for business until the following year.

With the completion of the railway, the whole technique of
taking out timber changed. The long river drives were gone, at
least for all new operations. Now the logs could be brought
speedily to the railways and shipped out on flat cars, or cut into
lumber by sawmills on the spot.

From the Egan Estate Station on the new railway, Booth built
a spur line to tap the rich supply of pine lying between there and
Opeongo Lake. The spur ran north to McAuley Junction, where it
divided, one track going to the left along McAuley Creek as far as
the Park boundaries, the other to the right into the Park, toward
Crotch Lake. When the pine was cut these tracks were torn up and
sold for scrap.

Whitney also built a spur line to his Opeongo limits from the
Whitney Station to Sproule Bay. The rails are gone, but the roadbed
has remained in use to this day, the road from the main Park

highway to Opeongo Lake passing along a section of the St. Anthony Company's original line.

The limits in the south and east of the Park were also opened up as the result of the building of the Booth Railway. Lumber companies in the southwest, operated by J. D. Shier of Bracebridge, by the Mickle and Dyment Company of Gravenhurst, and by the Gilmour Company of Trenton, all made .use of the railroad to bring in men and supplies. Most of these, however, found it was still cheaper to drive their logs to the original mills than to build new sawmills by the tracks.

The older outfits, such as Barnet's and McLachlin's, and the newer Huntsville Lumber Company, made full use of the new railway. Barnet had previously hauled his supplies for the White, or as it is now called, the Big Trout Lake limits along a tote road from Sundridge, but now a much shorter route was provided by a road running north from Brûlé Lake Station. This same route was used by the McLachlin Company when they purchased the limits in 1911. Both these firms continued to drive their logs by way of the Petawawa River to their mills in the Ottawa Valley, but some of the more recent companies have preferred to set up their mills right in the Park. The Huntsville Lumber Company operated at Brûlé Lake for some years, while J. D. S. McRae had a mill at Rock Lake in the 1920's, and another at Lake of Two Rivers between 1931 and 1943.

Many a story is told by old railroaders of the days spent on the Park railroad. Some of the older Park rangers remember the days when traffic was so heavy on this line, that there was a freight train every twenty minutes. Sometimes these trains transported as many as twenty million bushels of western grain in a single year. When the Canada Atlantic Company took over this section, many men who were to rise to a place of prominence in the business and railroad worlds, received their initial experience on the Park run. The "Canada Atlantic Old Boys" still have annual gatherings at Ottawa, where they recall the fine sense of comradeship amongst the men working on the old line. In those days, the trains were known by the names of their conductors; and "Gourlay's Special" or "McDonald's Run" passed along the tracks running through the Park. There was never an engineer too busy to wave at the passers-by, or to stop his train and pick up a ranger who needed transportation for himself and his canoe.

In 1903 the Canada Atlantic was taken over by the Grand Trunk

Railway, for a sum of something like fourteen million dollars. In 1923 the G.T.R. became a part of the Canadian National Railways, which found, a little over ten years ago, that it was operating at a loss in this section. As a result of an inquiry held in 1935, two decisions were made: that the section between Lake of Two Rivers (Mile 162.3) to Cache Lake (Mile 166.8) would have to be abandoned because one of the wooden trestle bridges had been condemned, and that the line would have to continue operating from both ends, because there was, at that time, no parallel transportation into the Park. Finally a wye was built at Whitney so that trains could turn there, instead of going up to Rock Lake Station in the Park.

The second story mentioned at the beginning of this chapter, is an epic of misguided zeal.

In 1892, according to records of the Timber Division of the Ontario Department of Lands and Forests, one of the largest sales in the history of the province was held in Toronto. It was October the thirteenth, an unlucky day for the Gilmour Company that made the purchase. On that date, this Company won the bid for timber rights in what amounted to two-thirds of the Township of Peck, extending from Tea Lake, northward to include both Canoe and Joe Lakes. It was a rich property. To quote one of the old-time timber cruisers who travelled through the whole section: "the country was blue with pine."

Today, it is difficult to convince the visitor to Canoe Lake, that the flourishing village of Mowat, named after the Ontario Premier of those days, once stood on the west side of the lake; that there were thirty miles of siding by the station at the north end; most of all, that logs were floated from the lake before his eyes, 200 miles to the mouth of the Trent River, on the shore of Lake Ontario. True, the ruins of the old mill foundation are still visible down by the shore; and the springy ground tells of mill refuse rotting into the soil under the grass. The ruins of the old landing dock where the boarding houses used to be, can still be found. But a group of fine birch trees has grown up around the wreck of the old mill hospital; and of the stables, once large enough to house fifty teams of horses a night, there is little to be seen.

The vanished village contained a large warehouse, and a cook-house, and any number of shacks to accommodate the wives and families of the Gilmour employees. The shacks are gone; the two large buildings were preserved and repaired, to become the famous

Mowat Lodge, to be described in a later chapter. From the old warehouse to the station, all that the visitor may now see are a few surviving sections of corduroy, and the overgrown grade of the railway siding that once ran from the mill to the main line. Two substantial summer homes built for the Gilmour Brothers' families, later bought by Dr. T. A. Bertram of Dundas, still stand in good repair.

If the visitor is still skeptical as to the former existence of this ghost village, let him visit the graveyard on the hillside, back of the old road to Tea Lake. Here, Tom Thomson's body found temporary rest. Not far away lies the grave of a Mowat mill employee, killed by the limb of a falling tree, the grave marked by a stone which bears this record:

> In memory of Jas. Watson, the first white person to be buried at Canoe Lake. Died May 27, 1897, being one of about 500 employed at this camp by the Gilmour Company, aged 21 years.
>   "Remember, comrade, when passing by,
>   As you are now so once was I,
>   As I am now so you will be;
>   Prepare thyself to follow me."

At the foot of the inscription is added the information, "Engraved gratis by a comrade, D. W. McCain."

The story of the Gilmour operations has yet to be told. The skeptical visitor may accept the evidence of the village's existence in the old days, and still balk at the incredible story of the Gilmour logs. For experienced lumbermen to entertain the idea of transporting logs two hundred miles was improbable enough. That they should plan to float millions of cubic feet of timber *up* over the height of land between Lake of Bays and the headwaters of the Trent, was fantastic.

As a matter of fact, "float" is not quite the right word. Although this historic development took place outside the Park boundaries, it is worth describing here because the whole system was evolved as a means of getting logs out of the Park. The Superintendent, in his report for the year 1895, mentions the fact that the Gilmour Company had already been cutting on their limits for the past three seasons, but he went on to say that they had decided to postpone operations until the railway through the Park should be completed.

And no wonder!

From Archie McEachern, of Dorset, whose father was employed by the company during construction of their improvements in that district, has come the most vivid account of how the feat was performed. The Gilmour Company planned to float their logs down the Oxtongue River from Canoe Lake to the Lake of Bays. There they would be made into booms, and dragged by means of the steam alligator, still to be seen at Baysville, to the starting point of the haul over the height of land. The old stone pumphouse, situated about a mile from Dorset on the road to Baysville, marks the spot where an endless chain, designed to do the job, was to start.

Other companies had built costly dams and slides, but this Gilmour scheme was the most complicated, and costly, of anything yet devised. The pump down by the shore pumped water into the wooden trough, up which the logs slid. It also provided motive power for the chain, to which were attached a series of spikes, to stick into the logs and keep them in place. The first pump was supplemented by boosters along the trough, which were in some places as much as thirty feet above the ground. At the top of this first grade the logs were floated downhill for about a mile, where they arrived at the bottom of a second chain system. There, a second series of pumps brought them up the final rise to Raven Lake. This lake, which normally drains into the Muskoka system, had been backed up by dams, so that it flowed instead through the swampy district into St. Nora's Lake, at the headwaters of the Trent. The logs had to be driven through this swamp in booms, and you can still see, driving along the highway in the winter, when the leaves are off the trees, some of the old capstans that were used to secure the ropes for these booms.

Beside the problem of how to get the logs out of the Park district, there was the transportation problem. From Dorset, where supplies could be brought in by wagon or sleigh along the Bobcaygeon Road, there was a long haul to Tea Lake — and no road! The Gilmours cut one.

Rangers are still able to follow the course of this old road through the southwest corner of the Park, and at places both at Canoe Lake and in the Hollow Lake, now called Kawagama Lake district, it is still in use. The Park Superintendent, who took up headquarters at Canoe Lake during the summer of 1893, was delighted at the prospect of the speedy completion of this road. To him, it meant a handy way out and in through Dorset. As far as one can tell it was used by the company and Park officials during the winter of 1893-4, when supplies for the men working in the Park were toted in along its twenty-eight miles.

Jim Campbell, who travelled this road in Gilmour's time, and afterwards, when it was used by Shier and Mickle-Dyment, has stories of the stopping places on this road. The Gilmour Company had storehouses and a boarding house at Dorset, since this was the terminal of the part of the Bobcaygeon Road they used, as well as the centre for their tramway system. From there, the bush road ran out by Otter Lake, now Tock Lake, for a distance of about eight miles to the first stopping place, at the upper end of Fletcher Lake. There a man could get a meal if he needed it, and on the whole it was quite a respectable place, though it bore the sinister name of "The Pig's Ear". Ten miles farther on was a log house, and a barn capable of putting up fifteen teams of horses for the night. This place was kept by a not too respectable negro; "Dart's Den", as it was called, was a somewhat less savoury stopping place.

In 1895, spring came so early, that the men were able to break the log dumps at Potter Creek on April the twenty-second. Two days later they began the epic drive, and by the twenty-ninth the alligator was hard at work, towing the booms over the lakes to the Oxtongue River. All that time the water on the two lakes was held at a high level, destroying trees along the shore to such an extent, that the evidence is still there today. But the drive went on.

People are still living in the Dorset-Haliburton area who remember that drive. Tommy Archer is one of them. He recalls that a thousand men were employed in the construction of the intricate system of dams, troughs, pumps and chains, financed by the Gilmours. The company, he says, "spent millions of dollars" on it, out of a misguided faith in the cruisers' glowing reports. Down the Oxtongue went the logs, and up over the endless chains, into Trent waters. It worked!

Except for one little miscalculation. By the time the logs had finished their long, rough trip, many months had passed. When they finally reached the company's mills at Trenton, it was found that by the time they were ready to be cut into lumber, even the finest timber had begun to deteriorate!

In December of that year, the company stopped cutting in the district, explaining that there was a depression in the lumber market. Probably they had decided to change their method of getting the logs out, and were waiting for the Booth railway to come through. With the completion of the railroad in 1896, the Gilmour Company recommenced operations on more modern lines, building the mill and village at Mowat. But they still seemed to like doing things the hard way: the huge boiler from the Dorset pump-house, was hauled along the old road, in the depth of winter. Over this rough trail, the boiler was hauled by nine teams of horses, on birch rollers that wore out almost as fast as the men could cut them. By the time the railway was officially opened in the spring, the mill at Mowat was in working order.

When the Gilmour Company went bankrupt, the village and mill fell into the hands of receivers, who established a caretaker on the property. Some of the machinery, including the mill engine, was sold; but a great deal of the equipment was simply left where it had last been used. Axes, saws, and other odds and ends bearing the Gilmour name, may still be seen in workshops around Canoe Lake. With the exceptions mentioned already, there is today little evidence that the village of Mowat ever existed. When the name of the post office was changed to Canoe Lake, even that link with the past disappeared.

CHAPTER 7

To THE PIONEERS of the depot farms, to the Haliburton trappers, the railroad construction gangs, and the men who worked for Booth, Gilmour and the other big lumbermen, the reservation of Algonquin Park in the early nineties, when it came, was a fact — not an abstract idea. The idea was born in the brain of a clerk in the office of the Ontario Department of Crown Lands, a man who had never set eyes on the Park area, Alexander Kirkwood.

There was nothing phenomenal in Kirkwood's background. At the age of twenty-three he emigrated from Belfast, Ireland, to try his hand at wheat farming in New York State. In 1853, he moved to an obscure job in Montreal — probably clerical work, for shortly afterwards he was appointed to the staff of the newly formed Department of Agriculture, in the short-lived United Government of Upper and Lower Canada. After Confederation, in 1870, he became attached to the Ontario Department of Crown Lands.

But the restlessness that had brought him across the Atlantic still stirred in him, stimulated by paper glimpses, in his work, of the vast areas of virgin land that lay to the north. In 1878, he and a J. J. Murphy published a volume entitled "The Undeveloped Lands of Northern and Western Ontario", an estimate of the progress that had been made in frontier settlement in the previous quarter century. There is no question that Kirkwood later doubted the wisdom of the Government's settlement plans for the Huron-Ottawa tract; and it is very likely that while working on this book, he had his first glimmerings of the Park idea.

Gradually, one problem came to obsess him: if this height of land area should not be opened for settlement, what useful purpose could it serve?

Kirkwood's search for an answer led him into a wide field of reading and research. There was the timber, for instance, of the Huron-Ottawa tract, fast falling before the onslaughts of the lumber kings: what had other countries done to preserve their forests? There were the animal and fish resources: how could these be used without depletion? There were the rivers and lakes that would shrink into streams and ponds if the forests were cleared for settlement. All his research pointed to one answer, a conclusion that few men of his generation wanted to take seriously, at a time when it seemed that the country's boundless natural resources could never be exhausted. The answer was conservation.

In 1885, Alexander Kirkwood's idea was ripe, and he wrote a letter to his Commissioner, the Hon. T. B. Pardee. A year later, he published the contents of this letter in an eight-page pamphlet. Both letter and pamphlet set forth the idea of a "National Forest and Park", with specific reasons for the urgency of its establishment. Such a Park should be set aside

> "for the preservation and maintenance of the natural forest,"

and to protect

> "the headwaters and the tributaries of the Muskoka, Petawawa, Bonnechere and Madawaska Rivers."

Kirkwood suggested that within this region it should be unlawful to disturb or destroy any fur-bearing animals; and that its timber should be cut and marketed by the Government, rather than by private companies.

Proceeding with the case, he pointed out that some animals, notably the caribou, the moose, the white-tailed deer, and the beaver, had been hunted so intensively in that area of recent years, that they were in danger of extermination. Soon it would be too late to attempt to protect them in their native habitat. Then, with regard to forest management, he felt that if indiscriminate private cutting were allowed in the area, there might be dangerous consequences, not only to the water supply of the Province, but to the value of the district as a whole. If, on the other hand, the mature trees were cut under Government supervision, the young growth would in due time replace them. Such a policy would, further, provide a handsome source of revenue for the Government.

In justifying his choice of locale for the new Park, Kirkwood went on to describe the part of the Ottawa-Huron tract which he thought should be set aside for that purpose, namely, the headwaters of the four rivers already mentioned. He pointed out the evil effects, in the older parts of the Province, of "the wanton destruction of forests" by settlers who were anxious to clear their lands, and by lumbermen who were only interested in the immediate profit that could be derived from the forest growth. When the land had been denuded of its trees, these same settlers, who were dependent for their water supply on the rivers along which they had built their mills and villages, were the first to suffer. If this cycle of disaster were to be avoided in the Ottawa-Huron district, now was the time to act.

After the necessary precautions had been taken to protect both forests and game, Kirkwood thought that the Park should be thrown open to the people of the Province, so that they could make full use of its facilities. In a style that anticipated the lyricisms of later tourists bureaus, he praised the pure air and bracing climate of the highland region, eulogising the picturesque scenery and great abundance of fish. He visualised the day when

> "Seekers for health and pleasure in the summer season may be allowed to lease locations for cottages or tents along the shores of the great Opeongo Lake; and a site on that lake for a hotel and farm can be offered to public competition at annual rental."

The author of the Park idea recommended that the name of the proposed area be adopted from "one of the greatest of Indian nations" — the Algonquins. In the opinion of the commissioners "it is fitting that the name of a once great and powerful people, who in their savage manner held sway over this territory centuries ago, should bequeath their name to a part of it which it is now proposed to maintain, as nearly as possible, in the condition in which it was when they fished in its waters and hunted and fought in its forests." Finally, he referred again to the great natural beauties of the place. Here the traveller would be inspired by "the gloomy grandeur of the forest", could see for himself "noble pines and stately oaks bespeaking the growth of centuries", and could listen to "winds sounding solemnly in their branches". Even the arts were not neglected in this final rhapsody:

> "It is here that the imagination of the poet kindles into reverie and rapture, and revels in almost incommunicable luxury of thought."

Concluding, he assures the Honourable Mr. Pardee that:

> "The Commissioner of Crown Lands who establishes Algonquin Forest and Park raises a monument that will not crumble or decay, and his memory will be cherished in the warmest corners of many hearts."

No immediate action was taken by the Department, but Kirkwood either received some encouragement or was Irish enough to persist. Among his private papers a memorandum dated 1887 sets forth some practical questions that needed to be answered, before action could implement the idea. He wanted to know whether the setting aside of a permanent forest reserve was such

"a matter of importance and advantage as to warrant
any action on the part of the Government;"

whether it was in the public interest to close the area to settlement; and

"whether the conservation around the sources of these
rivers is a matter of Provincial concern?"

Exactly what percentage of the area was fit for settlement? How much was water? What areas were good timber lands? Finally, were there any property claims within the proposed Park limits?

There was one man better qualified than anyone else to answer these questions, a man who shares with Kirkwood the chief credit for the Park's establishment.

This man was James Dickson of Fenelon Falls, Provincial Land Surveyor, who had been conducting township surveys in the district since 1879. In the same year that Kirkwood published his open letter to Pardee, Dickson submitted reports for the townships of Finlayson and Peck. These reports included a summary of land and water areas, the arable acreage, extent of clearings; and such developments as depot farms, wagon roads, and lumbering activities. By a coincidence that the conditions of the area had predetermined, Dickson's reports completely corroborated Kirkwood's arguments in favour of setting up a park.

The following year action began. Only half the townships of the proposed area had been surveyed. The Hon. Mr. Pardee asked Dickson to take a trip through the unsurveyed Townships of Sproule and Preston, in order to report on them to his Department. Dickson made the trip and submitted his report.

Kirkwood, no doubt, read the report shortly after it was received early in the New Year. Although he knew of Dickson's sympathy, he must have read its first pages in a state of some suspense. Everything depended on these findings!

Dickson was not impressed with the necessity of forest protection — in that respect he was a man of his time. But he heartily endorsed the principal of conserving wild life, and fully agreed that a continued water supply for the surrounding districts, through control of the headwaters of the rivers that supplied them, was of prime importance. He says,

"The preservation from destruction of moose, deer and
beaver would, in my opinion, alone warrant the
Government in making this a reservation."

At another point, he states that if inexpensive dams were constructed
at strategic sites there would be

"a sufficiency of water held in reserve to enable lumbermen to drive on the Muskoka and Petawawa all the
summer."

Dickson's report recommended that eleven of the eighteen townships that were afterwards set aside to form the Park in 1893 be
so utilized, but he also outlined definite ways of developing this
region for the public good. Kirkwood had already suggested the
possibilities of the area as a holiday resort, but Dickson outshone
him as a one-man tourist bureau. Why not, he asked, publish a
guide book, generously illustrated with drawings made on the spot,
and a hundred pages or more in length, that would set forth the
attractions of the Park? A map, too, on a scale of a hundred chains
(one and a half miles) to the inch, would be an invaluable aid to
tourists. His suggested paths of access to the Park for such visitors
were impracticable, to say the least. To a seasoned bush traveller
like Dickson, who regularly carried out trips by canoe from his
home at Fenelon Falls to the scenes of his surveys, it never occurred
that the Madawaska and Muskoka river routes he suggested would be
anything more to tourists than the mere holiday jaunts they were
to him. Of course it must be remembered too that when he wrote
his report, the nearest railway stations to the Park were at Deux
Rivieres in the north, and Haliburton far to the south.

Perhaps it was his final rhapsodical outburst that clinched the
case for the Park.

"As we float along the streams or skim over the calm
water of the lakelets almost every stroke of the paddle
unfolds some new scene of rural beauty, seldom
equalled in any part of our fair Province, and to
paint them in all their pristine beauty would take the
most gifted pen or pencil of either author or artist."

Before this Park could be established, however, it was necessary
to convince the Government that the area really ought to be
withdrawn from settlement — that is, "reserved" for other purposes.
The total area of the eleven townships involved was about 866
square miles, of which roughly one-eighth was covered by lakes
or rivers. The remaining seven-eighths were made up of land that

was arable in places, but these arable pockets were so widely scattered that Dickson estimated there would be no more than one fertile township in the eleven. As for minerals, he reported that there was no limestone in the area, and with the exception of a little iron ore, there was nothing of value from a mining point of view.

In answer to Kirkwood's question about the timber, Dickson pointed out that most of the good pine stands, especially in the east, were already under license. However there were several valuable stands left, especially in the south half of Hunter and McLaughlin townships (around Brûlé Lake and Burnt Island Lake), and almost all of Peck (Smoke and Canoe Lakes), which could be reserved if the Government so desired.

The report outlined the extent of previous burnings, and the varieties of forest other than pine. The stands of hardwood, hemlock and yellow birch, Dickson was sure, would some day prove valuable. However, since he visualized the Park chiefly as a game preserve, he was not too upset by the prospect of continued lumbering in the region, seeing in the second growth a much better source of food for the wildlife than it had ever had in the past. As he said:

> "There is always a larger supply of young and tender shoots on which the moose and deer feed, and berries and cherries for partridge, than is anywhere to be met with in the original forest . . . and as to poplar and white birch, which are the favourite food of the beaver, they are always to be found in greater numbers where a second growth of timber has grown up than any other place."

The chief reason for the dwindling supplies of game in the district, was the wanton destruction by local hunters, interested only in the hides, and seeming to have no consideration for the season in which they killed the animals. In winter, travelling was easier for these hunters, and they ignored the fact that killing the deer at that time of the year threatened to exterminate them entirely. Dickson pointed out that the breeding season for moose was in September, and for deer in December. Winter hunting meant that mothers were destroyed before the birth of their young in the spring. To the settlers, he realized, one moosehide containing enough leather for twenty pairs of moccasins was worth forty dollars; but some measures had to be taken, if only for that reason, to prevent the disappearance of the animals altogether.

Although Dickson did not try to estimate the total beaver population, he gave the impression that there were many less than in former times. He reported that the beaver houses and dams were mostly old ones, and that indiscriminate trapping had greatly reduced the total. He felt that it would be worth while to take active steps to increase their number,

"First, because the skin furnishes us with one of our richest and most valuable furs; and, second, because from its natural habits it is in fact the greatest conservator of water that we have."

He went on to show that re-stocking would be comparatively simple, since the beaver usually had from four to six young each year. He maintained that it was foolishness to allow spring trapping, and strongly advocated closed seasons throughout the Province to protect the fur and game supply.

Dickson's attitude towards hunting in the future Park was explicit.

"I would strongly urge that neither moose, deer or any fur-bearing animals should be either hunted, taken or killed in the proposed Park for all time. By doing this, the Province will have a large breeding ground and harbour of refuge for her game. As the Park becomes stocked they would naturally spread out into the surrounding country and the whole Province would be better stocked than it is at present."

At the same time, he suggested that some effort be made to curb the wolf population, since their numbers would tend to increase as the other animals became more plentiful. A premium offered to the forester for the "scalp" of each wolf might check their increase.

As a practical man, Dickson set forth his recommendations for the best way of enforcing the restrictions:

"It will be necessary to have a game keeper and a few assistants whose duty it will be to see that the law prohibiting hunting and trapping is rigidly enforced and also to guard against fire . . . I would suggest that every game keeper be armed with judicial authority to punish transgression on the spot . . . and to destroy all traps and dead-falls whether found set in the woods or in the possession of any person in the prohibited area, and to confiscate all rifles, shotguns, furs or other game found with them."

His knowledge of the district made him foresee that it would take more than halfway measures to deal with trappers who were armed with an intimate knowledge of every inch of the Park.

Dickson's report spurred Kirkwood on to even wider studies. In his "Papers and Reports Upon Forestry, Forest Schools and Forest Management in Europe, America, and the British Possessions, and upon Forests as Public Parks and Sanitary Resorts, collected by Mr. A. Kirkwood", there is ample evidence that Kirkwood had as thorough a knowledge of what had been done in other parts of the world, as Dickson had of the area itself. Both of the men chiefly responsible for the future direction of the Park's activities knew what they were talking about.

So far things had gone well. Unfortunately, in 1889, the Hon. T. B. Pardee died, and four years elapsed in spite of Kirkwood's importunities, before the appointment of a Royal Commission promised real action. This Commission was

"To make a full report respecting the fitness of certain territory in the said Province, including the headwaters of the Rivers Amable du Fond, Petawawa, Bonne-chere, Madawaska, and Muskoka . . . with boundaries hereafter determined for the purpose of a Forest Reservation and National Park; the approximate cost of establishing and maintaining such a Park; and the ends to be attained by creation of such a Park."

The formal document setting up the Royal Commission and giving it the necessary powers to conduct its research, bore the signature of the Premier of Ontario, Sir Oliver Mowat. To the four men named in this document, a fifth was later added to make the following list:

Aubrey White — Assistant Crown Commissioner of Lands

Alexander Kirkwood — Senior Officer of the Lands Branch

James Dickson — Inspector of Surveys

Archibald Blue — Director of Mines

Robert W. Phipps — Clerk of Forestry.

The first formal meeting of the Commission took place in Toronto on November the fourth, 1892, by which date a great deal of ground work had been done. Eight months previously, James Dickson had submitted another report on the proposed district, duplicating some information already on hand, but mentioning the presence of squatters who had cleared patches of land in the township of Dickson, and at Booth Lake. Dickson reminded the Department that there had never been a formal survey of the Townships of Sproule and Preston; so during the month of August he was sent up to gather the needed data.

Returning with the information in September, Dickson advised that the time had come for action. In November the Commission met, with Alexander Kirkwood, appropriately, in the chair. At this meeting the Commissioners agreed that the territory outlined in Dickson's report was suitable for the proposed Park, but recommended that four more townships be added to the sixteen. Most of the points already mentioned were included in the Commission's recommendations, but a few highlights will interest the reader.

The Park boundaries were fixed to include eighteen townships in the District of Nipissing: Wilkes, Pentland, Biggar, Osler, Lister, Deacon, Devine, Bishop, Freswick, Anglin, Hunter, McLaughlin, Bower, Dickson, Peck, Canisbay, Sproule and Preston; a total area of 1,466 square miles, of which a little more than a tenth was water surface, and a fifth or less was land suitable for cultivation.

"Forest preservation and protection, (the report read) is, in almost every civilized country, one of the most pressing and vital of economic questions."

It mentioned the pine stands particularly

"which forest fires and the operations of lumbermen have greatly diminished."

When hardwood was fully mature it should be cut, and

"It might as well be cut by the lumberman, he receiving permission to do so."

The Commissioners believed that if the area were opened to settlement, its lands

"would soon be converted into a dreary and abandoned waste."

A peak of eloquence was achieved on the topic of the decline in wild life:

"Here not many years ago the moose, the monarch of the Canadian woods, roamed and browsed in great numbers . . . here herds of red deer grazed in the open meadows or quenched their thirst at the brooks or crystal lakes; here the industrious beaver felled his trees and built his dams on every stream; here the

Tom Thomson, Canada   Courtesy of Alan O. Gibbons

NORTHERN LIGHTS

GOLDFINCH.

wolf's detested howl startled the deer and the bear
pushed his black bulk through the undergrowth in
search of ripe nuts or berries."

The Commissioners suggested that streams be restocked with
native fish where these had disappeared, and other suitable varieties
might be introduced. Shrubs for deer and wild rice for ducks might
be planted in the Park.

A final summary stated that the proposed Act was intended to
provide

"a public park, and forest reservation, fish and game
preserve, health resort and pleasure ground for the
benefit, advantage and enjoyment of the people of the
Province."

The original name proposed by the Commissioners was "The
Algonquin National Park". In later years the word "National"
was changed to "Provincial", since other national parks in the
Dominion were under federal control.

CHAPTER 8

THE ALGONQUIN PARK ACT was passed by the Legislative Assembly of the Province of Ontario in the year 1893. Alexander Kirkwood's dream had become reality.

There is no better way of paying tribute to the achievement of Alexander Kirkwood, James Dickson, and those who supported and advised them, than to pause here, and view the rich legacy which their efforts secured for the people of Ontario, and their guests from beyond. What was there about the Park that inspired the founders, and has since claimed the devotion of a long line of Park Superintendents?

Size is scarcely the answer, although since 1893 eleven full townships and large sections of eight others were added, almost doubling its area into proportions greater than those of Canada's smallest Province.

Nor is it the Park's mineral wealth. One hesitates over what might have been the complications if rich mineral deposits had been discovered later. A character Mark Robinson knew of in his early ranging days, worked for the Gilmours at Mowat village, and was known locally as "Dirty Dick". He claimed he had discovered gold, but nothing came of it. Mica, it is true, occurs in quantities on the banks of the Bonnechere; and molybdenite, the soft blue-grey ore of molybdenum now used in steel alloys, has been reported from the Otterslide Lakes. No serious commercial mining has ever been attempted in the Park; and Dickson's original verdict has been maintained.

Perhaps only the total effect of a book such as this, can reveal the full reason for the fascination exerted on the Park by its visitors. One thing is certain however. Without the wildlife of the Park, it would hold little charm for any visitor. It is a land where even the vegetable life has a character all its own. Bright orange lichens display their colour on the sometimes grey, sometimes light brown, cliffs. The rocky headlands are clothed along their bare crests with pale grey-greens of humble mosses. Deep in the interior of the woods, one may run across beds of brilliant green moss. Swamp grasses, slender reeds, and lily pads grow in the stagnant water of the marshes; the beautiful white water lilies, and humbler yellow ones, dotting the surface decoratively. Willows, alders, and cedar thrive in the low ground, as well as hemlock, spruce, balsam, and the funeral black spruce. In old burned-over areas, or near the shore where the light is good, the paper birch and the poplar grow. As one ascends inland, the yellow birch is found in large stands, and on the well-drained land, often on the hill-tops, are stands of sugar maple.

Most typical of all the Park trees is the pine, even though the best of them were cut for square timber in the old days. In sandy soil the jackpine grows, with its rough, gnarled branches, and its rock-hard cones. In deeper soil stands the lordly white pine, aristocrat of the softwoods, its irregular, windswept branches reaching high. On the rock itself, thrusting its roots into every nook and crevice, is the red pine, seeming to thrive in spite of autumn gales and winter frosts.

The variety of trees is comparatively bewildering. Black ash and swamp maple, beech and ironwood, red oak, black cherry — even the occasional elm — all appear in the Algonquin woods. A dozen varieties of berry bushes, laden in summer with their ripe fruit, tempt the visitor to pause. Club mosses, ferns, and several species of orchids, are to be found. Nor are the woods lacking in flowers: the bunch berry or Canadian dogwood, the delicate creeping twin flower; violets, clintoia, starflower, foam flower, and the painted trillium.

But there is more than plant life in the Park to charm the visitor. In the shade of a stand of pine he can see gusts of wind flatten the wave peaks into white caps, and absorb the brilliant colours of sunshine and shadow that Tom Thomson has captured in his paintings of Park scenes. He hears the wind in the treetops, the waves that break on the beach, and the shrill call of the gull wheeling in the sky. Sweetest of all, if he listens for it, is the "sweet, sweet, Canada, Canada, Canada" of the white-throated sparrow.

It would be a disheartening experience to walk for a morning through Algonquin woods, or to paddle along the Park streams and lakes, without hearing or seeing a living creature. The rocks, water, and trees, would seem strangely empty. From the earliest days, the inhabitants of the Park have looked upon its life as necessary, if not for their enjoyment, at least for their sustenance and livelihood.

Night and day, the evidence of its wild life abounds in Algonquin Park. Here today, all but the wolf may seek sanctuary from, and live in friendship with, their one-time enemy, man. Here, uniquely, one may find in animals and birds, his friends.

Through the screen of the Park ranger's open window on a summer night, he may hear the lonely call of the loon, like distant hitchpitched laughter, or the uncanny hoot of an owl. At other times during the night, especially in the spring, he will hear the shrill song of the frogs. In the early dawn he awakens to the songs of innumerable birds; and all through the day, if he listens, he may hear the spiritual notes of the olive-backed thrust, the hermit, veery, and wood thrushes; the rarer gutteral croak of the raven, or caw of a crow, the comical cries of the Canada jay, or "whiskey jack" as the lumbermen call him. Here and there through the forest, the jewelled colour of a sprightly warbler catches his eye, or a covey of ruffled grouse whirrs suddenly out of the brush. At the lakeshore stands a great blue heron on his long legs, watching for minnows in the shallow water. In his canoe, the ranger may round a point to come upon a flock of mergansers, or fish ducks, two or three families, mothered by a single female.

One hundred and seventy-seven species of birds, according to Professor Dymond, Director of the Royal Ontario Museum of Zoology, have been seen at one time or another within the Park boundaries, and of these, a hundred and thirty are found regularly in summer.

Of all the birds, the loon and the Canada jay are the most characterful. In the Park one may come within a few yards of the handsome, black-headed, white-breasted loon, before he makes his sleek, leisurely dive, coming up an incredible hundred yards away. For all his wild laughter, he is a sociable fellow in protected regions, answering politely the weak human imitations of his call, even showing off with a ludicrous demonstration of how he can stand on his tail in the water. To see him flapping his wings, and vigorously paddling with his webbed feet to keep upright; and to see the lame duck tactics of his mate trying to divert one's attention from her young, are two of the unforgetable little intimacies of Algonquin Park life. The whiskey jack is the disreputable tramp of the woods, the cocky ruffian who snatches bread from the camper's fingers, or pecks insatiably at his cake of soap on the rock, one wary impudent eye on the owner. According to early Indian legends this bird had a superhuman intelligence, outwitting even the medicine man.

Curiously enough, as if they knew this wild life sanctuary was dedicated to man's friendship with animals, poisonous snakes do not occur. The harmless garter, red-bellied, ring-nacked, and DeKay's brown snakes are there, but seldom seen. Only the snapping turtle upholds the shady repute of his tribe. His painted cousin may be seen on occasion. The bull-frog, six other species of frogs, four different kinds of salamander, and the common toad complete the Park's modest list of reptiles and amphibia.

Forty feet down, in the deep water of hundreds of Algonquin lakes, lie the luscious lake trout, natives of these waters since the first Indian fished for them. These fish are pink in flesh, and sometimes vary so much in appearance, from lake to lake, that all but experts are deceived into believing there are several varieties. In the northern streams of the Park speckled trout abound, prize of the fly fisherman. A few lakes, notably Redrock Lake, harbour them, too. In the south, introduced into waters where they were not seen formerly, bass, pike-perch, and maskinonge are often caught today.

The greatest thrill the Park visitor gets, is from the larger land animals. Although usually shy, black bears soon grow bold if encouraged by being fed, even becoming a nuisance when they misinterpret the intentions of cottagers and campers who leave tasty food in tempting proximity to an open door. The huge, ungainly bull moose, as he stalks across the ridges in the autumn, the graceful deer bounding over a deadfall, the stately waddle of the bristling porcupine — are a few of the sights a visitor may see. Timber wolves, foxes, skunks, woodchucks, chipmunks, red squirrels, snowshoe rabbits, and the beautiful little native white-footed or deer mouse, are all found in the Park. So too are the rarer fisher and marten, trapped elsewhere almost out of existence for their beautiful furs.

The Park is full of stories about its animal life, many of which appear elsewhere in these pages. Of all the animals in the Park, none is so full of surprises, even for the old-timer, as the otter. Professor Dymond, in a paper on the natural history of the Park, from which much of the material for this chapter comes, has this to say about the otter:

"The otter, too, is commoner here than elsewhere. Many summer visitors count among their most prized memories the sight of a mother otter with her brood of kittens. Like every animal that kills any other animal that man himself wants to kill, the otter is often

condemned for its habit of catching fish. Ralph Bice
tells of an instance when the tables were turned and a
trout ate a baby otter. "Don't laugh," he says, "ten
men saw it." The trout weighed three pounds and the
otter was about ten inches in length from tip to tip
and there was no mistaking as to what it was."

Steve Waters, one of the original Park rangers, used to tell of
another unusual otter incident. One morning late in autumn, he
and his fellow ranger in that section were watching for poachers on
the shore of Opeongo Lake. The lake had frozen over only the
night before, and no snow had fallen. Suddenly, half a mile out,
fragments of ice shot up from the surface and fell again. As they
watched, it happened again closer to shore. A black speck appeared
in the hole, only to disappear before they could see what it was.
Not until the animal had almost reached shore did they recognize
it for an otter, breaking the ice at intervals with his head to get a
fresh breath of air. When they measured the ice it was three-quarters
of an inch thick.

G. W. Bartlett, who will be met formally before very long,
described another otter's antics on Fawn Lake:

"This grand otter came along towards us with one, two,
three, four, five jumps and a long slide. I measured
this afterwards and found it to be forty-five feet long.
Sometimes otters seem to take a great delight in
sliding down steep banks into the water. They tuck
their front paws in close to their sides and slide down
an incline like little toboggans."

One more example will suffice to illustrate the charm, and
sometimes humour, of the unexpected, which is perhaps the one
feature of the Park, more than any other, that accounts for the
spell it seems to cast on all who linger within its borders. Mark
Robson tells this one about a bear.

One summer, bears proved to be a particular nuisance to the
Munn Lumber Company, which was operating camps in the southern
part of the Park. It was bad enough having the animals devouring
your food supplies when you were in camp, but it was worse when
you were working out in the bush, and had no chance of doing
anything about it. Once, when a group of men had had their
mid-day meals stolen for several days in a row, the young foreman
decided to take action. He had heard that bears will not climb
small trees, so he hung the food on a branch of a tree with a

three-inch trunk. At noon it had disappeared as before. The next day he tried another scheme. This time he put the supplies in the stern of a rowboat that had been run up on shore, close to the spot where the men were cutting. When he had covered up the food, he went away satisfied that now it was safe. About eleven o'clock, when he went to get the lunch, he found that the boat itself had vanished from the place where he had left it. Then he saw it, away out in the middle of the lake, and what did he see in the boat, but old Bruin himself. Evidently he had smelt out the food in the stern, and had clambered in after it. As he moved down the boat, his weight must have served as a balance to lift the bow off the beach. Then a gust of wind would be sufficient to carry both boat and bear clear of the land. When sighted, he was just finishing the last of his meal. Once more the men had to go hungry.

There are other bear stories, tales too, of wolves and deer, even of the tiny chipmunk: these must wait for their time and place. Not a few of them, however, are tied up inseparably with the larger story of the Park, particularly that phase of it that concerns the rangers of the early days, and the way they met and solved the first problems of administration.

CHAPTER 9

IT IS SELDOM IN HISTORY, that such a large area of land as Algonquin Park, containing so much natural wealth, has been protected from commercial exploitation by any government, with so little opposition. Some friction was unavoidable: that there was so little is a tribute to the reasonable way in which the early settlers within the Park area, the lumbermen, the Indians, and the trappers were handled.

The most effective opposition should have come from the lumber and railway interests with stakes in the area. Indeed, had Kirkwood's original idea of Government cutting and selling of timber been followed, there would undoubtedly have been a battle royal before the Act ever came near the Legislature.

As a matter of fact, J. R. Booth was not too pleased to find that his railway would run through the southern end of the proposed Park; and wrote a letter to the Department, suggesting forthrightly that the Commissioners' plans be changed to keep the Park clear of The Ottawa-Arnprior and Parry Sound Railway, whose line was already surveyed.

It is extremely doubtful whether Kirkwood's fellow Commissioners ever gave serious consideration to the idea of reserving cutting rights in the Park, though they were all for some measure of control. The very contemplation of the complexities involved in such a step must have made Government officials shudder. Probably, in the long hours of discussion through the months and years that passed before the other ideas in his letter were put into effect, Kirkwood himself came to see that rigid control of the Park timber stands was impracticable.

Most of the lumbermen were in favour of the Park as proposed by the Commission. All of them were unanimously opposed to settlement projects in lumbering areas, involving, as they invariably did, an increased fire hazard. Furthermore, the new provincial fire ranging system recently put into effect, made them aware of the value of the fire protection their limits would have in the Park. Then, too, the move to conserve the headwaters of the streams, down which they floated their logs, was to their obvious advantage. Business men down along the Ottawa Valley, even as far away as the shores of Lake Ontario, were fully aware of the connection between the lakes and streams of the Algonquin highlands and their own busy sawmills.

On the other side of the fence, there were some misgivings among the Commissioners, whose chief interest in the Park was its function as a game preserve. How could trappers and poachers be controlled when the railway made the Park so easily accessible? The others pointed out that it would be an ideal means of supplying the rangers, and of keeping in close touch with the Department in Toronto, while the resort enthusiasts argued that the railway would bring visitors to the very front porch of the Park. So the south boundary remained as proposed.

That there would be difficulties in putting an end to trapping and hunting in the Park was self evident, and before long these troubles will be dealt with. The one remaining problem was what to do with the handful of people already living in the region. This problem was largely dodged for the time. The Dunfonds, for instance, were not disturbed, although they had a valuable holding in the very heart of the newly formed provincial game sanctuary.

Twenty-three years later, the case of the Dufonds was finally cleaned up, on the death of Ignace Dufond. On October the fourteenth, 1916, a letter was sent by Mr. Thomas W. Gibson, then Deputy Minister of the Department of Lands, Forests and Mines, to Mr. G. W. Bartlett, the Superintendent of Algonquin Park. The letter read as follows:

"Lot 25 in the 12th concession of Wilkes, Algonquin Park, was patented to Ignace Dufond in 1888. As the patent was issued under the Mining Act the land was subject to two cents an acre under the Mining Act. The taxes remained unpaid for a number of years, and in 1910 the land was forfeited to the Crown.

"This I think is the lot at the east end of Lake Manitou on which the Dufond family, or some of them live, and which has been occupied by them for many years. They have a small farm there with house and barn and some improvements. It would appear from correspondence which the Department has received, that the Dufonds would like to have the land re-granted to them, or that they would be willing to accept compensations from the Depart-

ment for their improvements and for the length
of time they have occupied the lot.

"Having been at this place it is my own view that it
would be advisable for the Department to retain the
title as there is always the possibility of it passing
into the possession of people whose presence in the
Park would be objectionable. The Department would
be willing to compensate the Dufonds to a reasonable
extent and to perhaps allow the old people to remain
in possession as long as they live, at a nominal
rental."

In response to this letter from Toronto, the Superintendent must
have replied to the effect that the whole situation was complicated
by the fact that there were other Dufond relations who were
interested in the farm besides this Ignace to whom it had been
granted originally. Writing on December 5th, Mr. Gibson referred
to such a letter:

"It is inferred from your letter that there are other
Indian relatives. Can you say whether Ignace Dufond
had more than one brother, Francis, who I understand is living with his (Ignace's) wife Susan?".

The third letter, dated December 19, 1916, was addressed to Mr.
Bartlett. It came from Peter Ranger who had been stationed as a
ranger at Kiosk since 1912.

"Replying to your letters that I receive the 16th I went
to the Indians on the 17th to get the name of all the
Dufond that I am sending you.

"Soc. Dufond is address is Mattawa but he live with
the old Francis on the farm this winter. Alex Dufond,
address Mattawa; Philamene Dufond; Catherine Dufond, Mattawa; Angelique Dufond—they don't know
if she is living, they did not hear from her since ten
years".

Next came a letter from Mr. Gibson dated December 29, 1916,
in which he pointed out:

"The Department would allow the old people to
remain in occupation as long as either one of them
lived, or desired to live there at a nominal rental of
say, $1.00 per year".

What actually happened as a result of this suggestion is a little
difficult to determine. The last and final piece of information that

this file provided came in the form of another letter from Mr. Gibson, dated a year later — December 14, 1917. This seems to have been in answer to a letter written by Peter Ranger, on behalf of the Dufonds themselves, because they were complaining that they were not receiving the full amount of the moneys that were to have been paid to them:

> "The arrangement made with these people (Susanne and Francis Dufond) was that they were to get $1,000 compensation for the improvements on the Indian farm at Kioshuque (Kioshkokwi) Lake, etc. This was to be paid to them in instalments of $75.00 every six months with interest at five per cent on the unpaid principal."

> "The money was paid over to the Toronto General Trusts Corporation, which makes the payments, and at the written request of the Indians, the installments were made payable through Mr. T. E. McKee, District Attorney, North Bay."

From this correspondence, two things are evident — one is that the Department officials had tried to treat these old Indians as fairly as they could, while realizing that eventually they must leave the way clear for the inclusion of this land in the Park itself; and the other, that Peter Ranger, who still lives in a ranger cabin at Kiosk, must know more than anyone else about the Dufonds.

It was promised, in connection with the story of depot farm days, that more would be heard of Dinney McGuey. The Department of Lands and Forests became interested in Dinney two years before the Dufond correspondence above, at a time when the last cutting had been done on the Bonnechere limits, and the Government planned to include the Basin Depot area, where Paddy Garvie had his depot farm, within the Park.

The following extracts from this correspondence explain themselves, and a good deal more:

Dated May 15th, 1914 — From Dennis McGuey to the Minister of Lands, Forests and Mines:

> "Mr. G. W. Bartlett came here and made agreement with me for my farm and buildings. I was promised two thousand five hundred dollars. Also he appointed me Fire Ranger . . . I have lived on the Limits for near forty years. I got permission from McLachlin Brothers to build where I now reside. I have been

Fire Ranger over twenty-five years. If only I could
be left here I would be quite content. As to going to
New Ontario if you put me in a place built as this
is built it would be alright enough . . .
P.S.—Don't put me too far from a station, let me have
five farms in a block for my sons and me."

Dated May 20th, 1914 — From the Department to Mr. G. W.
Bartlett:

"I must say that the Department for various reasons is
quite anxious to get these people away, and with as
little friction as possible. In view of lumbering being
at an end, there is no possible future for the settlement,
and the safety of the timber in that district would be
certainly more secure if squatters were removed —
including Mr. McGuey."

Dated July 7th, 1914 — From (Sergeant) Dennis McGuey to the
Minister:

"I write again to see what you intend to do with me.
It will suit me better to get the money for my place
than to go to New Ontario. It is all right for young
men to go there that have no care but themselves. They
can work and clear land and build themselves up. I am
too old to commence to make a home now. I have
worked for a long time for the Government and Limit
holders as Fire Ranger in the Township of Guthrie.
Same time I tried to build a home for myself. Please
let me know at once if I am to remain on here . . .
Or you might appoint me Park Ranger. I know this
country well. I know the hunters' trails, where they go
into the Park. This is a good place to watch them. I
can do my duty in that line all right."

Naturally, one cannot help feeling sorry for Dinney in his plight.
As he himself said, he had spent the best years of his life in the
Bonnechere country, and now he was being asked to move elsewhere.
He could see no rhyme or reason in the Government's request, but
there were other residents of the district who could appreciate some
of the reasons why this action was being taken. The children of
some of the Bonnechere families, now fully grown adults, could see
how their own backwoods isolation had handicapped them. Two of
the younger generation of the Bonnechere pioneers, Mike Garvie and
Mrs. Harry Stack, a daughter of the widow McCormack, recall the

difficulties they underwent to get any schooling at all, when they were children. These, and other people, felt that the Government was wise in moving the old families out of the district when the lumber companies had terminated their operations there.

Remembering the background of the Haliburton trappers, it is no wonder they resented what they felt to be intrusion on their own private property. They, who knew almost every leaf and stick on the Park trails, and depended for their livelihood on this knowledge, were now asked to trap in unfamiliar territory, outside the Park boundaries.

In the summer of 1893, Dickson had visited the Park and written concerning this problem. He informed Commissioner Hardy that he had procured a list of the parties who were trapping in the Park, and who would, in all probability, still have their traps in the area. He suggested that these men be notified by the Department that they would be expected to have their equipment out of the Park by the first of October.

Having made these constructive suggestions, he went on to comment on the most recent information available as to the game situation in the Park. He said that it was, at that time, abundant in the area, and that there was sufficient beaver there to restock the district in four or five years if the present population could be protected. To carry on this work, he thought that there should be two men employed immediately to locate the haunts of the wild animals, especially the beaver. Dickson particularly mentioned the threat to the moose in the area, since he said that he and other travellers had come upon a great deal of evidence pointing to the fact that hunters slaughtered these animals for bait for their bear-traps, as well as for their hides.

The list of trappers which Dickson furnished to the Department, contains the names of many of the Dorset and Haliburton trappers of whom we have already spoken. Those mentioned were: James Sawyers, William and Darling Radnow, John Archer, Isaac and Hamilton Bice, Frank Pokorny, Sam Vancleiff, George Ross, W. H. Sawyer and John Hoskin. Naturally, since before this time trapping in the Park area had been perfectly legal, some opposition was to be expected. It was all very well for the Department to talk about restocking the game in the region, but in the meantime what were they expected to do for a living? Dickson had foreseen this as far back as 1888.

To avoid friction as far as possible, he felt that the trappers themselves should be shown how they would benefit from the establishment of a game reserve, as well as being informed of the regulations for the new Park. The ranging staff, too, should be fully informed of the whole situation, and empowered with sufficient authority to deal with transgressors on the spot. That would mean that men appointed as Park Rangers would have to be expert bushmen, and should be permitted to bear firearms.

Acting on Dickson's suggestion, the Department sent to each man on the list, full information about the new order of things in the Park, enclosing a copy of the Algonquin Park Act, a copy of the Commission's report, and a map showing the exact location of the Park boundaries. The letter ended with the hope that the trappers would see the ultimate benefit to themselves of the Park's establishment. Though it did involve hardships for these men, at least the Government was doing its best to be fair and far-sighted.

No sooner had the Chief Ranger taken up his new duties in the Park than the first complaint arrived, written by a fire ranger employed on the limits of the Barnet Lumber Company in the north, by way of the Assistant Commissioner of Crown Lands, to whom it was addressed. The writer had just returned to his post on the Petawawa River, where, on the first of August, he had seen Indians from the Bonnechere, who were preparing to hunt in the district. They had located a camp between White Trout (Big Trout) and Burnt (Portal) Lakes, with the intention of killing moose for their hides. Moose meat was seen in their possession, as well as the skins of beaver and otter, caught in the area. The fire ranger had mentioned this matter to Mr. Barnet, who told him he should notify the authorities.

The Department's predicament at this time is made clear in a personal letter written by the Crown Lands Commissioner to Mr. Barnet:

> "It will be a ticklish business to prevent Indians killing wild animals in the Park where they have been in the habit of hunting, and their ancestors before them. I am free to say this Indian hunting did not occur to me at the time the whole matter was under discussion. Now I see nothing for it but to exclude the Indians as well as the white men. But great care and tact will be required to handle these people so as not to embitter them or leave them feeling they have a substantial grievance. They will be much more dangerous and

difficult to watch than a white man. They have not had a chance to know what we are doing or the object in view, and their being stopped will probably be the first intimation of a Park reserve they will have. Therefore, they should be told the whole history of the affair and what is intended, etc., and that they must not hunt in the Park."

At the same time, Mr. White wrote a letter to the Chief Ranger, telling him of the feeling of the Department on the matter. Perhaps a personal interview on the part of Mr. Thomson, and an explanation of the whole matter in a clear and kindly fashion, might help to prevent future trouble.

The first practical problem in the Park itself, once the paper problems of organization and policy had been looked after, was to appoint a staff, and to establish it on the spot. On June seventh of the same year, a meeting was called by Commissioner Hardy for that purpose. Director of Surveys Kirkpatrick, and Superintendent Wilson of the Niagara Falls Park, were called in to assist. After attending to details that will appear later, they decided to send in a party that summer, to be accompanied by Messrs. Dickson and Wilson, with the express mission of putting up buildings for headquarters and laying out canoe routes for ranger patrols.

Six weeks later, an Order-in-Council was passed appointing Mr. Peter Thomson first Superintendent of Algonquin Park.

"Upon recommendation of the Honourable the Commissioner of Crown Lands, the Committee of Council advise that Peter Thomson of Brussels, road and bridge builder, be appointed a Ranger of Algonquin Park, to be known as Chief Ranger, at a salary of $600 per annum; he also to be furnished with a small log house in the Park in which to live, and firewood from down timber, but not other supplies . . . "

Preparations had gone ahead for the first official expedition into the Park. On July 23rd, a party consisting of Messrs. Dickson and Wilson, not fewer than six men, and a cook, was to leave Huntsville by canoe for the journey up through Lake of Bays and the upper Muskoka waters (Oxtongue River), to the site chosen for headquarters. Some notion of the life they would lead is suggested by the list of equipment for the party.

4 canoes — 2 fiteen-foot, 2 twenty-foot; 30 pairs of twelve-pound blankets, 10 bed ticks, camp cooking

stove and Dutch oven, knives, forks, spoons, etc.,
grindstone, a box with four-pound axes, 1 broad axe,
2 hunting axes, a draw knife, a spokeshave, and a
supply of building tools.

Provisions — 500 pounds of long, clear pork, 500
pounds of flour, barrel biscuit.

Tents — 1 eight-man tent, 2 three-man tents.

Other articles — 2 rifles, 2 revolvers, ammunition,
compass.

Peter Thomson wrote from Canoe Lake, in the middle of August:

"When we left Huntsville, July 26th, Mr. Dickson wrote
you giving an account of proceedings up to that time,
also the number and names of the men who accompanied us. I then expected our mail accommodations
would be such that we would have communications
more easily with the outside world, but I find that it is
by a mere chance that we can either send or receive
letters once in two or three weeks at best.

We are installed in Algonquin Park and located at
Canoe Lake upon the Muskoka waters. Our journey
up the lakes and rivers Mr. Dickson will give you in
person. Upon my arrival at Huntsville I met Timothy
O'Leary of Millington, Stephen Waters and William
Gale, with instructions from your Department. I also
employed William Morgan and Robert Dinsmore of
Huntsville as labouring men. All of whom I am
pleased to say have so far proven to be first-class men
in every particular. It would be a very difficult task
to secure a more suitable lot of men for this particular
kind of work.

In company with Mr. Dickson we have made as extensive a tour in and around the Park as his limited time
would permit, but sufficient I think to give me a fair
idea of the limits and water courses of the reservation."

Apart from reports of Indians hunting in the north, things went
well for the Chief Ranger until October. Then he ran into trouble
that called for backing from the Department. On the 22nd he wrote
as follows:

"No doubt but you expected to have heard from me
before this time, but I started out the following morning
after my arrival at this place and at no time since

White Tail Deer.

WINTER SCENE, ALGONQUIN PARK.

have I been within two or three days' journey from the Post Office. We've not had any mail in the last month or more.

We started from Canoe Lake en route for Opeongo Lake and the southeast limits of the Park, cutting roads and trails over the portages, cleaning out all floodwood, etc., out of the creeks, and constructing camps at the following places: one at Cache Lake, one at Lake of Two Rivers, one at the southwest bay of the Opeongo Lake, and one at the southeast, at the head of Opeongo River cut a good trail four miles and built a camp at the head of McDougall Lake (now named Booth Lake), and cut good trails to the extreme east limits of the Park.

No doubt but you are aware of the fact that the Gilmour Lumber Company have commenced operations upon their limits in Peck. They have constructed a dam at the foot of Tea Lake, also a depot at that point and five large camps upon Tea and Canoe Lakes. I regret to say that in our absence they built a large camp alongside of our building, and a beautiful grove which I had hoped to preserve in connection with our head-quarters has been badly damaged. I saw their manager and he stated that he placed their camp at that place by the express orders of Mr. Gilmour. I find them very agreeable people and willing to do all they can to assist in preserving game . . . "

and so on. The Gilmour firm and the Department exchanged correspondence on the subject of the grove of trees, in which Commissioner Hardy made it very clear who was in control of the Park.

Peter Thomson's 1894 report gave an account of the work that had been accomplished during the first year of the Park's existence. He listed the Park Staff as follows:

    Chief Ranger — John Simpson.

    Rangers — Tim O'Leary, Stephen Waters, William
        Geall.

    Temporary Rangers — D. A. Ross, James Sawyers,
        Daniel May.

During that year, the men had carried on the work begun by the work party that had gone in the summer before. In all, they had constructed sixteen shelter houses, and had cleared over eighty-three miles of portages. Some of the shelter houses had been made out of new logs, others had been prepared from buildings abandoned by lumber companies, who were no longer working in the district. Mr. Thomson also reported that the rangers had found time to plant some of the pine seed furnished by the Department, in the hope of beginning a programme of reforestation.

In reporting progress in protecting the Park's wildlife, Mr. Thomson compared his first impression of the region with his latest observations:

> "When I entered on my duties in July, 1893, scarcely a beaver sign could be seen, and it required close inspection to discover the presence of these animals; now we are aware of at least sixty places in the Park where families of beaver have located themselves, in a number of cases in places where there was no previous indication of their existence."

There is evidence, too, that both Mr. Thomson and the members of his staff had already fallen under the spell of the Park. Visitors to the district have always been delighted to find how enthusiastically the rangers talk about their encounters with the wildlife. The new Superintendent commented on this trait when he said:

> "In a district such as this where human companionship is almost entirely lacking, the presence of wild animals relieves the solitude of the forest and adds much to the pleasure of existence."

Then he went on to tell of some of his own experiences in the performance of his duties. On one trip made by the rangers, they encountered a cow moose swimming in a stream with her two calves. The rangers wanted to get close to the young ones, so they paddled towards them. The mother went up on shore into the bushes, but the little fellows proved to be quite friendly, and they finally condescended to take bread right out of the rangers' hands. Thomson recorded several other illustrations of the same sort of thing and then he concluded:

> "Though there is little harm to be apprehended from the wild beasts of the Park, there is just that spice of danger which is sufficient to give zest to the somewhat ardous tasks of the rangers."

With regard to lumbering operations, the Superintendent had certain complaints about the effect of their methods on the appearance of the Park. He found at many of the outlets of the lakes that dams had been built, to assure sufficient water for the spring log drive or for the use of alligators on the upper waters. When the water was held too long, the forest growth along the lake edges suffered. The earth was washed away from the roots of the trees, and the flooding left a ring of dead trees and deadheads along the margins of the lakes. As Thomson pointed out, this not only marred the beauty of the Park, but threatened to develop into a major problem, since the waterways provided the chief means of travel and the driftwood clogged up the rivers and streams.

This report was his last. Peter Thomson died at his Canoe Lake headquarters on September 5, 1895, stricken with paralysis.

CHAPTER 10

AFTER THE UNTIMELY DEATH of the first Superintendent, Algonquin Park entered a critical period. For a time, it seemed that Alexander Kirkwood's dream would turn into a Government nightmare. Dickson, in advising the Department as to ways of handling the ousted trappers, had done his best to forestall what was perhaps inevitable.

The annual report for the year following Peter Thomson's death was drawn up by John Simpson, his Chief Ranger, who succeeded him. This report mentioned the progress that had been made on the Booth Railway, then under construction. During 1895, twenty miles of track had been laid west of Whitney, and men were now working nine miles inside the Park. The work of the rangers increased with the consequent fire hazard, and strict game supervision was made that much more difficult.

Mr. Simpson made special mention of the work that the rangers were doing in marking out the southern and western Park boundaries. The authorities were particularly anxious to blaze out a clear border line in that region, so as to give trespassers no excuse for overstepping the limits. The Department had prepared a supply of signs printed on linen posters, that were to be erected at key spots, to set forth the penalties for hunting and trapping in the region.

During that year, the rangers had marked out about twenty miles along the west border in the section opposite the Dorset-Haliburton country, from which most of the poachers were likely to come. There they had come upon frames used for stretching skins that had been used the previous winter. On the other hand, some progress had been made: several of the trappers had asked the rangers' permission to remove their traps from their old grounds in the Park. These men had been escorted into their camps and out again by Park Rangers.

Thereafter, Park records are obscure until the appointment of Simpson's successor. Judging from subsequent events, and the scattered correspondence of the period, it seems that a few of the rangers became involved in dishonest practices, and that the Park had consequently fallen into disrepute. As information filtered down to Toronto, the Department became alarmed and decided to appoint a new Superintendent. In the Spring they approached George

Bartlett, and persuaded him to accept the post. By August, he was installed in the new headquarters at Cache Lake.

Mr. Bartlett describes his appointment in these words:

"I was down in Toronto on business when I was first approached for the Algonquin Park job. My business was with the Government over some timber limits and I was asked if I would take over Algonquin Park. I was then forty-seven years old. I became Superintendent of the 3,000 square mile tract. The job included the position of Postmaster, Commissioner in the High Court of Justice, Police Magistrate, and Chief Coroner in the district of Nipissing. The Premier of the Province told me that the Park had been a blot on the Government and asked me to make it a credit."

To this new undertaking, Mr. Bartlett brought an excellent background of experience in lumber camps and in rural Ontario. As a boy of eleven, he had been brought out from the Old Country to an uncle's farm at Springtown in Renfrew County because of illness, but he grew into a healthy man of more than average strength. At the age of twenty he married and established a home in Orillia, where most of his family of seven sons and three daughters were born and educated. His work took him frequently into the north country. At twenty-one he worked as a labourer on the Transcontinental Railway. Afterwards, he was put in charge of a gang of men who were clearing the bush for the construction of the C.P.R. from Mattawa to Sturgeon Falls. While with the railway he qualified as an expert culler of lumber, which gave him background for his future work. After leaving the railroad, he worked on the J. R. Booth limits on the Upper Ottawa, where he had charge of several camps and a total of some five hundred men. There is a Park story that Booth himself recommended Bartlett to the Department.

The news of Bartlett's appointment made little difference to the old trappers, or to the Indians in the north, who continued to hunt moose and deer. In their experience, the Government was far away, and the Park Rangers were easily persuaded to wink an eye at poaching. Some of them, they had seen, were not above doing a little illegal trapping themselves.

George Bartlett changed their ideas and behaviour, but not overnight. His first step was to increase the Park ranging staff from four to nine. The easy-going life under Simpson was gone. Going out in pairs the rangers kept the Park under fairly constant supervision. Five canoes and seven pairs of snowshoes were added to the equipment, and the Cache Lake headquarters improved. Following Bartlett's indefatigable example, the spirit of his men leapt to meet the challenge, and before his first year was done trespassers were aware that here was a new force to reckon with.

An example of how Mr. Bartlett dealt with these men, and of the way his earlier experiences bore fruit in his new work, is the story of three poachers brought into his office by the rangers. Immediately he recognized them, but they didn't realize who he was, because he had worn a beard when they knew him. When the charges were read in English they shook their heads. They didn't understand. The charges were read in French. No, they still didn't understand what this was all about. Finally Mr. Bartlett turned to the man who seemed to do most of the headshaking for the trio.

"Come, Antoine," said he, smiling at the look of amazement on the man's face, "don't you remember one time when you and I had to stay overnight and all the next day on a little island on Sturgeon Lake, when there wasn't enough wind for our big sail boat?"

Antoine's face cleared, and then fell. He walked up to the desk and said sheepishly, "Say, boss, don't be too hard on us for this first steal!"

Their offence was serious, and Bartlett committed them to three months in jail, hoping that this sentence, and his own fair treatment, would prevent a repetition of the offence.

The manuscript of an article prepared by him, and describing how he and Steve Waters spent twenty-two days in crossing the Park from north to south, affords an excellent picture of how he supervised the vast area under his control. This trip, taken probably in 1902, seems to have been the first that Mr. Bartlett took through the northern area of the Park, in his official capacity. The plan was to circle around to the north by rail, and enter from Eau Claire on the North Bay-Ottawa Line of the C.P.R.

This railroad trip was far from dull. Going west on the Canada Atlantic, still within the Park boundaries, the train ground to a stop. The wooden bridge at Rainy Lake (Rain Lake) had just finished burning down. Fortunately, another train was waiting beyond the wrecked bridge; Bartlett and Steve unloaded their canoe, packed in their dunnage, crossed the water, and continued their journey.

When they finally reached Eau Claire, they were able to get a wagon to take them for twelve miles alongside the Amable du Fond River towards the Park boundaries. This was the road used both by the Dufond family and by the lumber firms in the district, and they found it passable, though very rough. At length, at the halfway camp, they were able to put their canoe in the water. Mr. Bartlett's own words continue the story.

"We began our journey up the river — our destination for the night being Koish-Koqui (Kioshkokwi) Lake. After we had gone about two miles along our way and when we were still outside the boundaries of the Park, we sighted an Indian camp and ran ashore to investigate. We found a squaw and two young Indians, and judging by the moose shanks that we saw lying around they were living on the fat of the land.

"When we reached the shelter house which was our destination, we stopped for the night. After tea we heard the dip of a paddle and as we were now in the Park, I had the right to inquire, 'Who goes there?' I blew my whistle and hailed the passing canoe. Ah-ha, we found it was the Indian from the camp we had visited earlier in the afternoon. The poor chap was very uneasy, and explained that he had been in the Park getting roots and bark for medicine. This statement was corroborated by the contents of the canoe and by his own appearance. We warned him and let him go, telling him we had noticed the moose shanks in his camp.

"On the next day, after a portage, we reached the Indian farm on Manitou Lake (now called Wilkes Lake). Here live a family of the Dufond descendants after whom the river was named. They had quite a clearing, a large house and barn, and they kept horses, cows and poultry. They were not disturbed by the Government when the Park was established. Mrs. Dufond kindly invited us in and treated us to some maple sugar of which she made 450 pounds. It was exceedingly good. After a smoke in which the old lady joined and a chat with Dufond, we pushed on up the lake to Pine Island, where we had a shelter house. Incidentally, when we inquired of the Indians how the lake got its name, they told us that long ago, when their great-grandparents first visited it, there

was a huge serpent seen in the lake, and the Great
Spirit was in the serpent — hence the name.

"We retraced our steps once more to Kiosh-Koqui
(Kioshkokwi) Lake and went from thence down to
Mink Lake. There we met two of our rangers who
had come through from Rainy (Rain) Lake. They
reported game very abundant. They also found the
carcasses of two bull moose in the lake at the foot
of a huge bluff. An examination showed that they
had had a battle royal at the head of the bluff and
had fallen over, killing them both. Our shelter was
built among some old lumber camps and during the
night, hearing a noise, we got up to find a fine old
buck that had gone into the old meat house to lick
the salty block where meat used to be cut. He had
been trapped by the door blowing to and he was
making desperate efforts to get out. When we gave
him the chance, he did not wait to thank us.

"We spent four days at the shelter on Cedar Lake.
Sunday we stayed quietly in camp. Monday the
other rangers went on to Great Opeongo Lake (now
Opeongo Lake). Tuesday Steve and I fished along
the rapids on the Petawawa River, where choice
speckled beauties are to be found, and then before we
left, we crossed over to the Depot Farm, where we
had some baked beans with the drivers and posted
our letters written on birch bark. Then we were forced
to stay in camp all day because of a change in
weather. The day before it had been beautiful and
mild with just sufficient ripple to make the lake appear
one sheet of diamonds. Today, its foam-capped waves
came piling in upon the shore covering the trees with
ice until the branches hung with long icicles. What a
sight it was a little later when the sun burst forth —
the trees appeared as if decked with silver.

"Saturday morning we started for Catfish Lake. There
is one very interesting thing on this lake — Turtle
Rock. It is on one of the islands and it looks like
some huge prehistoric animal. It is said that the
Indians used to worship it. It resembles a huge turtle
and is estimated to weigh thirty-five tons.

"At Burnt Lake (now named Portal Lake) we spent the night at Barnet's Depot at the head of the lake. We were welcomed by their fire ranger, Mr. Leblanche, who treated us to the very best his larder afforded. Those interested in reforestation can find a very encouraging field in the splendid growth of young pine on the Gillies' Limit there.

"The shelter house at Misty Lake had been broken into —by a porcupine who had taken possession of it. He had eaten a hole through the door and had destroyed door and window frames. These apparently harmless animals are a great nuisance in this way and will cut your canoe gunwales and paddles, if left where they can get at them.

"Finally, after continuing on down through the chain of rivers and lakes, we reached the railway once more at Rainy (Rain) Lake. We had covered a good part of the western section of the Park and I was satisfied that things were pretty well in order there."

In after years, Mr. Bartlett found that it was much easier to make his inspection trip in the winter by snowshoe. Then he would set off with two rangers — his son Jim and Mark Robinson were frequently his companions — and would be gone for many weeks. A dog team would haul the supplies, and they would get around most of the Park in this way. Each night they would plan to stop at a shelter hut where they would be warm and comfortable, and where they could stay if the weather were unfavorable.

On some of the earliest trips the dogs were driven by one of the pioneer rangers, Albert Ranger, whose two sons, Telesphore and Peter, joined the staff at a later date. "Albair," as Mr. Bartlett and everyone else called him, had a great love for his two dogs, Jack and Judy, and they, in turn, would obey him in a way that they would no one else. Everyone who remembers Albair and his dogs agrees that he thought the world of them, and that they thoroughly enjoyed their winter outings in the Park. In spite of that, the story of the tricks they played on their master, and Albair's reproachful prophecy, "That dog Jack, he got some bad plan in hees head," came to be a stock saying at headquarters. George Bartlett's picture of "A Six Weeks' Snowshoe Trip Through the Park", quoted with the permission of his widow who now lives in Ridgetown, shows some of the difficulties encountered by Park administrators in the old days:

"We had been several days upon our way when we saw some snowshoe tracks near dusk as we struck across the country. Since they were evidently not those of our rangers, we talked the matter over and decided that our first move in the morning would be to look the parties up in case they should prove to be trappers. This meant an extra early start and we planned to turn in before long. There were certain signs of warm weather that caused us a little anxiety — we heard the call of the Acadian owl for one. He makes a noise like a saw-whet and usually he heralds a change. However, we decided not to worry. We had little moccasins for the dogs' feet if their feet started to ball up. These were made of a small piece of deer skin in the form of a bag with a drawstring on the top to tie around the dog's leg. We rolled up in our sleeping bags and it seemed only an hour or so when Albair's 'Levez, levez' roused us to a hearty breakfast.

"As I had decided to follow the tracks we had already seen, we retraced our steps with that end in view. However, we soon found that our men were not trappers but were in the bush on legitimate business. We had only gone a little over two miles when we met the two men who had been responsible for the tracks. They proved to be two bush rangers who were looking over some timber for the limit holder.

"At one of the other shelter houses we went out with the rangers who were staying there to see how they were getting along with their trapping of beaver for the Government. Each year these skins are bundled up and taken to headquarters where they are marked Algonquin Provincial Park and stamped with the Government's registered stamp — a King's crown. These are sold at auction and represented an annual income of many thousands of dollars.

"We had an interval of soft weather, but finally we were on our way again. It was below zero at last and the slush on the lake had frozen sufficiently to carry us — truly wonderful travelling. The wolves were on the alert, too, making the woods ring with their howls, but did not come out into the open to give us a chance for a shot. Our dogs were rested and keen, but as we came out to the second lake, to use Albair's expression, 'One of Jack's bad plans got in his head'. The result of this was that, when the lead tightened up the harness, he held back. Since the harness was not buckled as tight as usual, he backed clean out of it, and before we could stop him, was off across the ice as fast as he could go. We could do nothing, so Albair lit his pipe and sat on the load until Mr. Jack condescended to return and be harnessed. This was not until he had explored the lake to his entire satisfaction. Albair's reproaches seemed lost on him, for he only wagged his tail and pulled, evidently satisfied that he had had the best of it. Despite his 'bad plan' we made twenty miles that day, and early in the afternoon we joined the other rangers."

As Mr. Bartlett pointed out in this account, the rangers covered a great deal of territory during routine game patrols of the Park. On that particular occasion, the travellers suspected of poaching were proved to be there on legitimate business, but at others, the rangers were forced to take into custody poachers and traders who were trespassing on the Park game preserve. Mark Robinson tells many different stories about the work of the old rangers, who moved about in pairs to patrol the whole Park area.

One of these incidents must have taken place about 1908, when both Mark and his ranging partner, Zeph Nadon, were quite new to the district. They were living together at the old cabin at Canoe Lake, when Mr. Bartlett gave them a difficult assignment. He knew that furs were being smuggled out of the Park, and he felt that he could learn who the culprit was if only he could discover how he was disposing of his catch. If they could find out how the furs were being transported out of the Park to the buyer, action could be taken to clear up the whole matter.

It was some time before the two rangers were able to get the slightest clue as to how this poaching ring was working, but the Park had a grapevine system all its own, and after a while they learned that a stranger by the name of Black was paying frequent visits to the Rock Lake district. At that time the Park boundary came just to the head of Rock Lake, the railway station itself was outside the limits, and therefore out of their territory. However, they determined to see what was going on. They had heard that Black was adopting a very hail-fellow-well-met attitude to everyone in the area, and they thought they'd like to have a chance to see what he was up to.

One day Mark and Zeph managed to be on the station platform when Black got off at Rock Lake. Sure enough, Zeph recognized him as a fur buyer whom he had known in the Temiskaming country. Still, they knew that they could not pin anything definite on him unless they caught him in the very act of dealing with trappers in the Park, or receiving furs which they could prove had been taken in the Park. They decided that they would wait around until he had departed, and then search the place where he had been staying. Just as they had expected, they found a fine supply of furs on hand. There were many skins of animals that could be found only in the Park — such as mink, marten and fisher.

Even with this knowledge, they were still powerless to do anything but make a report to Mr. Bartlett, and they were not too sure that he would be pleased with their investigations outside the actual Park boundaries. The letter of the law said that their jurisdiction extended outside for a distance of one mile, but Mr. Bartlett felt that they should confine their efforts to the Park itself. When they reported to him at headquarters, it was late in the afternoon. He listened to what they had to say, and told them that he would consider the matter the next day. Soon after supper, he called them back into his office. He had been reading their written report, and the name of Black caught his attention.

"Who's this man Black?" he asked, "surely you don't imply that poor old Jimmy Black, who isn't quite right in his head, is mixed up in this?"

Mark and Zeph explained that the buyer was no relation to old Jimmy, but that he had likely taken the same name to throw people off the scent of what he was really doing.

Finally, when this whole matter came into the open, it was found that there were a number of people linked up with the marketing of the furs. Not only was Mr. Black involved, but some of the railway employees were taking part in the racket, too. One man lived near a railway trestle not more than half a mile from Park Headquarters. He was paid by the railway company for acting as a fire warden, and for keeping the bridge in repair. In addition, he was augmenting his income by loading stolen furs on passing trains.

However, locating and charging trappers in the Park was only one of the tasks undertaken by the rangers in their work of protecting the wildlife of the district. Sometimes it was very difficult to catch the trespasser in the act, and clever poachers devised many schemes to obtain the fur they were after. Sometimes the rangers found that they had to be content with safeguarding the lives of the animals by simply destroying trapping equipment picked up within the boundaries.

At one time, when the poaching was particularly widespread, it became known to the staff that certain trappers had evolved a new system that was hard to beat. By hiding their traps off the regular ranger patrol routes, these trappers could cross the Park boundaries early in winter with a small pack of supplies, and bury themselves in the very centre of the Park without the rangers' knowledge. This type of poaching was very difficult to combat with the limited staff at the Superintendent's command. But Mark tells of one trip which he and Zeph took through an out-of-the-way section of the Park. In between Opeongo Lake and Burnt Island Lake, is a rough section that travellers usually avoid. There, he and Zeph found a great hoard of traps which they gleefully disposed of by tossing them in the lake. They failed to catch the poacher, but at least they had the satisfaction of knowing he would take no pelts out of the area that season.

In spite of the rangers' vigilance, however, poaching activities actually increased. The reason for this was a new Government policy whose repercussions were so widespread that it is worth looking into.

Bartlett's first report, for the year 1899, quoted two authorities to the effect that the beaver population had already increased to a gratifying extent. Ranger Jim Sawyer believed that the beaver population had more than trebled in those sections of the Park where he had set his trap lines in the old days when he travelled into that district from the Haliburton country. That same year Mr. Bartlett had received a visit from the Indian Chief, Big Canoe, who claimed that Canoe Lake had been named after him, and who told the Superintendent that he had trapped in that area some forty years before. Since Big Canoe belonged to a band of Ojibwas who had previously claimed the whole of the Park area draining into the Georgian Bay as their hunting grounds, it is quite possible that he had hunted along the Oxtongue River in the early days, although it is improbable that his name had been given to Canoe Lake, since the first record of this name goes back to 1853. In any case, Chief Big Canoe toured all through the region, and reported to Mr. Bartlett that he was delighted to see how much the beaver had multiplied since his last visit.

In his 1908 report, Mr. Bartlett stressed the fact that the beaver in the Park had become so numerous that he felt the Department would be wise to allow the rangers to do some supervised trapping. By 1909, the work had already begun, and over three hundred beaver had been taken in a comparatively small area. Two years later, the annual catch stood at 402 beaver skins, while a small number of otter, marten, mink, and muskrat, had also been taken. The total value of these furs was placed to $3,340.00. Each year from then until 1920, when the project was given up, the Superintendent's annual report gave the amount that had been realized from the Department's fur sale. In that last year, the total revenue had risen to $14,179.00, but even that was not sufficient to compensate the authorities for the amount of trouble that this activity caused, or the amount of criticism that they had to meet.

The Department, in adopting the scheme, had reckoned without the effect that this policy would have on the ranging staff, or the antagonism that it would arouse in the trappers of the surrounding district. The increase in poaching on the part of both these groups was tremendous. On the ranger side, it was hardly fair to expect men to devote their energies to game preservation, and yet to ask them to trap in order to build up a revenue for the Government. Critics accused the men of taking one animal for the Government, and one for themselves. It was not difficult to market the pelts privately, and the rewards were great. Not all the rangers were involved in this game, but there were enough to lower the reputation of the whole staff in the eyes of the general public.

Then, too, the trappers in the surrounding country began to redouble their activities, and occasionally a ranger would work with them. The trappers felt that the Department had been unfair to them, and that they were quite justified in taking their revenge in their own way. The Government had set aside this territory as a reserve in 1893, and had deprived them of grounds over which they had been trapping for many years. The boundaries had been marked out, warning signs had been posted, and fines meted out to offenders. Now the Government itself had taken to trapping, an act which was tantamount to the Government poaching on *their* grounds. This train of thought led to a period of illicit trapping that, in the long run, must have cost the Government much more than it realized from the sale of fur.

Many an ingenious scheme was devised by the poachers to outwit the rangers. There was the Indian in the north of the Park who approached the boundary for two miles on stilts, and into the Park a good distance before abandoning them. There is the tale of another trapper who padded the heel of his moccasin and then walked with his snow shoes on backwards, so anyone finding his tracks would follow him the wrong way. One perfectly innocent attempt to outwit the rangers will particularly interest any who have heard of the writer Grey Owl, or better still, those who have read his books.

By 1908, poaching in the Park had reached the point where an investigation was ordered, and some rangers, implicated in aiding and abetting the poachers, were dismissed. The news spread far and wide, bringing to the Park one day a lean, hawk-nosed young man, by the name of Archie Belaney. Archie had been born in England, but had read so voraciously about bush life in Canada, that he came out, while still in his teens, to learn his woodcraft the hard way. By the time he showed up in the Park, Archie had been around a bit, and fancied himself as a woodsman. In fact, he was rash enough to make a bet that he could cross the Park from boundary to boundary in the middle of winter without being caught.

The rangers' intelligence service was good: Bartlett got wind of the bet. Albert Ranger, Zeph Nadon, Mark Robinson and Bud Callahan were all put on the alert, and instructed to keep a sharp watch along the railway tracks, which Archie was bound to cross. Mark Robinson had recently been stationed at the old shelter house on Canoe Lake, while Bud Callahan was living at Smoke Lake. Both spots were on the main poaching trails into the Park.

Bud figured that Archie would likely come in along the old Gilmour Road from Dorset, and then strike north through the Crown Lake District, to hit the border of the Park at Porcupine Lake, now known as Big Porcupine Lake. Sure enough, he was right! It was late in the afternoon that Bud came upon his tracks, and just as it was getting dark he caught a glimpse of him ahead.

Belaney smiled hospitably when Bud showed up, ranger badge and all, at his fire. After all, he had just entered the Park; he *was* travelling without a license, but beyond that he had not infringed on Park regulations. The two men had a friendly chat, fixed their beds for the night, and went to sleep.

But not Archie Belaney; he wasn't going to lose a wager as easily as that. While Bud slept he got up, put his things on his pack, and slipped away into the darkness.

In the meantime it had turned bitterly cold. In territory entirely new to him, and barely enough light to see by, Archie must have wished more than once that he had forgotten his bet, and stayed snug and warm in his sleeping bag under the brush shelter. Some time early in the morning he fell into a shallow beaver pond at the west end of Ragged Lake, and lost his pack. Now he was in a real jam: he had no dry matches to light a fire with which he might dry out his clothes.

While this was going on, Bud had awakened after a good night's sleep, to find his companion gone. Muttering uncomplimentary remarks, he had followed, increasing his pace when he came to the broken ice in the beaver pond, thinking, no doubt, that it served him right for putting him to all this trouble, but realizing that Archie's predicament in that weather was no joke. When Bud caught up with his fugitive, he found him in a wretched state, with both feet frozen.

This time Bud was in no mood for pleasantries—nor was Belaney. Callahan decided to take him along to the Superintendent's office, with all possible speed. They stopped to cook a meal at the shelter house left by the Mickle Dyment Company at the south end of Smoke Lake, and then went on up to Mark's place at Canoe Lake.

When Mark examined Archie Belaney's feet that night, he shook his head gravely. They were badly swollen. He bandaged them up, and loaned Archie a change of clothes. When it came time to leave for headquarters in the morning, Mark felt that the trapper was in no shape to leave, but Bud was inexorable. They took a train through to Cache Lake, and after the interview at the office, Belaney went back to Mark's place to stay until his feet had healed sufficiently for him to be on his way.

For three weeks Mark nursed him, doing everything in his power to save Archie's feet. Even after the flesh had healed, Archie had trouble walking. Finally, when he was well enough to go, Mark performed the last act of the Good Samaritan, and loaned him enough money to take the train back to Timagami.

Thereafter Mark lost track of him. Trappers reported that he was still living in the Timagami District, and Tom Thomson came upon him once when he was working over that way as a fire ranger. Mark never saw Archie Belaney again.

But he did eventually hear from Archie, in a most unusual way. When Grey Owl's first books were published, Mark was very interested in the stories told by this man, who seemed to have such an intimate

TIMBER WOLF.

Veteran Park Ranger, Zeff Nadon.

knowledge of the habits of the beaver. One day, in 1935, an Indian came into the Park Headquarters while Mark was there. He walked up to Mark and said:

"Grey Owl sends you his greetings."

"That's very kind of him," replied Mark, "but I don't think I've ever had the pleasure of meeting him. That's one thing I've looked forward to."

"Oh, I think you must have met him," responded the visitor. "He told me that you had once nursed him for three weeks in your home in the Park, when he was suffering from severely frozen feet."

With that information Mark realized that his acquaintance with Grey Owl had been made many years before, in the days when he was still Archie Belaney. Grey Owl had remembered.

To return to the chief cause for the increase in poaching, Mr. Bartlett could hardly have foreseen the complications that his policy would bring about, when he first sponsored its introduction. From his point of view, the receipts from the fur sale would help reduce the expenses of running the Park, and would assist in publicizing the Park. As far as he could see, it was simply an extension of a policy that had already gained renown for the Park in many different parts of the world. From zoos, and from collectors scattered all over the United States and Europe, had come requests for live animals from Algonquin Park. Beaver, especially, were shipped in specially marked crates, to many distant spots.

From the files of Mr. Bartlett's correspondence, it is apparent what a great deal of time both he and his ranging staff spent in this shipping of live animals. The beaver is a very sensitive creature, and on many occasions when shipments were made to England or to the Continent, the animals died on shipboard, because they didn't receive proper care. Then, when the animals did arrive, there was frequently a great deal of trouble before the cases were returned to their owners. Mr. Bartlett must have often wondered whether the work involved was worth either the cash returns or the publicity that it brought to the Park.

One by-product of this activity was a steel trap, perfected by Jim Bartlett, the Superintendent's son, for capturing live animals. The trap proved so efficient, that it is in common use in many parts of Canada to this day. It consisted of wire netting over a frame, in two sections, that opened out like a suitcase. These two sections were joined together along one side by a very strong spring, which allowed them to open out flat under tension, but closed them together with terrific force when the spring was released. To catch the beaver, the trap was opened out and put in the water at the top of the dam. When he swam up to investigate, the beaver's chest released the spring, and he was caught. Pictures of this invention, with others to show the Algonquin Park shipping cases, and the fine beaver skins taken in the district, are included in the Park reports for the years 1915 to 1918.

Experts from many parts of the world came to see how the Government Game Reserve was run, evidence that the Park was becoming well known as a successful venture. Among the visitors, was Mr. V. Generosoff, of the Russian Department of Agriculture, who came during the summer of 1914, to observe methods used in Ontario for preserving wild life, his own government contemplating similar action.

The attitude of the Park authorities to wolves, was always of particular interest to such visitors. Administrators of game reserves have always had difficulty making up their minds as to whether predatory animals should be exterminated or whether they should be offered the same protection as other wild life. From the first, it had been foreseen in the Park, that the increase in the deer population would likely lead to a corresponding increase in the number of wolves in the area. Some naturalists argued that a percentage of predatory animals was needed to keep the other species in a healthy condition, since the weaklings were killed off, and only the sturdy stock survived. The Park authorities, however, decided to exterminate the wolves, and, in spite of a great deal of discussion, this has continued to be the policy to our own times.

Starting about 1903, the rangers were supplied with poison for use in their war against the wolves in the Park, but as time went on this method came under severe attack. For one thing, there was no way of making sure that the poisoned bait set out for a wolf would not be eaten by another animal. Then, some people claimed that the wolf's stomach was so strong that it could disgorge the poisoned meat, and suffer no ill effects. The practice of using poison in the Park was finally discontinued, and the rangers fell back on setting snares, and on shooting the wolves whenever possible. The bounty, which stood at fifteen dollars for many years, has now been increased to twenty-five.

Many stories are told by the old rangers, about the tricks they have used in trying to kill wolves which they knew were prowling about in the neighbourhood of their cabins. Mr. J. Edwin Colson, who first came to the Park as a ranger in 1905, claims that wolves are too smart for traps, but that they can sometimes be taken in snares. He recalls one time, however, when a wolf was killed, that it had several different wire nooses about its neck. Each time he had been caught, he had broken free by the simple expediency of turning his head around in order to bite through the wire. One wolf is reported to have been captured, that had bitten through a steel wire made of six strands of metal.

The man who claims his bounty for wolves in the Park, works hard for it as a rule: but not always. Peter Ranger tells how he once claimed the bounty for a wolf which he had killed on Maple Lake. That year the snow had held off at the beginning of the winter, so that in January, the lakes were a sheet of ice, and it was much simpler for the rangers to make their rounds on skates than on snowshoes. Peter had put on his skates one day when he planned to cross the lake in the north part of the Park. Far out in the centre of the lake he caught sight of the carcass of a deer, and as he approached it, he noticed two wolves advancing out of the woods at the shore, towards the deer. Since Peter had his gun with him, he was determined to get close enough for a shot. He dropped to the ice and began edging closer to his quarry. In the meantime, he found one wolf was staying close to the shore, but the other was making his way very slowly towards the deer. Peter saw that the ice was so slippery, the wolf couldn't get a good grip on it with his claws.

All this time, Peter was inching along the ice as quickly as he could. At length, when he was still several hundred yards away, the wolf looked up and saw him approaching. Peter fired, then skated towards his quarry. The wolf was hit, but the bullet did not strike a vital spot. As if he knew that he couldn't move across the ice as quickly as Peter, he dropped and started to roll towards shore. However, Peter soon got close enough for another shot, and finished him off.

The next time he went to North Bay, he took the pelt with him and went to see Mr. Parks, the game warden, to claim the Government bounty. The girl in the office heard him telling how he had killed the wolf, and asked if he would repeat the story for one of the reporters from the "North Bay Nugget". Peter said that he didn't mind, and gave all the information to the newspaper man. What was his dismay when he saw the report in the next issue of the paper headed "Another Wolf Story", and told as if the whole incident had been the product of Peter's imagination.

Peter had another tale to tell about wolves — and this one had a witness to vouch for its authenticity. One day in September, 1941, he was paddling across Crooked Lake in his fifteen-foot canoe. There, well out in the middle of the lake, he saw a wolf swimming after a buck. This time he didn't have a gun with him. There wasn't much chance of killing the wolf, but he didn't want the wolf to get the deer. Consequently, Peter edged the canoe close enough to the pair so that he could take a crack at the wolf with his paddle. The buck swam off when it found that it had a chance to do so, but Peter kept the canoe in place between the wolf and the shore, and hit the wolf on the head whenever he had a chance. One time the wolf took a snap at the bow of the canoe, and it swung right around like a top, but still the struggle went on.

Finally, after about half an hour of this battle, Peter saw another ranger, Dan Stringer, coming down the lake in a motor boat, towing two canoes. As Dan got closer, he could see what was happening, and he began to shout to Peter to paddle clear so that he could get a shot at the wolf with his revolver. Peter called out not to shoot because he knew that the wolf was heavy with water, and would sink to the bottom if it were killed. However, Dan kept right on coming, and when he was close enough he fired. Then, although Peter tried to slip his paddle under the body, the wolf was so saturated with water than it sank right to the bottom, like a stone. Dan and Peter tried for a long while to recover the body, so as to claim the bounty of twenty-five dollars, but all to no purpose. That was one time when the reward was not collected for a dead wolf.

In spite of the infiltration of wolves from surrounding areas almost as fast as they could be killed by the rangers, deer increased rapidly in the Park.

By 1917, when Canadian meat supplies, due to the First World War, had reached a low ebb, the deer population had so increased that Mr. Bartlett suggested the rangers be allowed to kill some of the deer for meat. In his 1918 report, it is stated that some 650 deer had been shipped to dealers in Toronto and Hamilton. According to rangers who were on the staff at the time, it was possible to shoot as many as twenty in a single day, in one section of the Park.

Today, although it is doubtful whether deer are as plentiful as in Bartlett's time, every visitor is almost sure to see a few. Even the early timber cutting has proved an advantage: deer thrive on the sweet young shoots of deciduous trees in the succulent second growth, and the lower branches of the young cedars.

A great deal more could be written about Mr. Bartlett and the long list of rangers who worked so faithfully under him. Of these many, Steve Waters, Tim O'Leary, William Gale, John Simpson, D. A. Ross, Jim Sawyers, Bob Balfour, Albert Ranger with his two sons, Telesphore and Peter, Zeph Nadon, Dan Stringer and Ed. Colson are a few that have been mentioned so far. More will be met with later, but it is impossible to name them all. They were a fine group of hardy bushmen, proud of their work, loyal to their chief, and full of enthusiasm for all that the Park stood for; full of tales, too, about their experiences in it.

We leave them for the time being, with three of their stories that convey, better than any other means, the new sense of comradeship between animal and man, so typical of Algonquin Park under George Bartlett.

According to both Ed. Colson and Mark Robinson, the beavers built a dam one year across a railway culvert, at Joe Creek. This dam caused the water to back up, so that it flooded part of the tracks. Every time the stationmaster pulled the dam to pieces, he was greeted the next morning with a brand new dam. The railwayman was nonplussed. No doubt he had a gun, but this was Algonquin Park! Finally, he tried to frighten them away by leaving two lanterns burning, one at each end of the dam. All night the beavers watched these strange, bright visitors that seemed to be alive, but never moved. In the morning, the harassed stationmaster came skeptically over to see what had happened. Nothing! The dodge had worked.

The next night he took to bed and slept longer and more soundly than he had slept for weeks. That light idea was certainly a smart one.

But in the morning he met with a rude shock. His ranger friends had a very simple explanation. During the day those brainy little beavers had discussed the two lamps long and earnestly, finally deciding that they could only have been placed there for one purpose. And to show their gratitude to the man who had put them there, they built a bigger dam than ever, by the light of his lanterns.

Mark Robinson had another story to tell about the Joe Creek beavers, and their contest with the railroaders. Charlie Ratan, one of the section men, had many a quarrel with them. One of these came about because of the loss of his pick-axe, a tool he frequently needed in his work, and one which he sometimes used against the beaver themselves when he tried to clear out one of their dams. One day he came storming along to Mark; his pick-axe had disappeared and he was sure that Mark, or someone else close at hand, had hidden it as a joke. Mark knew nothing about its whereabouts, and neither did anyone else. The next time they broke down the dam to avoid the flooding of the tracks they found it — firmly lodged in the masonry at the very bottom of the structure.

Once, according to Mr. Colson, when the beavers found an old storm door, near where they planned to construct a dam, they built it into the dam itself. The glass window of the door was still intact. However, in the course of the building operations, the beavers pushed a heavy stick against one of the panes of glass and broke it. Until it was filled with mud and other debris, the beavers took turns in tobogganing through the chute that this open window in the old storm door afforded.

CHAPTER 11

FROM ALEXANDER KIRKWOOD'S REFERENCE to "noble pines and state-ly oaks bespeaking the growth of centuries", it is quite clear that up to the time he wrote these words in his proposal for the Park's establishment, he had never been near the place. Yet there is an unconsciously wistful note in the language he uses, that reveals an urge common to most of us. To business and professional people particularly, hemmed in as they are by office walls, and tied to the grey monotony of routine tasks, it is impossible to think of a place like Algonquin Park, without wanting to go there.

All the founders of the Park agreed that it would be a waste indeed of the wildlife and natural beauty of the area, if no people went there to enjoy them. Dickson, it will be remembered, strongly urged that a guide book be published, and was almost prepared to set up a tourist bureau, so enthusiastic was he over its charms. The Ottawa-Arnprior and Parry Sound Railway had been welcomed as a means of easy access to the Park, and from first to last, every Park Superintendent has gone out of his way to welcome visitors.

And yet, apart from the native hospitality of the north, no rigid policy has ever been worked out with regard to the type of activity that should be encouraged in these Park visitors. Happily, this lack of any plan has resulted in a wide variety of both accommodation and recreative facilities.

To seasoned surveyors like Dickson, and to the long line of superintendents and rangers, it has always seemed that the ideal way of enjoying the Park was to travel, not merely to, but *through* it. George Bartlett's first trip across the Park from north to south in 1902, gave him the idea of marking the portages with the name of the lake to which they led, the route, and the length of the carry. Today, such signs strengthen discouraged tyro trippers all over the Park; in some places canoe docks have been built, and everywhere there are fireplaces at the permanent camp sites. Even the rangers' own shelter houses may sometimes — with permission from head-quarters — be used by visitors.

Two campers who had such permission, were spending one very rainy day in the rangers' shelter house at Lake Louisa. When they had fed themselves, and played cards for a while, there was nothing else to do, so they dozed off for an afternoon's sleep. One of them woke when he heard a small scratchy noise on the floor. He lifted his head sufficiently to see that the sound had been made by a chipmunk, which had come up through a knot hole, and was having a look around the cabin. When he saw that all was well, he clambered up the wall to a shelf where there was arranged a collection of old bottles — souvenirs of many fishing trips to that district. The chipmunk looked as though he knew what these bottles had formerly contained, and was prepared to get his full share of enjoyment from them. As though performing a round trip over a route he had travelled many times before, he scampered along a scantling just above the shelf, and paused at the mouth of each bottle to enjoy one lingering whiff of its former fragrant contents. Having completed the tour, he whisked back through the hole in the floor, and was seen no more.

But a majority of the early visitors were less prepared for canoe trips, than the Park was prepared for them to take trips. Rather than spend their time on an extended jaunt through the Park, they preferred the comfort of hotels, and were content with the shorter excursions; or wanted merely to bask in the summer sun on the verandas of their own summer cottage.

The houses built on the island at Canoe Lake in 1893, for the families of the Gilmour brothers, were undoubtedly the first summer homes to be erected in the Park area. In 1905, these houses, known to the Gilmours as "Loon's Retreat", were purchased by Drs. T. A. Bertram and A. J. Pirie, and stand to this day, still used as summer homes. To those with families, this was the ideal way to use the Park, and while it has never been possible to buy land in the area, from the first, visitors have been allowed to lease land and even build under certain necessary Park requirements.

A majority of summer visitors in early Park days, however, seemed to prefer the accommodation of the hotels and lodges, which began to appear not long after the Park's establishment. The earliest of these was Highland Inn, the story of which is inseparably tied up with that of Mrs. Edwin Colson.

In May, 1900, when Mrs. Colson first came to the Park from Ottawa, she was still Miss Molly Cox. During the previous winter, she had been working so hard that the doctor told her she must stop nursing for a while, and take a complete rest. When her Ottawa friends, Dr. and Mrs. Wm. Bell, heard of this, they wrote to her from the Park, where Dr. Bell had recently joined the staff as a ranger, urging her to visit them for the summer.

After a few weeks in the Park, Molly Cox regained her old vigour, and then began to look around for something useful to do, to keep herself busy. When she discovered that they needed a new house-keeper for the rangers' boarding house, she decided to take over the job. How successful that proved to be appears in a report written by Mr. Bartlett at that time, during an investigation by the Depart-ment. A member of the ranging staff who had been dismissed for incompetence, pointed an accusing finger at the recent changes at the boarding house, and Mr. Bartlett was called upon to report just what had taken place there.

According to the Superintendent, the rangers had never been so well looked after as they were under Miss Cox's direction. One of the complaints had been that the rangers had been required to cut hay along the railroad tracks for a cow imported into the Park, and said to be milked for the sole benefit of the families of Mr. Bartlett and Dr. Bell. Mr. Bartlett pointed out that the men themselves had all the fresh milk they could drink as a result of the cow's presence.

But not all Molly Cox's time, during those early years in the Park, was spent in hard work. She was wise enough to take advantage of the pleasure that the woods and the lakes had to offer, and frequently joined her friends, the Bells, in expeditions to different places in the district. Mrs. Colson, in later years, used to speak of the good times they had with their Ottawa friends who came to holiday in the Park. On picnic trips, she and Mrs. Bell used to startle the other women by appearing in breeks, instead of the long flowing skirts that were then in fashion. Sometimes they were joined by Mrs. Bell's brother, Mr. R. C. W. Lett, a member of the ranging staff at that time, and later Publicity Director for the Canadian National Railway. Two well-known places in the Park received their names as the result of these expeditions. Molly's Island, on Smoke Lake, was called after Mrs. Colson, then Molly Cox; and Kootchie Lake was named for a little dog belonging to Dr. Bell's sister. The little dog had tumbled overboard one day when a picnic party was paddling through the lake, and the dog's name was given to the lake to commemorate the rescue.

In all probability a number of the lakes in the surrounding district received their names from Dr. Bell and his friends. For many years he made a special point of exploring the Park in order to complete a canoe trip map which he had drawn up. This map formed the basis for the one printed by Arthur Brown of Toronto, which was sold for many years to visitors at Highland Inn. Even today a revised version of Dr. Bell's map is sold in the Park, and is regarded as one of the best for canoe trips.

Mr. J. Edwin Colson had come to the Park from Guelph when he joined the ranging staff in 1905, and sometimes he went along on picnic excursions planned by the Bells.

It was the case of Pinonique Dufond and the hired man, Baptiste, all over again. But Molly didn't have to hide her attachment as Pinonique had from "the old Susanne". In 1907 Molly Cox became Mrs. Edwin Colson.

Today, the original Nominigan Lodge is Mr. A. G. Northway's summer home, and Minnesing Hotel is a unique camp of which more will be said later. Only guests of theirs who have gone in by road will have an adequate idea of what the "stage" journey must have been like in the early days.

The stage was simply a wagon with a built-on top. Mrs. Colson, after one of her trips to Nominigan Lodge, insisted on removing the top; better a few scratches from the swish of overhanging boughs than the risk to life and limb involved in travelling the road in that top-heavy contraption. Frequently, by other accounts, the guests would fall out of the stage at the end of a voyage in the vehicle, and embrace the firm earth, singing doxologies of praise and thanksgiving.

If this was the reaction of natives, one can imagine how others felt, especially visitors from overseas. The memory of Minnesing Road was still strong in one couple who revisited the Park recently for the first time since their honeymoon there in 1914. The lady laughed as she recalled their earlier visit. Her husband had come to Canada a few years before she came over, and they had been married in New York when her boat docked there. Then he whisked her away to this highly advertised summer resort. She was terrified. Her friends had warned her that Canada would be primitive, but never in her worst dreams had she expected anything as wild as that road. As the wagon strained in every jolt, tilting now left, now right, she thought of all the lovely clothes in her trousseau. To add to her discomfort, it rained in torrents. Once there, they found it very comfortable, but her whole visit was haunted by the horrible fear that the whole of Canada would be as primitive. Things had changed in the interval between their visits: originally they arrived by train; this time they arrived in their own car, on a modern highway.

In the same year that Highland Inn was built, the Hotel Algonquin, at Joe Lake, was begun by Mr. Tom Merrill. This hotel was also convenient to the railway line through the Park, and was popular from the first. Because of its choice location, it was a frequent rendezvous for fishermen, and a favourite base for fishing trips. In 1917 the Colsons, who had given up their connection with Highland Inn five years earlier, bought Hotel Algonquin, which they continued to manage until it was bought by the present owner in 1943.

Once during the Hotel Algonquin days, the Colsons were visited by a bear which, according to Ed. Colson, had called for a particular purpose. It was rather late in the evening, and as Ed. sat alone in his office smoking a last pipe before turning in, he heard a noise from the pantry. Flashlight in hand, he went to the pantry door and flung it open. The room was empty, but the window was open and the screen was missing. Also missing, was a great jug of milk that had been sitting on the table. Mr. Colson found the jug set down intact outside the window — empty. He used to claim that a bear can use his front paw just like a hand, when he wants to carry something.

During their long sojourn in the Park, first at the rangers' boarding house, next at Highland Inn, then at Hotel Algonquin, and finally at the mill office, which they remodelled, at the head of Canoe Lake, Mr. and Mrs. Colson came to be known to many hundreds of Park visitors. Not only did they contribute to the welcome and comfort of the travellers in that region, but both of them made a very real contribution to the life of the people who lived all year round in the Park and nearby district. Mr. Colson, as lay reader in the Church of England, conducted church services and Sunday School when there was no qualified clergyman available. Mrs. Colson was frequently called upon to nurse the sick. As one of her Park friends said of her, she did everything for her neighbours but marry and bury them, and her husband could perform these services if necessary. Mrs. Colson advised young mothers before the arrival of their first-born, and helped to bring the baby into the world; pulled teeth when people had a toothache; put broken bones in splints; and travelled about the country in all kinds of weather to bring cheer and comfort to the sick and lonely.

Mrs. Colson herself has stories of some of her adventures in those days. One time when there was no doctor available, she and her husband were called in to look after a man at the Munn Lumber Camp, then operating close by. The man's leg was fractured and needed a splint before he could be moved. Mr. Colson fashioned a rough one out of a piece of board, and his wife set the bone and bound the splint to hold the leg rigid until he reached a doctor. The man was taken to the company's headquarters at Whitney.

That was the last they saw of him — except one day years later, when they were standing on the platform of the Algonquin Park Station, looking for some guests who were due.

"My God, you're the woman I wanted to see!"

Mrs. Colson was overwhelmed by a huge lumberman who had suddenly burst out of the crowd and dashed over to where she stood. The stranger bent down and hoisted up his trouser leg excitedly, pulling down the sock to reveal the limb in all its hirsute beauty.

"There's the leg you mended," he bellowed triumphantly for all the crowd to hear. "Doctor said it was a compound fracture, but he didn't have to touch it."

Incidents like that made life sweet for Molly Colson.

Another time she received an urgent message from a man whose wife was expecting a new baby. The couple lived in a wretched little shack down Rock Lake way, and the husband, apparently a section man, had rushed up the tracks on a three-wheeled "speeder" to bring Molly back to help. The doctor from Whitney who had been out to see the woman only a few days previously, was now himself in bed with the flu. A black storm was brewing, but Mrs. Colson gathered a few things together and set off on the ten-mile trip. As they whizzed down the track, lightning crackled in the sky and the wind roared through the trees. All the while the man kept moaning, "Ma God! Ma God," and exclaiming that his wife and child were dying.

When they reached the shack, Molly found that man had not exaggerated. The new baby had died, the mother was in a very serious condition, and one of the other children was having convulsions. For four days she stayed on the spot, until the worst danger was past, and then arranged for the family to move into the rangers' house, where the woman could have better care.

Finally, feeling she had done all she could and that it was time to go back to Cache Lake, she told the husband she was leaving, and got her things ready. As she sat downstairs waiting for him, she was startled by sudden blood-curdling screams from above, as if the man had suddenly decided to murder his wife and was in the very act. As Mrs. Colson stood trembling in the room the man came hurtling down the stairs past her, out the door, and down towards the tracks. One of the neighbours explained that he was subject to these fits, which worked themselves off if he was left alone. Mrs. Colson doesn't say how she got home, but it is safe to assume that she preferred flagging the next freight train to taking another ride with the Rock Lake madman.

Another woman who helped to make the Canoe Lake district well known, both to tourists and to people in the surrounding district, was Mrs. Shannon Fraser. She first moved to the derelict village of Mowat when her husband was appointed by the receivers to take over supervision of the mill estate. Up till then, from the time when the mill ceased running, Bob Gallna had been the caretaker, and for years afterwards his name and friendly presence were recalled by old-timers pausing at Canoe Lake to look over the old mill-site. The Frasers carried on for some years, then purchased some of the old buildings for their own use, and turned the place into a flourishing holiday resort.

At first the Frasers lived in the old Gilmour hospital, up on the hill, but in 1913 they purchased the building that had been used as kitchen and boarding house for the mill hands, back in the days when Mowat had been a thriving village. Then, in addition to their post office duties, the Frasers opened up a boarding house for summer visitors. Mrs. Fraser turned out to be such a successful manager that in the following year, the old company storehouse was bought and fixed up to take care of expanding business. These two buildings became known as Mowat Lodge. In 1920, the original buildings were destroyed by fire, but until then, Shannon Fraser's was a favourite place for Park visitors. Shannon was a jovial soul with a gift for playing up a good story, and his wife was an excellent soul and a kindly one, who knew how to cook. Many a Park visitor today, who once slept and ate under the roof of Mowat Lodge, remembers the sociability and the food of the Frasers.

Sometimes Shannon found it difficult to get people for help at the post office or boarding house, and would persuade his guests to stay on and work for him for a while. Tom Thomson always headed for the Frasers when he came to the Park, and often helped out; usually as a guide for fishing parties, but often, especially in the spring and fall, he would turn his hand to anything, from drying the dishes for Mrs. Fraser, to patching the roof for her husband.

One of the standing jokes in the Canoe Lake community was Shannon Fraser's optimism about the number of guests he expected on the next train. His neighbours loved to ask him how many guests he was going to pick up, whenever they saw him on his way to the station, driving along the old mill road.

"A big party comin' in today," he would invariably tell them. Returning later with an empty wagon and a broad grin on his face, he would explain: "I guess they must have missed that one."

From all accounts, Shannon had his troubles with some of the Canoe Lake residents who worked for him off and on. Two of these, George Rowe and Larry Dickson, were well known to Dr. Bertram, Mr. Hayhurst, and other summer cottagers who came into the district after 1906. Rowe and Dickson lived in little shacks on the old mill property, and made some extra money in the summer by acting as guides for Park fishing parties. Larry's cottage, up on the hill near the site of the old hospital, later became famous as the subject for Tom Thomson's "Larry Dickson's Shack", now in the National Gallery of Canada at Ottawa.

Apparently both of these men, in spite of Park regulations, used to take a drop too much. When that happened, Shannon's business would suffer and he would fire them. It made things difficult for Shannon. In a written complaint to Mr. Bartlett, he asserted that someone had given George Rowe "licker", with the result that "the missis had to take the mail". Before long, however, all would be forgiven and forgotten, and George and Larry would be back at work till it happened again. Incidentally, these two handymen must have been fairly tough: Larry Dickson once told Mr. Hayhurst that he swore by horse liniment as a cure-all; any time you wanted to clean up a hang-over, he would tell the summer visitor, all you had to do was just take a few drops on a lump of sugar!

When the original Mowat Lodge burned down, the Frasers built another hotel by the lakeshore, on the site of the old sawmill. That, too, was burned in 1930, and the family moved out, first to Kearney, and afterwards to Huntsville. By this time, the post office name had been changed from Mowat to Canoe Lake, and was taken over by the clerk of a lumber company working nearby. Mr. Everett Farley succeeded him as postmaster. Today Mowat and Mowat Lodge are only names; but always, for old-timers, they will be names whose memories will be all the warmer for the sojourn of the Frasers at Canoe Lake.

In the twenties and thirties numerous other camps, lodges and hotels, were opened up. Some of these will be mentioned to show how well distributed such accommodation has become in the Park, and how accessible the Park now is to visitors by road and railway.

On the Canadian National Line between North Bay and Ottawa, near Government Park Station, stands Kish-Kaduk Lodge, opened by Mr. and Mrs. Edward Thomas in 1928. Mr. Thomas worked for the railroad both north and south of the Park previous to this venture. The new King's Highway No. 60 gives access to Opeongo Lodge at Sproule Bay, opened in 1934 by Mr. and Mrs. Joe Avery, winter residents of Whitney. This lodge is a favourite haunt of those who come to fish on Opeongo Lake. Just opposite the highway, on Lake of Two Rivers, at a point commanding a fine view of the lake and surrounding hills, is Killarney Lodge, built by Mr. and Mrs. B. W. Moore in 1935. Guests for the Arowhon Pines, an adult camp for parents of young Arowhon campers, and others, travel north by launch from the highway at Portage Creek — or from Joe Lake railway station — to Baby Joe Lake. This camp was opened by Mrs. M. Kates of Toronto in 1942.

When George Bartlett retired as Park Superintendent in 1923, his son, Mr. Alfred Bartlett, opened a lodge on Cache Lake opposite Park Headquarters, making use of the old buildings there, and adding others. Bartlett Lodge has entertained many family holiday groups and fishing parties since that date. Mr. Bartlett tells a story of how the local beavers co-operated with him to display their skill to some of his guests. Two of these guests were particularly anxious to see a beaver at work cutting down a tree. They had seen the animals swim past the lodge dock each evening just at sundown, but they had yet to see one in the act of tree felling. Mr. Bartlett, like his father, was a man of action, and went to work. During the afternoon he selected and cut down a healthy young specimen of the beavers' favourite food — a small white birch — and moored it upright in the water just out from the shore by means of guy-lines. That night, the visitors were close at hand when the beavers swam by on their nightly cruise. But when they sighted the tree growing in such an unusual place they stopped, swam in to investigate, and then without stopping to enquire who had placed this tasty banquet in such a convenient spot, got busy and cut it down. It was a sad blow for them when they discovered they could not tow their prize away, and had to go home without it. The next day the shortened tree was set in place as before, the guests took up their places again, and the beavers obliged with a second performance. On the third night, what was left of the tree was up again. The beavers swam up, took one look at the pitiful remnants — and probably another disdainful look toward their audience — and swam sedately on their way without so much as a nibble. What did these visitors think they were, anyway, cheap entertainers?

Not all the lodges in the Park are devoted to pure holidaying, however. The unique camp already mentioned as occupying the former Minnesing Hotel was begun in 1923 by Dr. Henry B. Sherman of Carmel, California, a retired scientist of repute, who decided to devote his life to a study of the records of the life of Jesus as set forth in the four Gospels. In 1925, Dr. Sherman's group moved into the old log cabin Hotel Minnesing, purchased from the management of Highland Inn. There, in the solitude of the Algonquin wilderness, classes and discussions are carried on each morning until one o'clock, then the rest of the day is free for the enjoyment of the lakes and woods, and for conversation with others of this stimulating group of students. Inspiration and instruction gained in this seminary is taken out to every corner of the world, by men and women who go forth to their chosen professions in America, in Europe, and in the Far East.

All these resorts have been built by private individuals, on sites leased from the Government for that purpose, but of recent years, the Department of Lands and Forests has taken steps to assist in making provisions for visitors who wish to holiday in the Park. When the highway was constructed, a large camp-site was set aside at Lake of Two Rivers for an auto-camp. Family parties sometimes make this their headquarters for several weeks at a time, since the fine sandy beach is ideal for youngsters. Visitors from far distant parts come to this spot to pitch their tents and to enjoy an Algonquin Park holiday.

Doubtless, in years to come, new lodges will open, and new living conveniences provided in conformity with Park standards. But the most significant development of summer life in Algonquin Park has yet to be mentioned: there were some far-seeing people who believed that the Park should offer even more than fresh air, sunshine, good fishing, glimpses of wild life, and contemplation in seclusion. There, as the reader will see, developed a new idea in summer holiday life.

TOM THOMSON, CANADA   Courtesy Art Gallery of Toronto

BATEAUX

YOUNG BALD EAGLE.

CHAPTER 12

THE NEW IDEA, like all other new ideas, had its roots in old. From the beginning of the century, men like the late Sir Robert Baden-Powell in Britain, and the late Ernest Thompson Seton in America, had been sponsoring a new kind of education, based on the feeling that the formal schools took too little account of the primitive kinship with nature common to all young people.

The hotels and lodges in the Park catered largely to adults, who determined their own forms of amusement. Boys' and girls' camps in Algonquin Park were to develop a unique kind of camp program based partly on the tendencies mentioned above, but even more on the environment of the Park itself.

Not a few of the early camp visitors, urged on by the lure of distant fishing spots, or the fascination of the faraway, had left the comfort of hotels and lodges to sleep under canvas, and paddle along the water highways of the Park.

An example of this type of visitor occurs in one of Mark Robinson's favourite stories, incidental to telling how he met the famous Tom Salmon. Tom Salmon, he would explain on the rare occasions when it was necessary, was an old-time Lake of Bays trapper so well known as a snowshoe expert, that he was once commissioned to make snowshoes for an Arctic expedition. As a fly-fisherman, he was looked upon as a top-ranking expert by rangers and Park visitors alike. However, for the present purposes, Tom Salmon is incidental. Mark's own words tell of the visitor, and how through him he realized his own ambition of seeing Tom Salmon in action.

"This happened during old Mr. Bartlett's time when I was stationed at the Cache Lake rangers' house. For several days I had been away from headquarters on a trip out into Canisbay Township with a timber cruiser. The weather was hot and when we finally flagged a freight train to take us and our canoe back home, I was tired out.

"No sooner had I stepped off the train at Park Headquarters than I heard someone say, 'There's Robinson now'. Immediately an Englishman — you wouldn't mistake him anywhere — stepped up to me and said, 'You'll do!' I didn't know what he was talking about, and since I was hot and tired and wanted nothing better than a wash and chance to finish the report of what we had been doing, I told him that I wasn't free. He simply repeated, 'You'll do!' and I walked off. Then, because I thought I'd better find out what it was all about, I called in to see Mr. Bartlett. He explained that he was an English writer who was travelling across Canada and who wanted to be taken on a fishing trip. Mr. Bartlett said not to bother about his insistence that we start before noon, but to go ahead and finish my other job first. He said that I would find him an interesting person if I went on a trip with him.

"When we started after dinner we were provided with plenty of grub and with a seventeen-foot birch bark canoe. Once more I flagged a freight and it set us down seven miles along the line at Canoe Lake. By this time I had found out that my companion's name was Joseph Adams, and that he really did know something about fishing. I think he was supposed to be one of the champion fly-casters in England — at any rate, as he showed us later, he was very good.

"That night we camped at the island in Canoe Lake where Taylor Statten's camp is now, and the next morning we went on down through Tea Lake into the Oxtongue River. Since it was towards the end of July, I knew the water was too warm for trout in most places, but that we stood a good chance of getting some where the main course was joined by a small stream that would bring in a fresh supply of cold water. In spite of my knowledge of the district, Mr. Adams was sure that he knew better than I did about the best places to cast his fly. 'I've fished in almost every country except Canada', he kept saying, 'and I always like a little riffle on the surface of the water'. If that 'riffle' was there he would try the spot, if not, he would pass it by. I'll say this much for him, though — he certainly was an expert at casting. He could bring his fly down on the exact spot where he wished it to land — it was beautiful to see.

"When we reached the Whiskey Rapids he seemed a little nervous of going down them in a canoe. 'Is it safe, Ewie?' he asked (he had told me at the beginning of our trip that he would call me 'Ewie' if I didn't mind because Robinson was such a long name). 'Is it safe, Ewie?' he repeated. I told him that he could get out and walk along the bank if he wished, but that I intended to stay in the canoe. He decided to save himself a wetting, as he put it, and I was waiting for him by the time he arrived at the end of the path. 'You went through very lightly', was all he said, but I noticed that he never got out of the canoe again.

"Finally he decided to give up for that day. He had had very bad luck but it was his own fault. Every time I would suggest a likely spot he would say, 'Ewie I've fished in all the important waters of the world except Canada and I know you'll never catch a fish there'. We stopped that night in the old shelter house at Camp Four. The rangers had taken it over when the lumber companies moved out.

"Next morning, when we started out again, I decided that the best place for us to try was Salmon's Pool farther down the river. I knew that Tom Salmon had driven a balsam pole into the mud at the bottom of this pool and had found that it was fourteen feet deep. There would be fish there if there were any at all in the river. When we reached the place where the pole was sticking up, I caught hold of it to steady the canoe and told Mr. Adams to try his luck. Once again he protested, 'Oh, no, Ewie, we'll never catch anything there'.

"Well, I was getting tired of this attitude, so I decided that at least we'd give the spot a try. I hooked my leg over the pole and announced that here we would stay. Mr. Adams looked at me in surprise, but I just stared back silently. For about two minutes neither of us spoke, and then I knew that I had won out. 'All right,

Ewie', he said, 'if we must fish here you shall make the choice of the flies that we shall use'.

"Now that put me on the spot, because the chap had a a whole book full of flies and I didn't know one from the other. However, I was not to be outdone and I started to thumb through his collection. As we had come down stream I had noticed that the trout seemed to be rising to a little mauve midge that floated on the surface of the water, so I picked out one that looked something like that. 'A very good choice', remarked my companion, 'now pick out two others'. I selected a March Brown which I knew would often draw trout, and one other. He proceeded to tie all three on the leaders at once. I've said before that this man knew how to cast, and no sooner had the flies touched the water than there were two on, both at once.

"The problem was how to land them. 'May I stand up?' Adams asked, and since I had my leg around the post I told him to go ahead. I offered to lend a hand, but no, he was determined to finish the job himself. The result was that these two got away. Later, however, he hooked two others and this time he handled the landing net like a veteran, holding it in one hand and the rod in the other. He was pleased with himself, for the fish were beauties, and we stayed where we were all day long. Once he had a triple catch and he landed them all — not one of them was under twelve inches long. Finally, when he had thirteen, he decided it was time to go back to camp. As we returned he remarked with a happy sigh, 'My cap is full'.

"But that wasn't the end of our good fortune. Since we had a good supply of grub we decided to stay over for another day to try out our luck again. That night we played host to a couple of fellows who had lost their grub when their canoe upset. Adams admitted to them that he had had most remarkable fishing. 'It took some effort to persuade me', he said, 'but it certainly was *most* unusual'. On the next day we had the good fortune to fall in with Tom Salmon himself. He had been off on a trip with some of the members of his family and we stopped to compare our luck.

"Well, the two men got talking — you'll remember that Tom was a famous fly fisherman, too, and they decided to have a contest to prove which one was the more skilful. I'd often heard that Tom had been taught to cast in England, that he could cast while standing with his back against a barn door. That day we certainly saw something that I'll never forget. Tom's daughter and I were to act as judges. Our job was to float chips of wood down stream to test their accuracy. I've never seen anything like it — both of them could land their flies right on the chips — just as neatly as you please, and at ninety feet. As far as I could see there was no difference between the two fishermen, although my sympathy was naturally with the local man. Finally the two shook hands and we set off on the return trip.

"We had been gone four days when we finally got back to headquarters, and by that time Mr. Adams was convinced that Algonquin Park was as fine a place for fishing as he had ever seen. I don't know whether you'll see anything about this in the book he wrote, but there's one thing certain, he knew how to fish, and Salmon's pool had the fish to give him."

Joseph Adams returned to England in 1912 and published a book entitled "Ten Thousand Miles Through Canada", which was sufficiently popular to pass into a second edition within a month of its publication. It contained a twenty-five page chapter on "The Trip to Algonquin National Park", with an account of this same incident that tallies for the most part with Mark Robinson's version.

Other early visitors like Adams left the hotels and lodges to camp in the choicest spots of the Park. Some of them travelled out of a pure love of movement, paddling through the day, and pitching their tent at night wherever they found themselves, recapturing the charm of the life of the old voyageurs, and of later canoe trippers like surveyor Dickson. To these the Park revealed the innermost secrets of its nature.

Significantly, a few of them took their families on these trips, and unconsciously led the way for a new wide sphere of activity within the Park. Dr. Lester Scott was one of these, and how rich were his rewards will be seen in the final chapter of this book. Gradually, the idea grew that the ideal way of enjoying the Park was through camp life in its wildest parts, and that even small children could share this life under experienced care.

As early as 1908, a stout-hearted pioneer in women's education, Fanny L. Case, of Rochester, New York, appeared in Algonquin Park with a group of American girls, and the firm conviction that classroom walls were not the ideal background for the learning process. Superintendent Bartlett's eyes would undoubtedly have dropped open with amazement but for the fact that he knew she was coming. During the previous two summers, Miss Case had already taken a group of students north to the Magnetewan River with such success, that she decided to establish a permanent camping headquarters in Canada. When she approached Mr. Bartlett with the idea, he welcomed it with enthusiasm; and so the Northway Lodge campers spent their first summer at Cache Lake.

Campers and leaders alike were pioneers at that first camp. Miss Case had brought with her from the United States an expert swimming counsellor, a musician, a craftsman, a naturalist, a nurse and a cook, but none of these had had previous experience in living under canvas in the Canadian wilds. From Ernest Finlayson, who had worked in the Park previously, and who had just graduated in forestry at the University of Toronto, they learned the camping arts. As Miss Case recalled in later years, "His knowledge of growing things, his enthusiasm, and integrity of character, made him for us the ideal guide."

Under Ernest Finlayson's direction, a programme of canoe trips was set up. This scheme proved to be so successful that it has been the basis for Northway Lodge trips up to the present time. Elsewhere in Canada, and in the United States, canoe trips had been looked upon as too strenuous an occupation for girls' groups, but Mr. Finlayson made himself responsible for drawing up rules and instructions to safeguard the health and welfare of all taking part in these excursions. Canoe trips were popular from the first, and they rapidly became the very core of camp life. Food lists were tacked up on the walls of the Picnic House, while regulations were laid down about the packing of supplies and the loads to be carried by each girl. Day outings, and canoe trips, became the acme of the camping experience.

The Northway camp site was in a rugged state when the campers took over in the summer of 1908. During that year, everyone had such a good time helping to put things into shape, that Miss Case decided that half the fun in camping came through having to fend for oneself. Throughout the years, she has tried to preserve that aspect of camping. That first summer the campers helped Mark Robinson, then newly appointed to the Park Staff, and some of the other rangers, to clear the fallen logs and underbrush from the point. Campers and staff chose the spots for their tents so that each would command a view of one particularly fine section of the lake or woodlands, and they named each tent according to the location chosen for it. These names were handed down by the first occupants to those who followed in succeeding years, so that even now most of the seventeen tents at the camp still bear their original titles. Tents, as sleeping quarters, have been retained until the present time, but other buildings have been erected as the need arose. Always, Miss Case has tried to interfere as little as possible with the natural beauty of the campsite.

Before long several boys' camps were established, but these were replaced in time, and only Northway has a continuous history from early days down to the present.

To-day, at Northway Lodge, the morning work hour has always been one of the camp traditions. Although in other things the camp schedule is kept as flexible as possible, this period is set aside each day as a time that is spent in an activity assigned to improve some aspect of the camp as a whole. Sometimes the project is a big one, such as the construction of a craft cabin or a sleeping hut in the woods, sometimes it is the repairing of canoes, or the chopping of wood. All the tasks are undertaken in a fine spirit of co-operation, so that the workers feel that they are making a valuable contribution to the good of the Northway community. In this way the campers' initiative and skill is brought out, while at the same time their loyalty to the camp and their pride in their forest home is fostered.

One attitude that Miss Case has tried to stress at Northway Lodge all through the years, has been the point of view that camping is "well spent leisure". Always, she has felt that the girls should find in the Park, sufficient time to carry on the activities that they are unable to perform in the city. Paddling, swimming, and nature rambles, play a large part in the the camp program, while fine musicians on the staff lead in evening musicales. Campers have come to realize that the knowledge they have gained at Northway Lodge in the constructive use of leisure time, has provided a basis for full and spontaneous living, then, and in after years.

Writing of this camp, Miss Case has set forth her own feelings on the success of the Northway experiment:

"We could not have anticipated the degree of lasting joy and satisfaction which many a camper, almost all, has found in this way of life. These results have been expressed in chance meetings, sometimes after twenty years or more, and by the presence of daughters of former campers who have joined us at Northway Lodge. The connections through the years with many fine people, both assistants and campers, have brought rewards to those responsible and the camp is a composite of these contributions."

Most of the early camps for boys were "school camps", run in conjunction with particular schools in the United States. Such were the short-lived Long Trail Camp for boys at Joe Lake, and Professor G. G. Bowers' Waubeno Camp on Cache Lake.

Mr. George Bartlett wrote numerous articles for nature magazines during his tenure of office, and in one of these describes a day with the boys of Camp Minnewawa, the camp school of Bordentown Military Institute, New Jersey, on Lake of Two Rivers. Under Professor W. L. Wise, boys from this school came up to Algonquin every summer between the years 1911 and 1930. According to Mr. Bartlett, a group of twelve boys returning from a day's outing, came upon a mother beaver and her three kittens. They paddled their canoes silently closer, but the mother heard and, slapping her tail on the water to warn the young ones, dived beneath the surface. Two of the kittens followed, the third stayed up. The boys gave chase, caught up with it, and lifted the little animal into the canoe. Evidently there was something wrong with him. They decided to take him in to camp and call a council to decide what to do next.

The next morning, some of them paddled this little friend Pat, as they now called him, up to Park Headquarters to give him to the Superintendent. Mr. Bartlett gave the boys a little talk on the beaver and its habits, then arranged for a lady at one of the nearby cottages to take Pat and see if she could nurse him back to health. The boys learned about the engineering skill of the beaver, about the construction of his house, about the young who are born with all their teeth and their eyes wide open, how the castor is used for perfume, and how in the old days, Hudson's Bay Company employees used to serve them stuffed instead of turkey for Christmas dinner. Finally, they were sent on their way with the Superintendent's concluding moral:

"Boys, we could learn a lot from the beaver. He never gives up once he starts a job, no matter how difficult it may prove". To finish off the story, it must be added regrettfully that little Pat did not respond to treatment, and was buried near his own kin at the edge of a neighbouring marsh.

The second oldest camp in the Park is Camp Pathfinder, at Source Lake, which has been running ever since the first year of World War I. In the spring of 1914, two residents of Rochester, both teachers, formed a partnership to establish a camp. Franklin Gray, a native of Barrie, Ontario, who taught physical education in Rochester, was one of the pair, and came up to the Park to pick the site. After a wide search, they decided on the island in Source Lake, for its accessibility to the railway line, its vantage point for canoe expeditions, and its isolation from other Park settlements. In the first camping season the following year, eighteen boys enrolled. This number was increased to twenty-four and twenty-eight in the next two years. In 1917, because of the ill-health of his partner, Mr. Bennett, Mr. Gray took over full ownership. It was in that year that the present owner and director, Mr. Herman J. Norton, first visited Camp Pathfinder. Between 1918 and 1925 he and Mr. Gray were joint owners, but since that time Mr. Norton has held the sole interest in the camp.

Under Mr. Norton, the "Chief", as the boys at Pathfinder call him, the camp has carried on a wide and varied programme. The staff is made up of experts in many different fields, in order to provide the finest leadership that can be procured. Mr. Norton has made sure that each camper is taught carefully all the skills and crafts necessary to make him secure and self-sufficient in the camp situation. Through the years a credit system of awards has been developed, to encourage each boy to strive for success in both camp activities and on the trail. Before any camper may leave headquarters on a canoe trip, he must pass rigid tests that cover swimming ability, canoe tipping and righting, and trip knowledge. The expert canoe-manship of the Pathfinder campers who traverse the district in their red canoes, is well known to other trippers who have encountered parties in remote corners of the Park.

Slowly, the idea was developing. First-hand knowledge of wood-craft and canoe-tripping, as a means of developing initiative and self-reliance, came to be the keynote of Algonquin camps.

With the first Canadian camp organized by Taylor Statten of Toronto, the further idea of reviving native handicrafts developed, even to the point of re-enacting under the fascinated eyes of teen-age boys, an anciently familiar scene under Algonquin skies: the construction of a birch-bark canoe.

The story of how Camp Ahmek, at Canoe Lake, came into being, is worth telling. During the summer of 1912, Colonel J. J. Gartshore had camped for several weeks with his own boys and girls on Big Wapomeo Island. When he heard that the Statten family was looking for a place for a holiday, he suggested that they take over his equipment, which had not yet been removed from the Park. Mr. and Mrs. Statten were so delighted with their Canoe Lake visit that they made arrangements during the next winter, while staying at Highland Inn, to lease Little Wapomeo Island for their own summer home.

To their island in Canoe Lake came many friends for camping holidays, and the enthusiasm of members of this group began to lead into a new development. For several weeks, in the summer of 1917, a group of men interested in Y.M.C.A. work camped on the island, to develop the Canadian Standard Efficiency Tests for boys. The programme initiated at this gathering became the official programme for boys' work of several Protestant churches under the name Tuxis Boys and Trail Rangers.

A second camp was held in 1920, under the auspices of the Boys' Work Committee of the National Council of the Y.M.C.A., intended as a centre for training leaders for the Tuxis Boys and Trail Rangers organization. To it were invited some one hundred and thirty boys' work leaders, from all sections of Canada. It is not possible here to mention all the important boys' work executives present at this important event; but of the prominent Canadians invited to give instruction in natural history, some significant names were: Professor J. W. Crow of the Ontario Agricultural College, C. A. Chant, Professor of Astronomy at the University of Toronto, W. D. Hobson of Woodstock, Jack Miner from Kingsville, Dr. W. E. Saunders of London, and Stuart L. Thompson from Toronto.

As part of their training in campcraft, staff and students alike lived in tents pitched on the shores of Canoe Lake, where the present Camp Ahmek is located. This was a new experience for many of the group, and their initiation into camp life was not made any easier by the fact that it rained continuously for the whole day on which they were setting up camp. However, the work party was revived by hot coffee and sandwiches, prepared in advance by Mrs. Statten and some of the women at Mowat Lodge. By nightfall, everyone had a shelter over his head. The camp had been designed as a training ground for future camping leaders, and the experience gained at this time had far-reaching effects on camping in many different parts of Canada and the United States.

Two of those who had taken part in the 1920 camp returned in the following year, when Taylor Statten established his own camp for boys at the Canoe Lake campsite. C. E. (Chick) Hendry, and George Chubb were at Camp Ahmek during that season, and both returned for many subsequent camping seasons. "Chubby", as the latter is affectionately called, has continued as business manager of the Taylor Statten Camps until the present time. Dr. Frank Wood, of Toronto, was co-director with Taylor Statten at this first boys' camp.

The first season at Camp Ahmek brought its own problems, and many are the stories of difficulties encountered, and overcome, at that time. One of these stories has to do with how Pete Sauve came on the staff as camp cook. Pete's predecessor at Ahmek was a man who did not like bears. Now the Canoe Lake bears had discovered that the camp storehouse could furnish them with supplies gratis. The cook was continually complaining about these raids, and he threatened to pack up and leave if some steps were not taken to get rid of these visitors. Finally, one day after train-time, Taylor Statten learned that the worst had happened — the previous night a bear had clawed his way right into the cook's own tent. This was the last straw; the cook de-camped, and it was necessary to search for a new man to take over the job. Fortunately, at that moment, Pete Sauve stepped into the breach. Pete had been in the Canoe Lake district off and on since the time when he first cooked for the Gilmour Lumber Company, some twenty-five years before. His good-natured disposition, and his ability to make first-class pies, soon made him a favorite with staff and campers alike. Pete Sauve has continued as an Ahmek institution to the present time.

In 1934, after the boys' camp had been running for three years, the companion camp, Wapomeo, was established for girls by Mrs. Taylor Statten. Camp Wapomeo's first season was spent on Little Wapomeo Island, where there was sufficient room for the forty-five girls who made up the first group. However, the camp soon outgrew its original quarters, and in 1927 the site was moved to Big Wapomeo Island. A further expansion was made possible in 1937, when Senior Wapomeo Island was included in the camp property. In addition, the girls were able to use certain facilities, such as the riding stables on the mainland. At the present time the two Statten Camps have control of four islands in Canoe Lake, and stretch along about a mile of the shoreline of the bay on which Camp Ahmek was first located. Each year about four hundred and fifty boys and girls, as well as a staff of two hundred young men and women, spend the summer months at these camps in the Park.

Camp Wapomeo and Camp Ahmek have been called a brother and sister type of camp, and in this way they differ from other Park camps. While each camp has its own headquarters, and its own staff, there are a number of activities in which campers from both units join. Under the supervision of their counsellors, sailing races, swimming and canoe regattas, musicales, plays, concerts, circuses, and many other programs, can be shared by the two groups. In this way, campers from both camps, and their leaders, have an opportunity to work and play with members of the opposite sex in the healthy atmosphere of the camp environment.

This co-educational feature is carried into the September camp, held each autumn at Camp Ahmek. Here, camp leaders, former campers, their families and their friends, gather each year in an adult camp for several weeks. The full facilities of the camp are made available to these young people who have learned the Algonquin Park way of life, through many visits to the region.

Two outgrowths of the Taylor Statten Camps are worth noting here as having affected camping activities in other parts of the world. In 1929, a book, "Camp and Character", was published by H. S. Dimock and C. E. Hendry as the result of four years of experimental work conducted at Ahmek and Wapomeo. This book has been used widely since that time as a textbook for courses in camping, given in many different parts of the United States and Canada. Another outcome of the work at these camps was the establishment of a camp for boys and girls near Madras, India, set up by the Taylor Statten Camps, and directed by Wallace Forgie.

Guests at Camp Ahmek are always curious to know why the main dining hall is decorated with a series of very large posters that ornament both sides of the long room. When they ask about their significance, they learn that each depicts the most outstanding event of one camping season. The younger campers are always delighted to regale the visitor with the whole history of the camp, by recounting the story that lies behind each picture.

From the "Chief" himself, as Taylor Statten is known to campers, counsellors, and visitor alike, we learned what lay behind the scenes set forth in two of the most unusual posters. Actually, the two pictures must be taken together because, before you can understand about Lord Willingdon's narrow escape, you must know about the visit which the Bishop of Birmingham had paid to the camp in the previous year.

The most outstanding event for the year 1930 appears to have been the visit of the Bishop of Birmingham to Algonquin Park. The poster for that year shows him in complete regalia. His full-faced portrait reveals a very large gentleman, wearing the traditional bishop's hat and "dog-collar". Certainly, His Grace, the Bishop of Birmingham, did pay a state visit to the camp, the campers did receive him with due respect and reverence, but before his departure — however, that would spoil the first half of the story. It is sufficient at this point to say that word reached camp that the Bishop of Birmingham, and a group of English friends, were touring Canada, and would very much like to have an opportunity of seeing how young Canadians disported themselves in the northern woodlands. They hoped that it would not inconvenience the camp authorities if they paid a visit to Canoe Lake in the immediate future.

On the appointed day the guests arrived by train, and were welcomed to the camp by speeches delivered in the dining hall at noon. The party was made up of His Grace, the Bishop of Birmingham, his friend and travelling companion, the Earl of Essex, and Jeeves, their personal servant and butler. All day long these eminent gentlemen toured the camp, seeing all the regular activities, and making suitable remarks about the wonders of the Canadian scene. By nightfall the campers were becoming more and more suspicious, but they waited until morning to take their revenge.

In the morning, the Bishop and his entourage were transported in state across the lake to see the girls' camp, Wapomeo. They travelled on the pirate ship, which was towed by one of the camp launches. But the girls had been forewarned — and the phoney Bishop of Birmingham, a Toronto friend of the Chief's, was dumped overboard, together with his practical joke, into the cleansing waters of Canoe Lake.

But the strange thing about the posters in the Ahmek dining hall is that the Bishop of Birmingham appears smiling and serene in the 1930 edition, but it is the gentleman of the next year, 1931, who appears to be falling into the lake. When he asks about this unfortunate personage, garbed in morning coat and tall silk hat, the visitor is amazed to learn that he is none other than the former Governor-

General, the King's representative in Canada, Lord Willingdon himself. As you look at the picture for a second time, you find that he is not quite *in* the water, he seems to be sitting on top of it. Then you learn how he was saved from an ignominous ducking in an Algonquin Park lake.

In 1931, the campers had been told once again that they were to be honoured with a visit from one of the great of the land. Once more they had been informed that this visitor wanted to see how the young people of Canada worked and played in Algonquin forests; and this time they, too, would have a share in the fun. This time they would not wait until the second day. Even before the visitor arrived, they had their plans carefully worked out. They would receive the gentleman with all politeness and deference. Then, at the first opportune moment, they would toss the so-called Governor-General into the lake.

Fortunately, for the Governor-General, and for the campers, too, the Chief got wind of this carefully prepared scheme. He and his staff did their best to persuade the campers that this really was a visit from the Vice-Regal party — but they were not convinced. They had been fooled once, and they were not going to be caught again.

When the day of the official visit dawned, the camp leaders were not too sure what the outcome would be. They had warned the campers that everyone must be on his best behaviour, but they had the uncomfortable feeling that the plan might be put into action in spite of their precautions. As an added measure of safety, a special bodyguard of trusty seniors was assigned the task of watching over the safety of their distinguished visitor.

Lord Willingdon must have acted his part to the full satisfaction of the campers; one shudders to think what one little gesture might have cost him. To the intense relief of the camp directors, the visit passed without incident. The Governor-General liked the camp, and the campers approved of him. That is why the Ahmek poster for the year 1931, shows the tall gentleman in formal attire, within a hair's breadth of being ducked below the waves of Canoe Lake.

It is unfair, in a Park where dozens of excellent camps exist, all featuring canoe trips and the outdoor life, that only a few should be described in detail.

Camp Tanamakoon, for instance, deserves a chapter by itself. This first Canadian girls' camp was organized in 1925 by Miss Mary G. Hamilton, Principal of Margaret Eaton School in Toronto. Tanamakoon Lake, then called White Lake, was an ideal place for such

a camp. The camp stands on the shore of a sheltered bay with a
sandy bottom. The lake is small, with an old lumber camp clearing
nearby that is ideal for riding. Here, in close relation with training
courses in physical education at the University of Toronto, young
women specialists in that subject learn the value of outdoor life, and
go out to all parts of Canada as leaders in camp and health activities.
A lodge, theatre, infirmary, craftshop, workshop, offices, cabins, and
tents, all contribute their share to the varied activities.

Tanamakoon campers have learned, by bitter experience, that
stories about the proverbial curiosity of bears have a foundation in
fact. Some time ago, the camp adopted the habit of allowing canoe
trippers to make use of canoes that had been left for them at the
end of some of the longer portages on their regular routes. These
canoes were simply turned over on the ground, and the camp
authorities felt sure that in the Park, where people are accustomed
to respect one another's property, they would be perfectly safe.
However, what was the dismay of one group that had counted on
using such a canoe, when they found that a passer-by had deliberately
landed a smashing blow on the keel of the upturned canoe, and had
bashed it right in. It was not until the campers had finished their
trip that they received the probable explanation of the destruction.
One of the veteran guides told them that it had likely been caused
by a bear, whose curiosity had gotten the better of him. Seeing this
object lying in his pathway, he had taken a swipe at it to find out
what lay underneath. From that time on, Tanamakoon campers
followed the example of rangers and other experienced bushmen,
and erected simple frameworks at the ends of the portages, in order
to raise their canoes off the ground. These structures allowed wandering bears to look underneath for themselves, instead of crashing
through the bottom to satisfy their thirst for knowledge.

Each week, groups of girls go out on canoe trips, and one of the
sights of the Park is a flotilla of Tanamakoon canoes, rounding the
bend of the lake towards the main dock on a Saturday afternoon or
evening, in triumphant formation.

Camp Arowhon enjoys the distinction of being the only camp
where boys and girls live on the same campsite. These are grouped
into, children under five, the "independents" — between five and
sixteen, and the older "privileged campers". In each age group, all
possible activities are enjoyed by boys and girls together. Under
Mrs. Kates and Mr. Harry Homes, the two sexes learn to take each
other for granted, and establish a healthy comradeship.

The most recent addition is Camp Tamakwa, founded in 1937 by Mr. Lou H. Handler, of Detroit, a graduate in Forestry, and with broad camping experience in the States. This camp lies on the north shore of Tea Lake, and has at present accommodation for 125 campers.

Of recent years, new emphasis has been placed on other aspects of the camping programme in all the Park camps. Youth leaders have come to realize that camping provides an ideal laboratory for the training of democratic citizens. In no other situation are the same opportunities for co-operative living possible. The campers live in small units, huts, tents, or cabins, and each individual finds that he is expected to make his own contribution to the well-being of the group. For twenty-four hours a day, the camper is in an atmosphere where his own decisions will help or hinder the happiness of the group with whom he is living. Friendships made in camp are lasting ones, and the character development that takes place during the summer months, often turns a wayward, adolescent, boy or girl into a straight-thinking, responsible individual. At many of the camps, discussion groups are formed, either informally around the evening campfire, or in Sunday evening sessions, where the young people are encouraged to talk over the troubled problems of school, family, and community, that each sooner or later encounters. The campers bring to the Park a wide variety of backgrounds, and they are being encouraged to use their Algonquin holiday as a training ground for constructive thinking.

While a friendly rivalry exists between the camps, the boys and girls all found a common cause to work for when, in 1943, due to the necessities of war, the ranging staff was reduced, and a system of Junior Park Rangers was inaugurated. Mr. Maurice Kirkland, a high school teacher who had once been a ranger, worked out the details. By the middle of the following summer, every large camp was co-operating. Groups from the camps went into the adjacent regions to clear portages, to build landing docks and fireplaces, to construct shelters and camp tables. At the same time they carried on routine fire patrols, reported fires, and on several occasions extinguished small blazes that had been left by careless campers. Some of the senior boys laid out trails through the lesser known district to the west of Canoe Lake. The construction of portages to link up some thirty small lakes, made adequate fire patrol of this region possible.

Algonquin Park has gained a reputation, through the years, as

PORCUPINE.

RUFFED GROUSE.

an ideal location for summer camps. The connected chains of small lakes make canoe trips possible for young people who can manage short portages, but for whom longer carries would be injurious. The sheltering hills, and the small lake areas in the southern districts, mean that trips seldom run the risk of being storm-bound. The telephone communications, and the availability of the Park aeroplane for emergencies, safeguard the health and safety of the campers. Parents, leaders, and campers alike, appreciate these advantages that the Park has to offer.

At the same time the Park provides opportunities for real adventures in the art of living. Stripped of the artificial amusements of the city, the camper learns to fall back on more permanent pleasures. He finds the joy that comes from the performance of difficult physical feats, he learns how to make himself warm and comfortable with the minimum equipment, he learns to be self-sufficient. At the same time, he comes to appreciate the wildlife which he discovers all about him. Birds, mammals, insects, flowers, trees, the sky above, and the rocks beneath, become real, tangible, and fascinating. The Park holiday experience in camp has provided many boys and girls with a background of friendship and interest that has been carried on through life, besides fostering a spirit of international good-will with our neighbours from the United States, and from many other countries.

CHAPTER 13

The Eight Superintendents, and the two Acting Superintendents who have been responsible for the Park, have all welcomed visitors, young and old, fully conscious of its possibilities for recreation and education. But always, their first concern has been to conserve the forests and animal life. It will be worth while here, to look back briefly over the years, to see the whole development of this vital activity since the Park's inception.

The contributions made by Superintendents Thomson, Simpson, and Bartlett, up to Mr. Bartlett's resignation in 1922, have already been noted. John W. Millar was Acting Superintendent for the following year, and was succeeded for the next year by Mark Robinson, in the same capacity. Two years passed before Mr. Millar was re-appointed as full Superintendent.

During the years when Mr. Millar was the Superintendent, the Department adopted a policy of retrenchment, so that the Park expenditures and services had to be curtailed. The official point of view seems to have been that the Park should pay for itself, and that the Department should not be expected to incur any new expenses through an expansion of its services. Mr. Bartlett had done what he could to supplement the annual budget by encouraging the rangers to trap fur-bearing animals for the Department's fur sale in Toronto, but when this practice was abandoned, there was a general feeling that expenditures on salaries and Park administration should be cut down as much as posssible.

For this reason, the period of the 1920's appears, in retrospect, to have been unprogressive. True, certain innovations were made during that time. Telephone communications were improved, boys' and girls' camps encouraged, and some new provisions were made for the benefit of tourists. But on the whole, very few changes were made in the Park. The Superintendent's annual reports reflect this inertia, since they become simply a catalogue of the number of rangers on the staff, the number of poachers convicted, and the extent of damage done by fire during the current year to the Park's forests.

Alexander Kirkwood's emphasis on an active policy of planned forest conservation had never been taken very seriously by the

Government, least of all in the 'twenties. But 1930 brought a significant change. With Mr. Millar's transfer to the head office of the Department of Lands and Forests, a new Superintendent was appointed.

J. H. McDonald was a trained graduate in Forestry and District Forester of Pembroke, a post now combined with the Superintendency. After his unfortunate death a year later another Forestry Graduate, Frank A. MacDougall, took his place.

The Park became a beehive of activity, reminiscent of the early days under Bartlett. The old concept of fire protection gave way to the active principle of prevention. For the first time, the Park Rangers combined their Park duties with fire ranging, which until now had been looked after by a separate staff. Assistant rangers were taken on for the fire season, an activity that gave seasonal employment to men of neighbouring villages, particularly Killaloe.

At Brent, Achray, and Whitney, new headquarters were built, and four Deputy Chief Rangers appointed for each quarter of the Park. A handsome building was erected at Achray in particular, of local stone; two rangers, MacFarlane and Mooney, happening to be expert stone mason and carpenter, respectively. For the first time aeroplanes soared over the Algonquin forests on regular fire patrol duty. Where Thomson once took twenty-two days to cross the Park in 1902, MacDougall could circle the entire area in two and a half hours. A rangers' hall and hangar were added to the buildings at Cache Lake; later another large hangar was built for the first Park plane — a Fairchild three-place machine with an open cockpit.

The Park telephone system has undergone great expansion and improvement since it was first inaugurated by Superintendent Bartlett, in 1911. In that year he obtained permission from the Grand Trunk Railroad to make use of their telegraph poles along the Southern Railway, for a telephone system that would link up the rangers in that district with Park Headquarters. With this improvement he was able to get in touch with the rangers at Rock Lake, Lake of Two Rivers, Joe Lake and Rainy (Rain) Lake, in order to give and to receive messages. The immediate value of this contact became apparent, because information connected with the prevention of trapping, with fire control, and with rescue work, could be transmitted quickly and accurately along the wires. When the Canadian Northern Railroad was constructed through the northern part of the Park in 1914, Mr. Bartlett arranged for their telegraph poles to be used for a line that would provide communication between rangers stationed in the district.

These first telephone lines were strung on poles erected for another purpose, but the setting up of the bush-lines was a different matter. It was about 1922 when the first of these was tried out in the Park. One of the earliest was a single line, stretching for twelve miles from Brûlé Lake to White Trout Lake. At about the same time two other lines were strung — one from Whitney to Opeongo Lake, a distance of sixteen miles; and the other from Killaloe to Bason Depot on the Bonnechere River, a distance of thirty miles. The method of running all these lines through was the same. The rangers did the "brushing out", while especially trained men fastened the lines to convenient trees. On the recent topographic map, called the Algonquin sheet, it is possible to trace the course of many of these lines in the Park. Now they have been extended to reach into most of the out-of-the-way corners of the area.

At the present time the telephone system combined with the fire towers, which are set up in key positions throughout the Park, aid in combating the forest fire menace during the summer months. When a fire watcher, stationed at the top of one of the towers, detects smoke in his area, he can telephone the information into his nearest headquarters. The man at the switchboard, who receives similar information from other watchers, can then plot the directions on a map, and determine the exact location of the blaze. Because of this speedy system of reporting, Algonquin Park has established an enviable record in the control of forest fires.

An article by Mark Robinson in the "Barrie Examiner" gives us a picture of fire ranging under the new regime:

"July 31st — the rangers were all beginning to show the effects of steady fire fighting through the month of July. District Forester F. A. MacDougall had been out on plane patrol all day, landing at different points to encourage his men who were fighting fires with the odds against them, yet managing to put out or keep the different fires under control. He returned to Head-quarters' base about 8.30 p.m. reporting a fresh fire on a small island on Ragged Lake.

"We won't do anything about it to-night," he decided, "but we'll have Jerry Kennedy get his men in readiness to leave early in the morning." In a few minutes

Jerry had his men around him. Fire pumps were tested, hose rolled and packed.

At the same time, in the office, the phone was continually ringing and every effort was made to keep up with the work. Soon after Mr. MacDougall got back, there came a call from Mr. Northway at Smoke Lake. "There is a fire at Ragged Lake," he reported. When I told him that we already knew about it, he replied immediately, "My motor boat and canoes are at your disposal. We will meet your men at the highway dock, Smoke Lake, at 5 a.m." I thanked him for his offer, for I knew that it would help a lot.

That evening everyone was more than busy. When Jerry and his men went to get a few hours' rest others were preparing their supplies. Food and cooking equipment for the fire fighters had to be assembled and gasoline had to be mixed with oil for the use of the gasoline pumps. In the office, too, there was much to be done. Anxious campers from around Cache Lake called in to inquire about members of their families who were out on trips in areas known to be threatened by the different fires. News of the progress of other fire crews had to be recorded. Bob Bowes called from his watchpost at Murchison Tower. While three local fires were reported out and another under control, the one at Lobster Lake seemed to be spreading and wanted more men. We couldn't do anything more that night, so we all planned to turn in to get a little rest.

Just as I was closing up at 10.30 the phone rang. It was George Homberg calling from the Whitney office. "Those two pumps you wanted are repaired," he told me. I had wanted these pumps for another fire. "I have just returned from taking one of them to Lobster Lake and I brought back one of theirs that needed some repairs. It's in bad condition, but I may have it ready by daylight." I hung up wondering whether my good friend George ever got any rest.

August 1st — Sam, Jerry and his party left early in the morning, as planned, for Smoke Lake. Jock Walker took them in his car as far as the Smoke Lake portage, where Mr. Northway's launch picked them up. A phone call from the Northway's told us that they passed Molly's Island at 5.30 a.m.

The morning went by without any further upset, but just as we were packing up for lunch it came again. First it was Whitney Headquarters calling: "Murchison Tower reports a small fire in Airy Township. Ranger Holmberg and three men have gone to this fire. Holmberg will return." Then twelve minutes later it was another call: "Tea Lake Dam calling. Construction Company have let their fire get away. The fire is beyond control. Rush pump and equipment at once. The timing for that fire was pretty near a record. Eight minutes after we had received the message Jock Walker and Wib Behan had the car loaded with a pump, hose, gasoline, pack pumps, axes, shovels, and grub hoes and they were on their way. They had fourteen miles to cover along the gravel road but twenty-five minutes later the pump was in operation. Soon afterwards a party of thirty-eight Ahmek campers arrived with axes and pails under Dr. Ted Hayden. We had sent an S.O.S. call to the camp for some of their senior boys because we couldn't spare any more of our men. These boys and the men from the Construction Company, working under the direction of Alvin and Pete Ruddy, had the fire under control at 2.30 p.m. that afternoon.

In the meantime Jock and Wib had returned to Headquarters and we had fresh excitement there. At 1.30 p.m. a call came from Camp Ahmek to say that a fire had broken out in the centre of the camp and they needed a pump and a hose. Our last pump was in the hangar for repair, and it was lucky that Mr. MacDougall landed in from patrol just at that moment. He put in a call for the Pembroke Forestry Office, and they replied that they could leave in fifteen minutes with an extra pump so that we could have it by 3.30 p.m. In the meantime the Canoe Lake residents had come to the rescue of the camp. Thirty-eight of their older boys were down at Tea Lake, but everyone else helped to form a bucket brigade from the lake to the fire. At 2.45 p.m. the fire was reported under control and by 3.00 p.m. it was out. In the line passing the pails up the hill were a Roman Catholic priest and a United Church clergyman working side by side. Some wag remarked that for once the churches were working together to defeat a common foe.

During the afternoon calls continued to come into the office at Headquarters. At 3.30 p.m. Mrs. Gervais reported that her husband had left for a fire at the head of Burnt Lake that seemed to be working towards the Otterslides. Then, a moment later, came news of a fire at the head of Island Lake burning all along the north side of the portage. A number of nearby campers were trying to keep it from spreading.

Fortunately, we began to get some outside help, just about that time. The truck arrived from Pembroke Office bringing in two pumps, and Mr. MacDougall was able to get in touch with Tommy Higgins and his plane at Limberlost. Tommy said that he could be over at Headquarters in twenty-five minutes. Together they flew in the pumps and the necessary equipment, over a mile of hose, and tents, blankets and food on the spot. The report on the phone at 10.30 that night was: "It's a large fire and a hot one, but both pumps are working fine and I think we're gaining a little headway."

August 2nd — The first phone call came through at 4.30 a.m. It was Jack Gervais reporting on the Otterslides fire. "We have one pump on the lake with four streams of water going on the fire. Expect to be in full control of the situation by noon or earlier." "How are the boys standing up?" I asked. "They look black," he replied, "their fancy shirts are in rags and some of their trousers won't even make shorts, but they got the hose through the woods and they've done a great job. They're a hungry bunch, though, and we'll need more food and more gas and oil in another hour." In half an hour Mr. MacDougall was on his way with their supplies. Later, when he returned, he made another flight down to Ragged Lake to take in men to relieve the crew that had been working there under Jerry Kennedy.

That day things began to quieten down. Later in the day we heard that the Ragged Lake fire was out and that the Lobster Lake one was under control. Both the Tea Lake one and that at Ahmek had been subdued the day before so that left us with one only on the south side of the Park. When we closed up at 9.30 that night there were clouds in the west that looked as though they might bring rain. When it came in full force the next afternoon we were able to rest for the first time in more than a month."

The policy of conserving wildlife in Algonquin Park, maintained now for over forty years, has today borne rich fruit. According to Dr. C. H. D. Clarke, Mammalogist with the Department of Lands and Forests, the Park has played an important part in helping to keep three of Canada's most valuable furbearing animals from becoming extinct. The fisher and the marten have been trapped for so many years that without the sanctuary provided by the Park, it is likely that these animals would have by now disappeared from Southern Ontario altogether. Actually, although beaver and marten are found elsewhere, there are very few fisher to be seen outside the Park at the present time. It is said that because of the value of this pelt, an Indian trapper who comes upon a fisher's tracks will drop anything he is doing to follow the trail. A good skin will bring from one to three hundred dollars, and for that reason his returns would justify many days' travelling, and many hours spent without rest, from the time that the tracks are first discovered until he has captured his prize. The fisher, which in spite of its name is not a water animal, is the finest of all Canadian fur-bearers. It is not often seen even in the Park, since it multiplies slowly. However, in the winter, a short snowshoe trip in many parts of the Park will suffice to encounter some of these tracks. A good marten skin will bring up to sixty dollars, and higher prices have been known. A good beaver "blanket" is worth forty dollars In Eastern Canada, outside the Ontario Provincial Parks and the Federal Park on Cape Breton Island, these animals are not protected, and since they are quite easy to trap, they have become almost extinct. In the Rockies, marten are still common, and in parts of Western Canada there are other beaver grounds, but if it were not for the Ontario and Nova Scotian sanctuaries, the beaver and marten might have disappeared from the Eastern Canadian scene.

Park authorities and canoe trippers, with knowledge of the

conditions of the water routes through the district, have long been convinced of the great increase in the number of beaver in recent times. However, their knowledge has received confirmation from the results of the beaver survey undertaken by Mr. Donald L. Robb, under the auspices of the Department of Lands and Forests, during the years 1939 and 1940. In the report of his work in the Park, Mr. Robb made some interesting observations as the result of his beaver census. In sample areas of the Park, representing about one-tenth of all the region suitable for beaver habitation, he plotted, with the help of the rangers, all the locations of beaver houses and dams. Then he recorded whether these houses and dams were in present use or whether they had been built some time ago, and were no longer of service to the beaver population. As the result of his finding, Mr. Robb estimated that there were about 2,090 occupied beaver houses in Algonquin Park, or an average of three houses on every four square miles. These figures revealed the fact that beaver were thriving in those lakes and ponds of the Park where they were assured adequate protection and a good supply of the foods they like most.

The natural result of this increase in the number of beaver and other fur-bearing animals in the Park has been, as the Department foresaw from the first, the overflow of these animals into the surrounding countryside. This means, that at the present time, some of the best trapping ground in Ontario is to be found in the regions bordering on the Park. For some years trappers in the Haliburton area, as well as those from Huntsville, Kearney, North Bay, Mattawa, Pembroke and Golden Lake, have vied to see who could place his trap line in the most advantageous position close to the Park boundaries. As one would expect, this situation has brought its own difficulties. Quarrels and feuds have broken out amongst the local inhabitants who depend on trapping as their chief source of income; accusations have been hurled at one another and anonymous letters have been written to the Department about individuals who have stepped over the borders of the Park, to seize some particularly worth-while prize. There have also been frequent complaints about rank outsiders who have come in to raid these grounds, and who have departed to market the catch which was looked upon as the rightful property of the local people.

It was partly as the result of this that quite recently the Ontario Government took steps to set up a system of zoned trapping along the Park boundaries in the Huntsville and North Bay districts.

Having proved so successful, it is expected an attempt will be made to extend the system elsewhere in the Province. Because of the effects this new development may have in the border regions, as well as the protection it will give to adjacent districts in the Park itself, it is worth examining in some detail.

When it was decided to adopt a system of zoned trapping, all the trappers in the area who were accustomed to set their lines near the Park each winter, were called together. At this meeting, each man was given the opportunity to set forth his claims; that is, to describe which section of the country he considered to be his own trapping grounds. After everyone had been given an opportunity to speak, the area was divided into zones, and compromise boundaries marked out where necessary. This meant that in the future, each man would have sole rights in the particular area which was registered as his, and full permission, on the part of the Game Warden, to deal in a summary fashion with any stray trapper who wandered in to trap in his territory. In this way, a trapper would be encouraged to carry on his work in such a way as to give the highest yield of fur, by leaving enough young animals to safeguard the future supply. At the same time, he would have some assurance that these animals would later be caught in his own traps, and not in those set by some get-right-quick marauder who was only interested in the current season's catch.

This new system has met with the support of the local trappers, and especially with those whose zones extend right up to the Park boundaries. Ralph Bice, of Kearney, for instance, who works with his father and his son, values their combined trapping grounds, extending for nine miles along the west border of the Park, at something like $10,000. Each of these three men sets out his own trap line in the winter, and each takes in a good supply of beaver and marten, as well as the occasional fisher.

While on the subject of wildlife conservation, the perennial problem of the relationship between wolves and the deer population comes up. In spite of exaggerated statements to the contrary, there are actually only a few wolves in the region today. Proof of this lies in the record of wolves killed there each winter. Undoubtedly, the curtailment of staff during the recent war partly accounts for the decline, but even old hands like Peter Ranger and Jack Gervais do not kill as many as formerly. The following pre-war figures show the trend: One hundred and twenty-eight in 1931, seventy-six the following year, forty in 1933, twenty-one in 1934, an increase of nineteen the next year, but thereafter a steady decline down to a mere eleven in 1938. The present policy is to control rather than exterminate the wolves. In the National Parks of Canada and the United States, and in the famous Kruger National Park in South Africa, predators such as bears, wolves — and in South Africa, lions —are given the same protection as deer, antelopes, and other herbivores. It is only when individual animals become destructive to property or dangerous to human life, that they are destroyed.

In objecting to a full application of this policy in Algonquin Park, some have pointed out that wolves move in from other districts, attracted by the plentiful supply of deer in the Park, especially during the winter months. There is little doubt that some do cross the ice of the Ottawa from the Quebec side, or filter in from the Lake Nipissing country. Rangers stationed in the north catch more wolves than the others. On the other hand, any attacks on farm animals to the south of the Park are blamed on an overflow of wolves from the Park area. Even if it were true that wolves were pouring into the Park at the north, and out again at the south, which is far-fetched to say the least, a policy of immunity for wolves would be no solution.

Visitors to the Park today still see as many as six deer at a time from a car on the highway, and in the winter, a group of from fifteen to twenty cross over Cache Lake each evening just before sunset to feed at the kitchen door of the rangers' boarding house. They have become so tame that the neighbouring children give them nicknames — "Dirty Face" and "Rusty", according to their peculiar markings. There is certainly no dearth of deer in the Park.

Are they as plentiful or as healthy as they used to be? It is difficult to give a direct answer to this question. It may be that wolves are needed to weed out the weak and degenerate among the deer, and a full application of a survival of the fittest policy would have this effect. But there are other factors that influence the deer population. For instance, it is many years since greater portions of the Park were burned over or freshly timbered, and the young second growth on which the deer thrives is not as plentiful as formerly.

Another interesting point on which there have been differences of opinion, is the advisability of introducing non-native species of plant life into a Park of the Algonquin type. Latterly the tendency has been to keep the native plant life "pure". Actually, there are few foreign species of any kind in the present Park, although inevitably, along the old tote roads, a good many outside plants have taken root. The seeds of timothy, clover, heal-all, ox-eye daisy, yarrow, and orange hawkweed, came in with hay for the horses used in the lumber camps. Ragweed does not appear in the Park although native to its latitude and elevation.

The Royal Commission that drew up recommendations for the Park Act had no prejudice against introducing any species of plant or animal which would increase the public appeal of the Park. They suggested that new species of fish be introduced for the visitors' benefit; shrubs be planted for the deer, and wild rice for the ducks where these were needed. Simpson noted the absence of bass in the Park in his first report. At the turn of the century, Bartlett placed five hundred small mouth bass fingerlings in Cache, White, and Source Lakes; and later, in Opeongo Lake. Where these bass have succeeded in multiplying, it has been at the expense of the native trout, and the practice has been discontinued.

In 1909 and 1910, Atlantic salmon were planted in Source Lake, and perhaps in Cache Lake. A few were caught two or three years later, but so far as is known there have been no further signs of them.

In 1936 ten wapiti, or American elk, were released near Park Headquarters. Although they are known to have reproduced, their number is still small. So far, there has been no attempt to replace the one native animal that has disappeared from the Park, an animal fast disappearing all over the eastern north — the caribou.

Today, the original commissioners would probably be more than satisfied with the strides made in forest and game preservation, and in making the Park a place where people can recapture the values lost in the nervous strain of living in our cities.

Two developments have taken place which they never foresaw, and which remain to be described. Both were to be significant, not merely for Ontario but for the whole Canadian nation.

CHAPTER 14

In 1901, a party that included Billy Ross, a son of the Honourable G. W. Ross, made a canoe trip in Algonquin Park with Tim O'Leary, then Chief Ranger, as guide. Unconsciously, they paved the way for what was to become the most significant movement in Canadian art.

In Toronto that winter, three members of the Toronto Art Students' League heard such enthusiastic accounts of the trip that they wrote to Tim, asking whether he could perform the same service for them the following summer. O'Leary promised to meet them at the Canoe Lake Station with two canoes and the necessary supplies. Since they were all green campers, they could use the rangers' cabins for shelter.

The three men were W. W. Alexander, David Thomson, and Robert Holmes, all artists whose work was only beginning to be known in Ontario. It is not difficult to imagine their excitement at the prospect of going north to paint; but their wildest expectations, as they packed brushes, paint, paper and canvas for their trip, could not have foreseen its future significance.

When the three travellers arrived at Canoe Lake, O'Leary was there waiting for them. Immediately they started north through Joe Lake. Since the Art League motto was "Not a day goes by without a sketch," frequent stops were made at scenic spots along the way. Actually, their progress must have been very slow, for Mr. Alexander remembers one time when they were delayed for three days, because Robert Holmes was particularly anxious to complete sketches of some wild orchids that he had discovered.

At White Trout (now Big Trout) Lake, the party called in at one of the Lumber Company Depots. There the city artists were quick to transfer some of the local colour into their sketch books. Three of Mr. Alexander's sketches show different aspects of lumber camp life. One shows a pointer, the lumberman's general utility craft, with board sides and a flat bottom; another a well, rigged up with a suspended bucket at the end of a long pole, in order to bring the water to the surface; and a third depicts the camp barber's chair. This was a specially ingenious device, equipped with sleigh-runners so that it could be transferred easily from one cabin to another in the winter. Most of the lumber camps by 1902, were already fitted up with stoves and ranges, but occasionally the group came upon one with the old-style camboose fireplace. In every camp they experienced the warm welcome of traditional northern hospitality.

From the White Trout (Big Trout) district, the party proceeded on into Opeongo Lake by way of Green Lake (now Happy Isle). In this marshy district, Dave Thomson found many beaver dams as subject matter for painting, and they had a hard time persuading him to continue on his way. Frequently the group had to camp out, but now their guide was promising them an unusual treat. The ranger's cabin at Sunnyside, the old Dennison farm, had recently been·completed, and he was offering them solid comfort for their next stop. "A regular hotel" had just been completed. The title called up a vision of all kinds of luxury.

The Sunnyside shack is still standing, so it is possible to imagine their chagrin when they came upon this haven. The log cabin measures about fourteen feet by twelve feet. It has a low door, and a window commanding a view of the lake, two built-in bunks, and a small stove. When Robert Holmes entered the cabin which smelled of musty food, he decided to forego the pleasures of the "hotel" and sleep out-of-doors once more.

All along their canoe route, the party was delighted to find a great deal of animal life. Beaver, especially, seemed to be plentiful in this section of the Park. In one pond they surprised two beavers towing limbs for construction work. Another time they came upon a huge dam, eight feet high, which stretched right across their path. This dam was built in a horseshoe formation against the course of the stream, and it had all the appearances of a clever piece of engineering. Besides the beaver, the group had a chance to come very close to a cow-moose along the northern shore of Opeongo Lake. It was standing knee-deep in the water, feeding on lily pads.

At the south end of Opeongo Lake, the canoe trip came to an end. There, at the foot of Sproule Bay, they came upon their first signs of civilization since leaving Canoe Lake. The St. Anthony Lumber Company's Railway had recently been pushed through to that point, and they were able to make use of the line to journey down to Whitney. From there, they went back along the main line to Park Headquarters.

This trip was the beginning of a series of excursions by artists into Algonquin Park, which were continued until 1917. The three originals went back again and again, sometimes together, sometimes with other Toronto artists.

The late J. W. Beatty used to tell how he was first lured up north. Originally a Toronto fireman, he used his leisure to practice painting, saved his money, went over to Europe, and returned to support himself by his art. One of his first illustration jobs involved a story with a northern setting, that might have been inspired by Alexander's stories of the Park. In the illustration he had drawn a tea-pail over a campfire, showing the sides of the pail sloping like a bucket. A friend poured scorn on his drawing. Up north, Bill Beatty learned, a tea-pail has vertical sides. Then and there he resolved to go and see this peculiar country for himself, and followed the Algonquin Trail already blazed by Alexander, David Thomson, and Holmes. Tom McLean, a friend of Beatty's, was another early artist to make these northern trips. By 1912, Algonquin Park was well known in Toronto as ideal painting country.

Twenty years earlier, a young farm lad was growing up near Owen Sound. Like most youngsters, he did not know what he was going to do with his life. Probably he worried very little over the future, too intent on living for the day. He was passionately fond of the wilderness, and there was plenty of bush behind his back door where he could wander for hours in intervals between school and chores. A deep restlessness overtook him in his late teens. He took a routine job in Owen Sound and threw it over, went out to Seattle, where he worked at photography with his brother George. Dissatisfied, Tom Thomson came to Toronto in 1911. With his background in photography, and a quiet, competent manner which impressed all who met him, he landed a job at Grip Limited, a commercial art firm. That winter, he became interested in learning how to paint. There were plenty of experienced young artists to help him: J. E. H. Macdonald, Lismer, Carmichael, Frank Johnston and Varley were working under the same roof. Others, like J. W. Beatty, moved in the same circles; or rather, went on common sketching excursions whenever work allowed. Most of these men had learned to paint in England or Europe, but all of them were as ready to encourage as to criticize, and under their tuition his technique rapidly improved.

Unknown to any of this group, however, Tom Thomson had something the others could never acquire: the north was in his blood. Already, with his friend, Ben Jackson, he had gone up into the wilderness on fishing and sketching trips. He could not have been in Toronto long before he heard of Algonquin Park. So it is not surprising to find him, in the spring of 1912, camped with his friend Ben, also an ardent fisherman, at Tea Lake Dam.

The National Gallery has a sketch of Tom Thomson done at the time, and signed H. B. Jackson. It is entitled "A Rainy Day in Camp" and it reveals Tom in characteristic pose — absorbed in his fishing. Peculiarly enough, this early picture showing Tom's activities in the Park is like all the later ones. Sketches and photographs alike, all find him hard at work—fishing. Fishing was an occupation which could be carried on in the company of friends and companions who might want to stop long enough to take pictures, but painting was a solitary pastime, and no one was ever on hand to catch him in the act.

This Tea Lake sketch shows Tom clad in a conservative outfit, much more like the clothes worn by a city-born fisherman than those which he came to wear on subsequent visits to the Park. Here he has donned a broad-brimmed hat, a long-sleeved jacket, and high laced boots. He is seated close to the shore and is busy with his rod. He looks as though he is thoroughly enjoying himself, and is quite prepared to stay happily in camp throughout the whole of that stormy May day. Between his teeth he is gripping a sturdy pipe, and his whole attitude of concentrated absorption makes one feel that nothing pleased him better, than to have this opportunity of making the best use of a spell of gloomy weather. Although it is quite possible that Tom, as well as H. B. Jackson, did the occasional sketch at that time, there is no way of connecting any of his painting definitely with his first trip.

From an article written by Dr. James MacCallum, and published in the Canadian Magazine in October, 1917, we learn how Tom Thomson had spent the summer of 1912. It was in October of that year that Dr. McCallum first came to know Tom, when he met him at the studio of their mutual friend, J. E. H. MacDonald. Tom had just returned from a two-month canoe trip which he had taken through the Mississagi Indian Reserve to the northwest of Georgian Bay. When the Doctor heard that Tom had brought back a group of sketches made during the trip, he was anxious to see them, both because he had always taken a keen interest in struggling Canadian artists, and because he knew and loved the Georgian Bay country. Tom warned him that his sketches were rather the worse for wear, since they had been salvaged from the water at one point when their

TOM THOMSON, CANADA   Courtesy National Gallery, Ottawa

THE NORTHERN RIVER

Tom Thomson.

canoe had upset, but the Doctor insisted on having a chance to judge them for himself. When the Doctor had looked them over, he purchased several for his own collection, and encouraged Thomson to continue painting.

That winter was not only a milestone in Tom's career as an artist; it began a movement that was to create a milestone in Canadian history.

One of the sketches he had made during the previous summer had provided him with the material for a full-scale canvas, which was completed in time for the March show of the Ontario Society of Artists. When Tom learned that his picture, "A Northern Lake", had been purchased by the Ontario Government, at a price of $250.00, he was surprised at his own success. He must have turned northwards once more with renewed confidence in his own powers as a painter, and with the determination to set forth something of his own delight in the wilderness country, which he loved so well.

The twenty small sketches which he had brought back to Toronto made an indelible impression on Tom's fellow artists, corroborating Dr. MacCallum's shrewd judgment. Even though they could be dismissed technically as "moods smudged into panels", these paintings contained the essence of something every Canadian artist had been blindly groping for. "From them", says Arthur Lismer, "we saw that Tom not only was opening up as a painter, but that the north was a painters' country". Singly, and in groups, they went north — A. Y. Jackson, J. E. H. MacDonald, Arthur Lismer, F. H. Varley, Lawren Harris, and others, J. W. Beatty among them, after years of absence from the Park. All of them brought back paintings from the Park, and all were labelled, in the scathing criticism of the years between 1914 and 1917, as members of the "Algonquin Park Group".

The following summer, Tom Thomson went up to the Park alone —to paint. On his return to Toronto in the fall, he met an artist from Montreal whom Dr. MacCallum and Lawren Harris had persuaded to move to Toronto, an artist who, like Tom, had found that the north had something to say, and was learning to say it. The artist was A. Y. Jackson, known today from coast to coast as the "Dean" of Canadian landscape painting. Jackson and Thomson took to each other at once. Tom, who had decided not to return to an office routine in the city, was glad to accept Jackson's offer to share a studio in the new Studio Building that had just been built on

Severn Street overlooking the Rosedale Ravine. "In fact," as Jackson himself says, "we were so anxious to get to work that we moved in in January, before the building was really finished".

There the two artists discussed their work, and painted for the next two winter months. By that time, each had had a profound effect on the other. Jackson says he had become so tired of hearing Tom sing the praises of the wonderful part of the world called "Algonquin Park", he had decided to light out to see the place for himself; while Tom had learned a great deal about the techniques of painting — the preparation of canvases, the proper tools for the job, and the use of colours. Most of Tom's best work has to do with the vivid seasons of spring and autumn, while a great deal of Jackson's best belongs to winter, when he preferred to sally forth on snowshoes while the snow was still on the ground, in order to catch its varying beauty on canvas.

For two months in the early spring, while Tom was still in Toronto, A. Y. Jackson stayed at Mowat Lodge. When the cold was too extreme, he found that he could not work outside, but when it became a little milder, he undertook to do some good-sized canvases right on the spot, without preparing preliminary sketches to be used for studio paintings. It was in this way that "A Winter's Day" was painted. In order to get it, Jackson tramped across the lake each day to Hayhurst's Point. The picture now hangs in the Hamilton Public Library.

In a letter written at this time to his friend, J. E. H. MacDonald, and quoted by F. B. Housser in "A Canadian Art Movement", we get a first-hand picture of his reaction to this sort of life. There he wrote: "You don't notice the cold a bit. All you notice is your breath dropping down and splintering on the scintillating ground. At Canoe Lake Station it was forty-five below zero last night. Had a five-mile work-out this afternoon. The weather was milder and not at all penetrating. It was sunny but not colourful. The woods look very wonderful and full of colour motives; deer trails all over the place, and wolf tracks, too. I think if I have a scrap with a whole pack and get eaten up, it will be a great ad for the Studio Building".

J. E. H. MacDonald, whose sketches, after Tom Thomson's death, perhaps more than those of any other artist, were to carry on Tom's style of painting, caught the contagion of Jackson's enthusiasm. He was then living at Thornhill, where he had settled his family. When he had given his young son, Thoreau, full instructions as to how to keep the house warm, he, too, migrated to the Park. His "March Evening, Northland", was probably done at that time, and E. R. Hunter's catalogue of his paintings describes two other canvases that may have been the result of this early spring trip. These are "Snowflurries", showing an evening scene in the Park with snow-covered ground, and "Moonlight, Algonquin Park", also a snow scene in dull blues. MacDonald was in the Park on several other occasions; once when his friend Tom Thomson was there with him, and twice after his death, but it is likely that these three pictures were the product of this first trip.

It is difficult to discover when Tom went north to the Park that year, and whether his stay at Canoe Lake overlapped with the visit of either of these two artists, or with that of F. Horsman Varley, who also seems to have been at Mowat Lodge during the month of April. At any rate, he was there before May eighth when Arthur Lismer, then quite recently out from England, joined him for his first camping holiday in Algonquin Park. In the city, Tom had earned quite a reputation amongst his artist friends as a bushman, and Lismer felt satisfied that Tom would be able to look after them both on this occasion.

When Lismer arrived at Canoe Lake he found Tom had made arrangements for their camping equipment and their food supply. In fact, he had taken particular pains with one piece of equipment — his own canoe. Even before the ice was completely out of the lake, he had been conjuring up in his mind's eye just the right shade of dove-grey he wanted to paint it. However, when he tried to buy paint of that colour, he found that the paint-makers had nothing in stock that would come close to it. In spite of these difficulties, when Lismer arrived for the trip there was the canoe — resplendent in a fine new coat of the desired shade. Lismer wanted to know how Tom had managed to get that colour. "That was easy", Tom replied, "I just mixed in a tube of Cobalt violet to the standard grey canoe paint". Lismer knew "Cobalt blue" was worth two dollars a tube, but Tom was satisfied he had had good value for his money.

A photograph of Tom Thomson and Arthur Lismer frequently used for an illustration, was taken at this time — likely by the ranger, Bud Callaghan, at Smoke Lake. It shows Lismer in the bow of the canoe, nursing Bud's little dog, which looks more than contented to be paddling with this pair of campers. Lismer, too, seems to have made himself completely at home in this craft, to which he was unaccustomed. He has both long legs spread out, and his feet are resting on the gunwales of the canoe. On his head he is wearing a funny little round hat. Tom, in the stern, has a paddle in his right hand, while his left arm, leaning on a stump at the water's edge, holds the canoe steady and close into shore. Two fishing rods sticking out above the canoe, give the impression that the campers have been out on a jaunt to supplement their food stores. Certainly all three of them, including the dog, look as though they were enjoying the warm spring sunshine to the full.

Although they travelled about to many of the lakes down south of Canoe Lake, they made their main camp on Molly's Island in Smoke Lake. Lismer never failed to admire Tom's skilful way of handling the frail craft, upon which they were so dependent. Even at night, when it was almost impossible to pick out the shore-line, he seemed to be able to judge the right landing spot with unerring certainty, so that the canoe would graze gently along the sandy bottom instead of crashing into a shoal. Of course, Lismer was then a beginner in the art of paddling, so his friend's effortless stroke struck him as a masterly achievement. Everyone else who saw Tom handling a canoe remarked on his great skill as a canoeist.

For three weeks the two of them toured around through Smoke, Ragged, Crown, and Wolf Lakes, fishing and making sketches. That year they "saw the spring come in", and each day brought a change in hue and foliage. They lived in a state of enthusiastic delight, and everywhere they saw good painting material. However, in spite of their industry, Lismer says that very few of the sketches have survived. His own have been scattered and lost sight of, while Thomson's have mostly disappeared, too. In fact, Tom set small store on his ability as a painter, either then, or at a later date. He frequently gave away his latest sketch to any friend who mentioned he had a liking for what he had just done. Tom looked upon a great deal of his work as experimental because he was rarely satisfied that he had done full justice to the scene before him.

Later in the summer, Tom had gone up to Georgian Bay to pay a visit to the MacCallum summer home, near Go Home Bay. Dr. MacCallum had continued to encourage Tom since the time, two years before, when he brought back his Mississagi sketches, and for the five years intervening between that time and his death in 1917, Dr. MacCallum watched his progress and purchased sketches from time to time. Other artists were frequently invited by the Doctor to spend their summers in sketching holidays, using his Georgian Bay cottage as a headquarters, and the mural of Tom Thomson on the wall of the cottage was probably painted by J. E. H. MacDonald during this visit. When it came time to return to the Park, Tom once more set forth in his canoe. This simple acceptance of the wilderness way of life was something which never failed to fill his city friends with wonder and admiration.

Back in the Park, Mowat Lodge became the centre of an artists' colony in late August and September of 1914. The gathering had been planned in the spring, before the different individuals went off on their own painting trips, and now with the outbreak of war, all of them felt this might be the last time they would be together for a long while. In this they were quite right, as events proved, because at least three of this group were to join the Canadian Forces as accredited War Artists. Amongst those who were staying at the Lodge at this time were — F. H. Varley, A. Y. Jackson, Mr. and Mrs. Arthur Lismer, Percy Robertson and his bride, Beatrice Haggerty — while close at hand, in his own cabin, was Tom Thomson.

Mrs. Shannon Fraser remembers these artists, and others of their friends who made the lodge their headquarters during the next three years, as a jolly bunch of young people, who got a great deal of enjoyment out of traipsing around the country with their sketch boxes, sitting up till unearthly hours to discuss their new ideas, and were always so easy to please and so enthusiastic about the Park. The boarding house would overflow with their latest sketches, because they would have to be propped up to dry before they could be packed for the trip back to the city. Nobody minded that, and everyone shared in the friendly criticisms and the unstinted praise of the most recent experiment. There was a continual art show at Canoe Lake during the autumn painting season, and at one stage, the old hospital house at the top of the hill was taken over so that everyone could see what was being accomplished.

Mark Robinson recalls those days of artistic fervour at Canoe Lake. One day, when Mark was down by Tea Lake Dam, he came upon Tom and a group of his friends who had been spending the day painting and picnicing. As he passed by the island where they were camping, Mark was close enough to hear their conversation. Tom was pointing to one of the highly-coloured hillsides across the lake, and one of his friends had to admit, "Yes, Tom, it's all there. Your interpretation is not overdone." When Tom had first brought his northern sketches to Toronto, even his artist friends had doubted whether such clear, vivid colours could be found in the actual natural scene. Now that they were convinced, it was only a question of passing their conviction on to the rest of the world through their own painting of Canadian landscapes. However, at this stage in his development, Tom himself had not yet branched out into the startling use of colour that was to make his "Northern River" and his "West Wind" subjects of controversy.

When the other artists returned to the city, A. Y. Jackson stayed on in the Park with Tom until late November. Dr. MacCallum, knowing the two were working together, sent a message to Tom suggesting he was to continue to paint in his own style, and that he was not to allow Jackson to influence him too much. There were many things Tom could still learn from his painting companion. As always, he was quick to praise the work of his friend, and to see the faults in his own, but by this time he was beginning to get into his final stride, turning out sketches full of colour and action as the result of a morning's or an afternoon's work.

Together, Tom and his friend moved about from camp-site to camp-site, as the spirit and the changing forest prompted them. They started at a spot just north of Hayhurst's Point, near where "Spring Ice" or "The Opening of the Waters" was painted in a subsequent spring; they stopped down near Tea Lake Dam; and they went on down to Ragged and to Smoke Lake. Always "A.Y." was thrilled with Tom's camping and paddling skill — and Tom, in turn, gave the "city chap" a certain amount of credit as he learned some of the tricks and arts of the old camper.

When the leaves had all fallen, and the lakes were beginning to freeze, Tom and Jackson left the Park. Jackson went to Montreal to enlist, and this was the last he ever saw of Tom.

How long Tom stayed in the Park thereafter no one remembers, but it must have been late October when Dr. MacCallum received the news, "Tom is back". He had brought with him a collection of sketches which Dr. MacCallum describes as being full of "lightning flashes, moving thunder storms, and trees with branches lashing in the wind". Tom had not yet attained the perfection that he later achieved in the deft use of the simple line and the application of clear flowing colours, but he could catch the feeling and the moods of the changing pattern of the north country. The original sketch for the painting "A Moonlight Scene", which he exhibited the next spring at the Ontario Society of Artists Show, must have been done during that summer in the Park. This picture was afterwards purchased by the National Gallery in Ottawa.

By the spring of 1915, Tom's life had worked itself out to the pattern that it was to follow until his death. He had now given up any settled job, therefore, he had to earn his living by his painting in the winter, and by guiding and fire ranging in the summer. For the four winter months he would paint, and cook his own meals in the shack which he shared with Arthur Lismer, overlooking the Rosedale Ravine behind the Studio Building, in Toronto; while in the eight months of the spring, summer, and autumn, he would be up in the Park. There, too, he established a sort of routine. When he first went up in the early spring, he would stay at Canoe Lake, in the Trainor's little cottage near the outlet of the creek, and then during the fire ranging season from May to the end of September, he would travel to his post in the north of the Park near Achray at Grand Lake. In the fall, until the freeze-up, he would be back at the Canoe Lake cottage. In this way he could make both ends meet, and at the same time acquire a little ready cash to pay for the equipment necessary for his painting.

The National Gallery in Ottawa had already acquired a large number of Thomson's smaller sketches, as well as several of his larger canvases, before 1944, but in that year their collection was greatly augmented by the bequest of Dr. J. M. MacCallum's own private collection of Thomson paintings and sketches, valued at many thousands of dollars. Now there is a movement on foot to have a special Tom Thomson room set up where visitors to the Canadian capital may see at all times, representative paintings of this man who ranks amongst the foremost of our Canadian artists. In such a room, a person who knows the Park well could instantly recognize a dozen Park places. The fact that Tom insisted on painting scenes as he actually saw them, would help in recognizing these actual spots. He had no patience with artists who did not paint nature as it really was, but who combined two or more different scenes to get the effect they wanted. To him, the use of such methods was like telling a lie — when he painted, he must show things as they lay before him. He always insisted that his colours were not intensified, and that the patterns of his lines were there in truth. He wanted others to see the actual northland scene with the same magic eye that he himself possessed.

Although Tom Thomson seems to have left no records to tell either of where he painted actual scenes in the Park or when they were done, there are certain ways of establishing some information about the paintings that he left behind. The Accessions Book at the

National Gallery in some cases gives names and dates to identify the pictures with the Park; sometimes people who were on hand, remember seeing one particular sketch soon after it was completed; experts in tree growth and topography have identified certain sections in the northern districts as his painting grounds; and art critics have worked out the general sequence of his work, by the progressive mastery of style revealed in his sketches and full-sized canvases. But in spite of the research already made, there are still many of the sketches, in the MacCallum collection, in the collection of the National Gallery, and in the hands of private owners, having an Algonquin Park atmosphere, but that have not yet been actually identified with the Park.

In the National Gallery, there are some paintings whose titles indicate that they were painted in the Park. These include: "Petawawa Gorges", "Tea Lake Dam", and "The Artist's Hut". It is also quite probable that "Autumn's Garland", with its vivid maples in the foreground, and "Canadian Wildflowers" were done in the Park, because Tom nearly always managed to be painting there when the spring and fall seasons rolled around. The sombre "Moose at Night", and some of his northern lights sketches were likely done there, too. There were few other places frequented by Tom where he could have found the moose in their native habitat, and Mark Robinson recalls at least one occasion when Tom painted the Northern Lights while staying at Canoe Lake.

Many other paintings of Tom Thomson's have Algonquin Park moods or colourings. Some show the turquoise skies of spring, and the rich brown earth appearing through the melting snow. Others are early morning subjects, done in the summer time, when the sun turns the clouds over the lakes into masses of opalescent mother-of-pearl. Sometimes the titles of the sketches — "Hot Summer Moonlight" or "Burnt Country" have a Park flavour; or a campfire along the shore, birches on the hillside, or tricky river rapids; all these give characteristic glimpses of the country. All reflect the movement and the spirit of the Park.

At least two of his well-known lumbering pictures were done when he was ranging in the Grand Lake section of the Park. In his canvas "The Bateaux", now hanging in Hart House at the University of Toronto, a group of lumbermen's red pointers are moored close to the shore, while nearby is a log-boom enclosing the logs that are being moved downstream. According to Dr. MacCallum, the title "Pageant of the North" would have done better justice to the scope of this canvas. The sketch for the other picture, "Lumber Drive", was likely done in the north of the Park, when Booth's lumberjacks were driving down the Petawawa River. Pete Sauve, who went with the lumbermen as a cook at the camps that they established along the river course, says Tom was painting there one year when they went through. Mark Robinson, who was Deputy-Chief Ranger for some years in the district, identifies the place where this painting was done as being the narrows at the south end of Grand Lake, below Achray.

Tom seems to have spent at least one summer at the old rangers' cabin at Achray, which stood just to the right of the new stone building that is now the headquarters. Professor T. W. Dwight, of the Faculty of Forestry, University of Toronto, who spent eleven years there at the Forestry School's fall camp, feels sure that the canvas "West Wind" was painted from the place where Tom's cabin formerly stood. Professor Dwight took photographs of the skyline across the lake as it appears in recent years, and compared it with the hills in the background of the painting. Even allowing for changes brought about because of the tree growth in the intervening years, the similarity between the two is very striking. By using this same method, Professor Dwight decided that the picture entitled "Jack Pine" was painted from a nearby spot, the point stretching out into the lake to the left of the ranger's log cabin built by Ned Godin.

In both cases, however, while the land contours were almost identical, the trees in the foreground cannot be identified. There are white pines on the point shown in "West Wind", but there is no weather-beaten red pine such as the picture shows. There are a few trees and shrubs on the rocky Jack Pine point, but there are no jack pines at all along the shoreline of the lake, nor for that matter are they at all common in the district. However, Professor Dwight is full of praise for the accuracy with which the trees were painted in both these pictures. In the "Jack Pine", Tom Thomson was able to reproduce perfectly the drooping pendulous branches of the jack pine to give an impression of summer languor, and in the "West Wind" he has used the tough, hardy virility of the red pine to show how it has weathered the lashings of the winds from across the open expanse of the lake.

Men who have made a special study of the materials which different artists have used, such as sketching boards, paints, and brushes, can throw some light on the way Tom Thomson worked when he was in the Park. For many years, Mr. George Harbour has been in charge of the cleaning and repair of paintings in the National

Gallery, and he was able to show how Tom's sketch boards reveal the story of his painting methods. Other people have told us Tom often painted a sketch very quickly—Mr. Hayhurst at Canoe Lake, recalled how he used to be away for a few hours in the morning and come back at noon with a finished sketch, and artists have agreed that the original sketch for the "West Wind" could have been done in half an hour. The sketches in the National Gallery offer another proof of this speed. Frequently, they show indications of the paint having been flattened out, because it had not been given a chance to dry before the sketch was packed up to be carried elsewhere along the Park portages. Of course, where the paint was particularly thick, such flattened areas could have been the result of being stacked up in the Canoe Lake cabin before they were taken down to the Toronto studio, but it is a fact that a great number of the sketches that Tom did in the Park show this evidence of hasty packing.

It is interesting to note that Tom made use of all kinds of sketch boards for his Park drawings. Sometimes he was able to provide himself with a stock of the small-sized panels such as his friend, J. E. H. MacDonald, preferred for his outdoor work. Sometimes he could get special birch panels, that would be light to carry over the portages, but frequently, with the true woodsman's versatility, he made use of any substance he could find, on which to paint. There are some scenes done on the artists' boards brought north from the city, but there are others on millboard, on cardboard, on the flat side of corrugated packing boxes, and on cotton and wood panels. In some instances, pictures have been painted on both sides of the board, in order to conserve supplies.

In the winter, after his return to Toronto, he developed these same sketches into the full-sized canvases which were to make him so famous. In three successive years these great tableaux came out of the Park — "Northern River" in 1915; the "Jack Pine" in 1916; and the "West Wind" in 1917. All of them are associated with the Grand Lake district. Even if we had not known that this was the area where he had been working during the summers of 1915 and 1916, it would have been possible to identify them with this part of the Park. There the lakes are bigger and more wind-swept than in the southern sections, and the whole region is wilder, and more untouched. Old-timers are in general agreement that "Northern River" is Karishoo Creek, while the lake in the other two is Grand Lake.

After Tom Thomson's death, few of his fellow artists ever returned again to the Park. Surrounded by reminders of the friend they had lost, they would not have had the heart to paint. Many years passed before younger men and women, drawn by the influence of the Group of Seven's work, came up to see Tom Thomson's cairn, and paint the land he had loved.

Dr. MacCallum, the far-sighted friend who was the first to recognize his true significance to Canadian art, said of him afterwards, "Tom Thomson lived eight months of the year in Algonquin Park, often disappearing into its recesses for a month at a time. His sketches are a complete encyclopedia of all the glories of Algonquin Park, and aside from their artistic merits, have a historical value entitling them to preservation in the National Gallery."

Albert Robson, who worked with Tom and with the other rising young artists who were to band themselves later into the famous "Group of Seven", explains Thomson's chief contribution when he says, "He painted the lake country with fiery concentration, rarely travelling farther than his beloved Algonquin Park, where Canoe Lake was his regular headquarters. Other Canadian artists had painted the north country before Thomson; it is both unfair and untrue to say that he discovered it as paintable material. But it is true to say that he was the first painter to interpret the north in its various subtleties of mood and feeling, free from influence of European traditions and formulas. His personal knowledge of the country and his inherent honesty dictated its own methods of expression."

To those who know and love Algonquin Park, Tom Thomson's significance in the history of Canadian art is secondary. For them, it is sufficient to say, that of all the artists who have ever painted there, or may come to paint, to him alone belongs the title of "The Algonquin Artist".

CHAPTER 15

ON AUGUST 16TH, 1930, a totem pole was erected on Hayhurst's Point overlooking Canoe Lake, by the boys and girls of the neighbouring camps, under the guidance of two Ahmek leaders, Harold Hayden and Gordon Weber. At the top is the figure of a man; next a pair of wings — his aspirations; below that a group of tepees for his camping experience, a checkered area for his guiding career, a duck for his skill in swimming, a canoe for his expert paddling, a lynx for his woodsmanship, and a lyre for his art. At the base is carved the form of a palette, symbol of the art of painting.

So the youth of Algonquin Park have expressed their tribute to Tom Thomson.

In Algonquin Park today, Thomson has become almost a legendary figure. A recent documentary film was designed to show how magnificently Thomson was able to catch the colour and the rhythm of the Park in his paintings. Many are the stories told about Thomson around the campfires in the Park. One hears of a mystic ghost canoe, painted a shimmering magic grey, that glides across Canoe Lake at twilight, only to vanish into the mist. There's a story about a picnic group who followed after a swiftly moving canoe in the still of the evening, and who saw this craft land on a beach, where it left no mark or sign of its whereabouts. Someone else recalls a flaming comet which flashed across the summer sky one night a few years ago, on the anniversary of Thomson's death.

For the men and women of the Park who knew him best, Tom Thomson was neither a legend nor a totem. To them he was flesh and blood, human and real; shy perhaps, and not overly given to speech, but a generous friend with no pretentions, and a top-ranking woodsman. Tom Thomson was simply, to them, a man who belonged.

Of his first fishing trip to Algonquin with Ben Jackson, in the spring of 1912, there is no recollection among Park residents. It was his first arrival alone, a year later, that is remembered. Naturally, Mark Robinson was the man to remember that. Mark was then living at the rangers' house at Joe Creek, and he remembers being at the station one spring evening when the train came in. The stranger who alighted with his pack on his back, enquired of Mark where he could get "a decent bite and a good warm bed". It being early in the season, before the nearby hotel was open, Mark suggested he try Shannon Fraser's, and that was the first time that Tom made the acquaintance of the family with whom he was to have such a close connection during the next five years in the Park.

For several days Mark did not see anything more of this new-comer, but the sectionman, Charlie Ratan, reported that "this guy must be some sort of a queer fool" because he had seen him out back of the station several times, daubing bits of paint on a piece of board. Tom had discovered, with the coming of spring, the colour of the alders growing along the Portage Creek shore changed each day, and he had been trying to record this fact with his paints. One day, Charlie's sixteen-year-old sister, who was very curious about the actions of this stranger in the district, chanced to see one of his "boards". Immediately she exclaimed, "Why that's like the alders were a week ago!" Then Tom knew that he had been able to get the right colours. With the rare smile that always lighted up his face when he was pleased, he remarked that he must be "going places".

While making his rounds, Mark would often come upon this strange young man in out-of-the-way spots. Sometimes he would be tossing stones into the water from the bridge at Joe Creek to see how the ripples formed and broke; sometimes he would pace away from an object, and then return to it again and again. The rangers had seen a good many strange things in the Park, but probably the strangest of all was the sight of this lean young fellow, with the cut of a bushman about him, studying the tones of grey on an old pine stump, and explaining that until he could mix the same colour, and capture the exact value of a certain brown that showed up best in some kind of a fern, he couldn't make much headway. Perhaps they understood later, when they saw the subtle browns and greys revealed in his later sketches, sombre backgrounds for vivid splashes of autumn yellows or spring blues.

Mark makes mention of Tom earning his way in the Park during the summer by purchasing a guide's license, and taking parties of fishermen about the Park on trips. In later years, he seems to have made his headquarters at Shannon Fraser's, where he came to be looked on as one of the family. There were two other places where Tom made his home at Canoe Lake, but no one seems to know just when or why he migrated from one to the other. For several seasons he camped in a tent pitched on the east side of the lake, opposite

Mowat Landing, and just to the north of Hayhurst's Point. Sometimes, in the early spring and fall, he lived in a little cabin on the
west side of the lake, just below Potter Creek. This cabin was owned
by a lumber foreman, Hugh Trainor, from whom Tom received
permission for its use. It is interesting to note that one of the
Thomson paintings, "The Artist's Hut", in the National Gallery,
has recently been reproduced in colour. The picture shows this little
wooden shack on the edge of Canoe Lake, in the spring of the year,
while the snow is still lying in patches on the ground. In the foreground is a curtain of birch and poplar trees; two women, one
dressed in red, and the other in blue, are passing along the road that
leads north to the railway station. There is no date assigned to this
painting, but it was likely done after 1914.

Tom's second summer has been partially described in the account
of Lismer's stay with him. According to Mark Robinson, after Tom
had finished his painting in the spring of that year, he had taken out
a guide license, and had earned money in that way until mid-July.
He then embarked on a trip through the Park to Lake Nipissing, by
way of the South River. In making his plans he had told Mark of
his intentions to go on through to Georgian Bay, but that he would
be back at Canoe Lake by September fifteenth. Sure enough, he was
back on the day appointed, but he didn't seem his gay old self. He
pulled up his canoe, said hello, and immediately asked for the latest
war news. After supper, when he had read the papers, he went off
to his cabin without any remarks either on his trip or on the news
itself.

Later that fall, as already related, A. Y. Jackson and he painted
together after the others had returned to Toronto. In a large gathering
Tom had little to say, but in the company of one or two close friends,
he was a different man. Sometimes in their isolated cabin at night,
the glowing fire in the tin stove making a comfortable contrast within
to the frosty air without, he and Jackson would set up their week's
work, and pull it to pieces earnestly. At other times, Tom would
recall his own experiences in the Park: the night, for instance, when
his tent was pitched on the lake opposite the Blecher's, while paddling
to shore he had seen a wolf prowling between his tent and the edge
of the lake. Then, his hunger being stronger than his fear, he beached
his canoe and dashed up to the tent. He made his supper in the tent
that night, lighting all his candles, and wishing the walls were made
of wood instead of canvas. In the morning the wolf was gone.

When Tom came north to Canoe Lake in the spring of 1915, he

found Shannon Fraser had acquired a bookkeeper and assistant, George Chubb, who had come to the Park for reasons of health. "Chubby", who still returns to the Park each summer as the business manager at Camp Ahmek, recalls that Tom was accepted as one of the family in the Fraser kitchen. Everyone liked him for his kindly consideration for others, and his willingness to do the odd jobs which always turn up unexpectedly in a back country household. Chubby recalls two instances of this sort, while he and Tom were both at Canoe Lake. One of them happened before he actually got to know Tom. Chubby and a friend were camped on Little Wapomeo Island, and they had the misfortune to break the handle of their axe. They paddled over to the Lodge to ask Shannon if he could sell them one. Tom happened to overhear their request, and the next time they came around, he presented them with one fashioned by himself out of a piece of ironwood.

Another little incident, typical of Tom Thomson, took place while both Tom and Chubby were staying at the Frasers'. The old grandmother was sitting at the long table in the kitchen, where they all ate together when there weren't any guests. She had been brought up to say grace before meals, and always bowed her head as she sat down to eat. The others, who came in ravenous from their work, usually started right in without any preliminaries, but Tom always respected the old lady's custom, and waited until she had finished saying grace before beginning to eat.

It may have been that summer when the three tourists were caught on Canoe Lake in a sudden, dangerous squall. Whether Tom paddled out to them and shouted the instructions that saved them, or whether he actually pulled them out of the water, has not been told. But when Mark Robinson, the nearest ranger, found out about it and congratulated Tom, the latter merely replied with embarrassed brevity: "You rangers do that sort of thing all the time: forget it".

Tom's skill at fly-casting won him the admiration of the guests at Shannon's. They profited often from his success, too, because he frequently brought in a nice catch for Mrs. Fraser to cook for the household. Mark says that nothing delighted Tom more than to go out to a spot where everyone said it was impossible to catch anything, and to return triumphant with two or three good-sized fish. He made his own flies and "bugs", watching to see what insects made the fish rise, and painting his own imitations on the spot.

Although there is no date to indicate when the photograph of Tom Thomson fly-fishing at the bottom of a lumber dam was taken, there is no doubt that this shows one of his favourite pastimes in the Park. There are many stories of the good fishing to be found near the old dams, and certainly, the intent concentration expressed both in Tom's face, and in his stance on that particular occasion, are eloquent of his interest in the art of angling. In this photograph, in contrast to the Tea Lake picture, he is garbed in real north country outfit. The wool toque on the side of his head, and the flexible mocassins on his feet, show him dressed for warmth and comfort, in the fashion of any good woodsman.

During the summer of 1915, Tom came to know the northern part of the Park in the neighbourhood of Grand Lake and Achray, as well as he had previously known the Canoe Lake district. That year, he went north for the first time as a Park fire ranger, one of the temporary employees taken on to the staff at the time of year when the forest fires were most dangerous. This sort of work gave him a livelihood — Tom in his lifetime never sold enough of his paintings to make ends meet — and he could utilize the slack periods between fires to carry on with his painting. For days on end he would be out in the Park alone, observing the changes of season and mood taking place about him, while scanning the horizon for the first thin tell-tale column of smoke. When he wanted company, there was his fellow ranger, Jack Culhane, of nearby Killaloe, and his family, who always came up to the Park for the summer. Jack's son-in-law, Skinny (Leonard) McDermid, who worked on the railway, also knew Tom. Then there was Ned Godin, the ranger at Achray. On one of Tom's visits during the summers of 1915 and 1916, he painted a new sign for Ned's cabin, in old English lettering — "Outside Inn".

Amongst the other oddments painted in these latter years by Tom for his friends and neighbours, was an agate bowl, now to be seen in the National Gallery. This bowl, about ten inches across, Tom completely covered, inside and out, with a thick layer of oil paint. In a wheel at the bottom, surrounded by a conventional design of oak leaves, and woven into the pattern are the initials "T.T." These old friends of Tom agree that he set no great store by his skill. Frequently he gave them sketches they admired, which they, unconscious of their real value, left behind in the wintertime, in old attics or damp cabins. Some of these were later picked up and restored by collectors, but a great many of them have gone the way of the camboose camps.

One more summer of guiding, painting, and fire ranging, followed

before Tom Thomson's last. That winter he painted his final, and best
known canvas, "The West Wind".

Tom must have come north to Canoe Lake for the last time in
April, of 1917. Mark tells us of a special project that must have
been started two months before the lush greens of June ended the
spring painting season. This spring, Tom confided in his friend that
he had completed a series of sketches recording the changes in
Algonquin seasons and landscape for sixty successive days. There
has always been controversy over the amount of painting he did
that spring, for when his brother, George, arrived to take over his
belongings in July, there were only thirty-five spring sketches in
his cabin. The discrepancy between these figures has never been
accounted for.

That summer Tom decided to stay at Canoe Lake instead of
going north again to fire range. He had purchased a guide's license
once more, and seemed to be planning to take out groups of fishermen
on trips from Shannon Fraser's. His reasons for this change of
routine would be difficult to explain. Perhaps, with the sale of some
of his larger canvases, he felt it better not to tie himself down to
one section of the Park for the whole summer; perhaps health
considerations entered into the picture. Just why Tom was rejected
by the army when he applied for enlistment has not been recorded,
but he felt so badly about it that he did not even discuss it to his
friends. At any rate, on the fateful Sunday morning of July eighth,
1917, Tom was still at Canoe Lake.

Over twenty-five years later, there are still eight people who were
living at Canoe Lake at that time, who have their own versions of
what took place. The following account includes only those points
on which there is general agreement.

Nothing out of the way had happened in the Canoe Lake community in the preceding weeks. Mr. and Mrs. Colson had recently
taken over the management of the Hotel Algonquin; Shannon and
Mrs. Fraser were running Mowat Lodge; Taylor Statten had rented
Little Wapomeo Island for a few weeks to Dr. Goldwin Howland of
Toronto; Mr. T. H. Hayhurst was at his cottage on the point above
which is now the Tom Thomson cairn; and Martin Blecher was at
his house, formerly the Park Headquarters, at the outlet of Canoe
Lake Creek. Mark Robinson was the closest ranger to Canoe Lake,
as he was then living in the ranger's cabin near the railway tracks,
at Joe Creek.

Tom Thomson's actions on the morning of the day of his death are fairly well defined. Mark remembers having seen Tom passing his cabin early in the day. He was with Shannon Fraser at the time, and Shannon afterwards told Mark that they were talking about a large trout which Tom and Mark had both tried to pull out of Joe Lake Creek, above the dam. Each had hooked him several times, but the fish had always managed to get away. Now Tom had decided to play a joke on Mark by catching another large fish somewhere else, and leaving it on Mark's doorstep in the pretence that the object of their rivalry had been captured. Mark says both he and Tom knew a fish of that size was unusual, and that one of the best places to get them was at Gill Lake, a small, rather inaccessible spot to the southwest of Canoe Lake. For that reason Mark feels sure that Tom was headed towards this lake on the afternoon he was drowned.

Later in the morning, when Shannon had gone back to the Lodge, Tom dropped in at the Hotel Algonquin, where Mrs. Colson was busy at work. The Colsons had not been at Joe Lake for very long, and Mr. Colson had never met Tom. However, Mrs. Colson had talked to him on several occasions, and this time he came into the kitchen for a cup of tea. Afterwards, Mrs. Colson did not recall anything peculiar about him on that occasion. He seemed his normal self, and chatted in a friendly fashion. He left before lunchtime to return to Mowat Lodge.

About one o'clock that afternoon the guests at the Lodge saw him leaving his dock in his own grey canoe. He looked as though he were going off for a day's fishing, since he had his tackle and some food supplies in the bow of the canoe. That was the last anyone saw of Tom alive; what happened afterwards is an unsolved mystery.

Towards evening, Charlie Scrim, a young chap staying at the Lodge, and who was a particular admirer of Tom's, began to feel uneasy about his friend. No one else felt this uneasiness, because Tom often went off by himself and was sometimes away for weeks at a time. It was not till two days later, on July 10th, that news came of Tom's canoe having been found floating empty behind Little Wapomeo Island. Martin Bletcher, and his sister, afterwards mentioned having seen it between Mowat Lodge landing and the large island, when they had passed by about three o'clock on July 8th, but they had thought it to be one of the canoes owned by the Colsons and rented to guests at the hotel, which had come adrift, and they had done nothing about it.

When the canoe had been identified as Tom's, everyone started to search the lake. At first the rangers could not believe he could have drowned, because the canoe was found floating in an upright position. The paddles were lashed into place as if for portaging, and some of the food was still in the bow. However, his pack sack and his fishing tackle had disappeared, and these never were recovered. Acting on the supposition that Tom might have gone on foot through the woods to find a good fishing place, search parties travelled all through the surrounding country. Naturally, the area around the portage through to Gill Lake was covered very thoroughly, although it was considered nearly impossible for the canoe to have drifted such a distance from the time Tom had arrived there after leaving the landing, and the time when the canoe was first sighted by the Blechers.

When the news of Tom's disappearance reached his family in Owen Sound, his brother, George, had just come north to Canada from New Haven, where he had been studying art. As quickly as possible, he went by train to Canoe Lake, but on his arrival, there was still no further news of what had taken place — Tom's canoe had been found, and there still remained a slight chance of him having landed somewhere along the shore, and that he was still alive in the bush. George Thomson waited for several days at Mowat Lodge and then, because there seemed to be nothing that he could do, he decided to return to Owen Sound. Before he left, however, he took possession of the belongings which Tom had left behind in the shack, and made arrangements to complete the things that would have to be done in the event of his brother's death.

Soon after George departed from the Canoe Lake district, Tom's body was found floating in the lake. Old-timers in the Park say that a body frequently comes to the surface on the eighth day and the theory was confirmed on this occasion. On Monday, July 16th, Dr. Howland was sitting on the verandah of the cabin at Little Wapomeo when he saw an object come up to the surface of the water. He called to George Rowe and Larry Dickson, the two guides from Mowat, who were passing by in a canoe, and they paddled over to investigate. When they reached the spot, they found the object was Thomson's body. They towed it over to Big Wampomeo Island, and there decided that they should notify the Park Headquarters as quickly as possible. One of them stayed behind on the Island while the other paddled off to notify the Park authorities.

At Headquarters, Mr. Bartlett instructed Mark Robinson to go

over to the island and stay there until the coroner arrived from
North Bay. Since Dr. Raney, the coroner, could not possibly be
there until the next day, Mark took along supplies sufficient for his
sojourn on the island until Dr. Raney's arrival. Consequently,
Mark and one of the other rangers kept an all-night vigil on the
shore during the night of July 16th.

When the coroner reached Canoe Lake the next day, he was met
at the station, and Martin Bletcher offered the use of his house,
which was close by, as a place to hold the inquest. In the evening,
Dr. Howland was called in to assist in making the examination of the
body. They found no water in the lungs, and seeing evidence of a
dark bruise on the temple, they gave the verdict as one of "accidental
death". It is possible that Tom Thomson may have died from heart
failure, or he could have fallen and struck his head on a rock when
he landed his canoe, either at the place where he planned to portage,
or where he expected to eat his lunch.

According to the opinions of these people, Tom was a good swim-
mer and an excellent canoeist. As one of his friends said, he had a
short, low stroke like an Indian's, yet it was so characteristic that
you could tell it was Tom's canoe when he was still away down the
lake. He was a kind, likeable person, who minded his own business
and expected others to mind theirs. In this way he made himself
quite unobtrusive in the neighbourhood, and he was well liked by
those who did know him. No one is ever likely to know just what
happended after he departed from the Mowat Lodge dock on that
fatal Sunday afternoon.

It was impossible to notify the Thomson family in Owen Sound
in time for them to arrive for the funeral, and the decision was made
to bury Tom in the Mowat graveyard behind the Lodge, where several
plots, dating from the time when lumbermen were operating in that
region, had already been set aside. The funeral service was held on
the morning after the inquest, with a number of Tom's old friends
gathered at his graveside. Mr. Bletcher, senior, read the service
from Mark's Anglican prayer book, and the body was laid to rest.

Present-day visitors would like to think that Tom Thomson's
grave is still to be found in that Canoe Lake Cemetery, but the cairn
on the monument across the lake tells that "His body is buried at
Owen Sound". From George Thomson, his brother, we learn the
reason for this. On his arrival at Owen Sound he was informed his
brother's body had been found. As there was little else he could do,
he arranged for the body to be brought from the original burying-

place to the family plot at Owen Sound. In spite of the fact that many of Tom's old friends have always felt that he would have preferred to remain buried in his beloved Algonquin Park, there is really no reason to doubt that this change of burial place was made.

Some of Tom's artist friends travelled to the Park as soon as they heard of his death, but there was little they could do when they arrived. J. E. H. MacDonald and J. W. Beatty, who were there at the time, found that somehow the place had lost much of its charm for them — Tom Thomson had become so much a part of it in their memories that they could not even paint there. They decided to build a memorial cairn at the top of Hayhurst's Point — a height which overlooks Tom Thomson's beloved Canoe Lake district. Together they arranged to have the rocks hauled to the top of the hill, while J. E. H. MacDonald designed the bronze plaque with the story of Tom's career. There, to this day, visitors may read this tribute to the man whom many people in the Park knew as their friend, and whom other Canadians have come to know as a pioneer in Canadian art:

TO THE MEMORY OF

TOM THOMSON

ARTIST — WOODSMAN — AND GUIDE

who was drowned in Canoe Lake,
July 8th, 1917.

He lived humbly but passionately
with the wild — it made him brother
to all untamed things of nature. It
drew him apart and revealed itself
wonderfully to him. It sent him out
from the woods only to show these
revelations through his art — and it
took him to itself at last.

As one stands at the crest overlooking the dancing waters of the lake below, one has the feeling that Tom Thomson would have been content to know that the spot has been set aside as his own. From there in the spring, during the break-up season, you can look over towards the hills, for this point is close to where his own "Spring Ice" was painted.

Here in the heart of Algonquin Park, Tom Thomson found his real home: and here he died.

CHAPTER 16

THE INFLUENCE of Algonquin Park on Canadian life did not cease with the birth of a native Canadian art movement within its borders. Today we are witnessing a new development of which even the vision of Kirkwood hardly caught a glimpse, a development of practical value to the whole world.

Today, without in any way hampering its other activities, Algonquin Park has become a vast laboratory for study and research in natural science. Of recent years, scientists who wish to carry out controlled experiments on a wide scale have found the Park an excellent area for such work. Park authorities have given generous assistance to many different groups who have carried on field work within the Park boundaries. Experts in the employ of the Ontario Department of Lands and Forests, as well as from other different Provincial and Dominion Departments, from the various departments of the University of Toronto, the Royal Ontario Museum of Zoology, and other institutions, have found in the Park excellent facilities for carrying on their studies.

The pioneer move in this direction took place as early as 1908, when the first Forestry Practice Camp held by the Faculty of Forestry, University of Toronto, was held in Algonquin Park. In that year, three students, one of whom was T. W. Dwight, a present member of the Faculty, with two instructors. took over the rangers' cabin at the north end of Burnt (now Portal) Lake, in order to carry on field work in surveying and timber cruising. Barnet's Depot was then situated on the lake, and the students were able to gain a practical insight into the methods used by lumber companies at that time. The Forestry Camp was not held in the Park again until 1924, when it was established at Achray on the Northern Railway. There it continued until 1935, when it was moved to Haliburton County. During those eleven years valuable records were compiled by students and staff on the age and growth of tree life in the Park.

Typically, when this new field of usefulness for the Park had been opened up, others came to develop its possibilities. The Beaver Survey carried on by Mr. Donald L. Robb in the Park has been mentioned, but his was only one of several such investigations into the habits and peculiarities of different species of wildlife to be found in the area. Dr. D. A. MacLulich, known for his work on the rabbit cycle, used the Park as a laboratory from 1932 until 1936. In 1934 Dr. C. H. D. Clarke undertook a study of the Ruffed Grouse of the district in an effort to determine what disease was causing the death of many of these birds. A study of the mollusca was undertaken in 1935 by Messrs. Pritchard and LaRocque, of the National Museum of Canada. In 1939 and 1940, Mr. E. C. Cross and Mr. S. C. Downing, of the Royal Ontario Museum of Zoology, began a live trapping study of small mammals. While the last project has not been completed, reports on all the others are available to specialists in these different fields. Algonquin Park research has added much to the scientific data available to naturalists in other parts of the world.

Information compiled by the Ontario Fisheries Research Laboratory has been used by the Ontario Government and by other agencies interested in the results of their investigations. This work has been under the direction of Professor W. J. K. Harkness of the University of Toronto. From 1919 to 1934, the Ontario Fisheries Research Laboratory carried out studies on a great number of Ontario waters including Lake Ontario, Lake Nipissing, Lake Nipigon, the Trent Valley Canal, and trout streams of Southern Ontario. In 1929 the Laboratory first instituted investigations in the Park, when Mr. W. E. Ricker and Mr. F. P. Ide spent some time on Wolf and Ragged Lakes, the Oxtongue River; and on the Nipissing River in the northern part of the Park, for the purpose of studying the ecology of these trout lakes and streams.

At the direct request of Superintendent MacDougall, Professor Harkness visited many lakes in the Park to select the best site for a permanent laboratory from which to carry out fisheries investigations. In 1935, a field laboratory was established on Cache Lake. Five biologists worked here under Professor J. R. Dymond and Dr. E. B. Ide. Since then, fisheries studies in the Park have been carried on continuously. In the following year, a laboratory headquarters was constructed on Opeongo Lake, the largest body of water in the Park, and close to other important lakes and streams.

This laboratory has been the centre for fisheries research, which under the direction of Professor Harkness, has been extended to include studies of aquatic biology in all the important lakes and streams of the Park. Many students have here completed their field work leading to a Master's or Doctor's degree, besides the training gained in research.

One feature of this work is the creel census. By the distribution and collection of special cards to co-operative anglers in the Park, the biologists are now accumulating valuable records; asking such questions as, how long were you fishing, how many fish were caught, their size, and what specie were they? The cards are placed in boxes located at the ends of portages, at camp sites, and other convenient points. Distribution and collection of the cards is in charge of Fish Laboratory students who travel about the Park in the summer season.

At Opeongo and Cache Lakes, Fish Laboratory employees are on hand to assist in getting additional information about the fish taken from the lakes. If the angler is willing, his fish is examined to determine from its stomach contents what it has been feeding on, whether it is a female and would spawn during the year, and how old it was. The age of a fish can be determined by an examination of its scales. By reference to this tabulated data, the experts can determine the average length of time it takes to catch a fish, and the size of the average fish caught. Thus they know whether the number of fish is increasing or declining in any given lake. Few fishermen who fill in these census cards or bring in their catch to be examined, realize the importance of their co-operation. Records built up in this way have resulted in a new management policy concerning the lakes in the Park and has brought about widespread improvements in the fishing in these lakes.

Under this new policy, begun in 1938, a number of lakes are closed to fishing in alternate years. The experiment is in its infancy, but the creel census returns already show this technique will be of great value in maintaining fish production. A fact which illustrates this is that lake trout, which do not spawn in the fall, frequently reach regulation size during the summer, and though fishermen who catch them are within the letter of the law, next year's crop of fish is reduced.

At Smoke Lake, on the request of the Leaseholders' Association, a further step has been taken to maintain the fish population. Trolling from boats propelled by mechanical power has been prohibited. It was felt that when people have to paddle a canoe while fishing, they will stop when they have caught what they want, or even before if their muscles are soft. With a motor-propelled boat they will continue to circle around until they have caught their quota or have run out of fuel.

Research work in the Fish Laboratory has proved to have a much wider sphere of usefulness. During World War II, scientific studies

of the oxygen capacity of the blood, and of respiratory devices for
the use of Canadian airmen, benefited directly from the Fish Laboratory findings. Other branches of science have also benefited. Such
men as Drs. F. E. Fry, E. C. Black, W. A. Kennedy and W. R.
Martin have spent summers in fisheries research in the Park.

The work started here is now carried on in other Provincial Parks
in Ontario. In 1944 and 1945 Professor Harkness directed the
establishment of similar activities in Quetico, Sibley, and Lake
Superior Provincial Parks, all of which show promise of real assistance in the conservation of fish in these areas.

In the summer of 1944 the Park became the scene of an experiment
to test the possibilities of the use of DDT to eliminate forest pests.
Already this insecticide had proved its worth in war areas, and now
the authorities were anxious to know if it could be used to combat
the spruce budworm which was attacking the Algonquin balsam and
spruce forests. Professor Harkness offered the facilities of the Ontario
Museum Fisheries Research Laboratories in conjunction with the
Royal Ontario Museum of Zoology, in order to make a complete
study of the situation. The effects of the spray on the fish, insect, and
mammal life of the area were investigated. Dr. R. R. Langford, a
member of the Laboratory Staff, supervised this phase of the work,
while Mr. K. E. Stewart, entomologist with the Dominion Department of Agriculture, was in charge of the forest insect investigation
in the Park at that time.

This study showed that there would be certain indirect effects
from the spray on the other forms of wildlife which were dependent
on insects destroyed along with the spruce budworm. The food
supply of many birds and smaller mammals would be destroyed.
Amphibians and reptiles would also suffer a heavy death toll from
the effects of the spray, but it was felt that if the spraying was not
repeated too frequently, the natural fertility and the migration of
these animals would probably enable the population to recover.
Fish, with the exception of speckled trout, seemed to be unaffected
by the DDT, but, of course, they did suffer from the reduced supply
of insects for food. Many of the animals on which fish depend for
food, such as crayfish, were found to be seriously affected by the
insecticide. However, it was decided as the result of this work, and
on consultation with American authorities who were conducting
similar experiments, that it would be worth while to continue with
the aerial spraying program. In the Park, and elsewhere, with a
certain amount of care on the part of the pilots of the aircraft from

which the spray was being released, it was felt it would be possible to reduce the damages to other wildlife by shutting off the flow of the spray while passing over lakes and rivers. In this way the effect on water creatures could be reduced to a minimum.

Usually, Park visitors are unaware of the important scientific work being carried on in the area, but on this occasion, their attention was attracted by the ingenious markers used by the ground workers to guide the pilot to the special plot that was to receive the spray. At the top of lofty balsam trees near the highway, and close to the railway in the south part of the Park, the visitors saw cheesecloth bags mounted on poles projecting above the tops of the lofty balsam trees. From the air, the pilot could easily identify the rectangular plot to be sprayed by locating the four sign posts erected at the corners.

Another example of the way in which the authorities have encouraged the use of Park facilities for scientific research, is the action taken by the Department in 1944, providing for a Nature Reserve of thirty-one and one-half square miles within the Park boundaries. This research area was set aside as the result of a request made by the Federation of Ontario Naturalists for the reserving of an area where there would be no interference whatever with natural conditions as they existed at the time of its establishment. In the remainder of the Park, where fishing, canoeing, and lumbering are carried on, there will, of course, be no changes as a result of these activities, but in this reserve it is hoped to allow Nature to carry on in her own way over a long period of time. The area set aside for this purpose in the Park lies in a region readily accessible for purpose of study, being north of the highway and east of Canisbay, Linda, and Burnt Island Lakes. Authorities are hopeful of obtaining valuable information in future on the interdependence of the flora and fauna of the district as the result of the observations to be conducted in this region. These scientific activities, far from interfering with the holiday life of visitors, directly contributed to their enlightenment, and increase the value of their vacations.

A new item appeared on the Park program. Professor Dymond had been working and holidaying in the Park for several years, when in 1942, Mrs. A. G. Northway asked him to take a group of Boy Scouts, who were at that time visiting Nominigan Lodge, on a hike along some of the nearby trails, making use of the opportunity to tell them about the trees, wild flowers, birds, and anything else of interest found in the course of their ramble. Several adults, hearing of the proposed expedition, asked if they might join the party. The outing was such a success that the Smoke Lake nature hikes became a regular feature. Since then, these informal lessons proved so popular, they served as a general rallying point for all the campers on the lake. Young and old alike found the knowledge they acquired in this way made their Algonquin holiday all the more enjoyable.

This Smoke Lake programme had been under way for two years when the Department of Lands and Forests persuaded Professor Dymond to extend it to include other areas of the Park, so as to give other visitors the opportunity of learning something of the wonders of their surroundings. Only three of many ways of further-ing nature education were attempted the first year, but these reached many of the Park visitors. Conducted nature hikes were arranged to start from various points accessible to summer cottagers and hotel guests; a beginning was made in the planning of nature trails; and talks were given at the boys' and girls' camps. The hikes were similar to those conducted previously, but this time the participants were given mimeographed lists of the common plants and animals, so that they could carry on by themselves once they had the idea of what there was to be learned about their environment.

This is one final example of the unique way in which the Park exerts its influence on those who live within its boundaries. No visitor comes away without feeling that influence.

It is a far cry today from the time when swarthy Algonquin hunters stripped bark from its birch trees for their canoes, speared fish below its falls, snared the rabbit, slew the deer and moose. The Iroquois no longer holds up the bloody scalp-lock of his fallen foe in savage triumph. Trappers and settlers have come and gone; only a few piles of sand remain of the camboose camps of the great square timber days.

Yearly, the visitors increase in numbers and their Park activities multiply. Yearly, new ideas develop for conserving the wildlife and forest wealth; the fondest dreams of Alexander Kirkwood and the most practical expectations of James Dickson have been more than realized. Algonquin Park will go on expanding its usefulness. To rangers and residents and visitors, to all who know the Park for what it is, the intangible spirit of the Park that found such adequate expression in the paintings of Tom Thomson is the one value they cherish most.

No better words can be found than those of a visitor, leader of an early American youth movement, to express what the Park has meant to the thousands who love it. Dr. Lester Scott is more than a visitor. For twenty-five years he and his family made the Park their summer home in a manner that would have satisfied even the veteran surveyor Dickson. When asked to recall some of his experiences, Dr. Scott wrote the following words:

"Our friends in New York used to say that there were only two dates in our family, Christmas, and the day we left each year for Algonquin Park. That was perfectly true during all those years that we came north for our holidays in Canada. We took our son into the bush when he was only four months old and our daughter when she was ten months old. We carried them in pack baskets in the bow of our canoe while they were taking their naps. We went where we pleased, babies didn't stop us, they were part of the fun. Our youngsters have always talked of Algonquin Park as their other home.

"Once, some years ago, we figured that we had actually spent more than two and a half years camping in Algonquin Park, and two and a half years of living in any one place leaves a mark, especially when that place is largely wilderness. Remember that our impressions of the southern part of the Park were gained when there was no ranger's cabin at Joe Lake; when there were no buildings whatever, except the remains of an old lumber camp on Smoke; when there were no camps on Canoe; and when Ragged Lake was quite out of the world and not included in the Park limits at all. On our first cruise in 1911 south from Joe Lake through Canoe and down into Black Bear and Lake Louisa we saw only three people — and two of them were guides going home to Huntsville at the season's end. The Merrills ran the Algonquin Hotel at Joe; there was no railway station there; Shan Fraser was the postmaster at Mowat; and the Algonquin Indians from Golden Lake were still acting as guides for trips.

"In that day there was no railroad north of the line which ran alongside Cache Lake. There were no wagon roads into the Park, except for short distances, only a few hardy campers got as far north as Cedar

Lake and came out to Manitou and Tea Lakes to the line running between Toronto and North Bay. The building of the Canadian Northern Railway meant the opening up of the northern section of the Park to tourists, but that section has never been as thickly populated as the region now accessible by road in the south. The lakes are larger, the distances greater, and it had still preserved many of its original wilderness characteristics.

"Many of us prefer the northern section of the Park for this reason — there we still find many places where the 'trails run out and stop'. The zip and zing of the cold balsam-laden air of early August and the call of the loon were my first impression of Algonquin Park nights and they still mark that land as different for me. But there are many other things that mean Algonquin Park to me — the flying call of the loon, and that other characteristic call with its dropped terminal note; the sound of wings beating on the water as they take off in flight; the hoot and answering hoot of owls; the howl of the timber wolves, and cry-baby wailing of porcupines when they are not clicking their teeth at you in rage, and the distant (and for the sake of one's peace of mind keep it distant) odour of the woods' pussy — all these are part of the backdrop before which the camper acts out of his daily drama of cooking, woods housekeeping, fishing and cruising.

"There one learns, too, that all clowns are not human. Bears can be very funny and porcupines, while not actually rollicking, are not as stupid as their reputation. Then there was the time when camp was deserted and I was smoking my pipe while patching my canoe. I heard a movement close at hand, and glancing up, found a whole family of grouse sitting on a log watching my every movement. I blew a puff of smoke from my lips, but the whole family continued to squat there not an arm's reach away. I blew another puff and they ducked, but stayed right where they were. We kept up this game until I finally had to laugh out loud and then they slid silently off the log and melted into the bush. How often we watched the red squirrels busily knocking down pine cones only to have them stolen by rascally chipmunks who got well away into their burrows before the scolding red squirrels could get down from the trees. And then there's the story of the inquisitive bear at one of the lumber camps who wandered in the cook shack and had it all to himself, for the cooks piled out of the door in a hurry. That suited Mr. Bear very well, and he went about helping himself to an ample meal. Then he reached up to the top of the stove and hooked a pot of beans down to the floor. The fun certainly started then, most of the boiling contents of the pot smothered his head in transit, all hell broke loose in the shack, and the visitor beat a hasty retreat into the woods. They had to rebuild most of the shack afterwards.

"How often, when we were camped in the Park, have we thought of the great canoes that used to pass close at hand along the waterways leading from the far west. Their canoes were twenty-footers, while the largest we ever had was eighteen. We used that one for a long time, but my favorite craft was a thirteen-footer, a chestnut that weighed less than fifteen pounds—and that one was a canoeman's dream. This little fellow was brought from Mrs. Bell in Ottawa. It had been made for her husband, Dr. Bell, when he worked as a ranger in the Park in order to regain his health. To Dr. Bell, too, we were indebted for the famous blue-print map that all campers preferred to the Government issue of the time.

"Since that time there have been several maps and we old campers have always watched for new ones with interest. The early ones showed few lakes in the north part of the Park. Later maps showed many lakes that had been there all the time but just hadn't been located till later. What fun that was — finding a lake that wasn't on the map. We found many during our wanderings; it gave us quite a thrill of exploring in an unknown country.

"One day when the use of planes for patrolling was new, I was repairing a birch-bark canoe on the shores

of a little northern lake. I had built a small fire to
warm some pitch in a can when I heard the Ontario
Fire Patrol plane away off, and I knew they had
spotted my smoke. The plane kept getting closer until
the head came low and I saw the pilot waving at me.
He was doing his work in the Park with the newest
form of transportation — I was patching up one of
the oldest to carry me on my way.

"Now, although we are making our home in Arizona,
on the desert's edge, we still hear from some of the
rangers and guides, amongst whom we count our
very good friends. They tell us of the lakes where
the lumber companies are cutting and of the improvements in their methods. In the old days they
sometimes left disfiguring slash all through the district, but now the pine on the small islands is left
untouched and the shorelines for a distance of three
hundred feet are left intact. In fact, if one had not
known the land of old, he'd never miss the trees taken
out unless he penetrated the forest.

"In later years we established our headquarters at
Kioskoqui and it became the gathering place for all
the older youngsters — boys from college, classmates
of my boy's. They felt about our camp just as we
did — it was a place apart, a different place, a quiet
or a riotously gay place, as the spirit moved them.
We've had the thrill of having lads come over a
thousand miles just to be with us there for three
days. That says something for the forests and the
lakes that words will never say.

"After the war, all that are left of the old crowd are
coming back at least once more. They won't all come
— some of them are never again to handle a paddle
or to cast a lure. Their memory will be part of the
sweetness of the place to us who have shared the life
of the woods with them, the days of calm and rioting
water, the stars so close that they spoke to you, the
mystery of what lay around the bend of the stream,
the nights of glorious moon and the majestic sweep
of the aurora, the mud on your mocassins, the rain
down our backs, the flame of the maples after the